RESEARCH MONOGRAPH OF THE NATIONAL ASSOCIATION FOR THE EDUCATION OF YOUNG CHILDREN, VOLUME 6

Including Children with Special Needs in Early Childhood Programs

**Mark Wolery and
Jan S. Wilbers,
Editors**

A 1993–1994 NAEYC Comprehensive Membership benefit

**National Association for the Education of Young Children
Washington, DC.**

This monograph is dedicated to

James M. Mudd

– a good friend,

– a valued colleague,

– an investigator of naturalistic interventions,

– a long-time advocate and implementer of inclusive services for young children, and

– a courageous fighter against his own disabling multiple sclerosis.

Photo credits: Lorenzo Hilliard Photo Outreach Program, p. 4; The Creative Pre-School, pp. 10, 19, 100, 109, 123, 129, 134, 139, 164, 183, 194; Nancy P. Alexander, pp. 15, 40, 176; Subjects & Predicates, pp. 26, 35, 113, 171; Bm Porter/DonFranklin, p. 56; Lillis Larson-Kent, p. 67; Anne Crabbe, p. 75; C & W Shields, Inc., p. 90; Jim Bradshaw, p. 159; Marilyn Nolt, p. 190.

Copyright © 1994 by the National Association for the Education of Young Children. All rights reserved.

National Association for the Education of Young Children
1509 16th Street, N.W.
Washington, DC 20036-1426
202-232-8777 or 1-800-424-2460

The National Association for the Education of Young Children (NAEYC) attempts through its publications program to provide a forum for discussion of major issues and ideas in our field. We hope to provoke thought and promote professional growth. The views expressed or implied are not necessarily those of the Association. NAEYC wishes to thank the editors and authors, who donated much time and effort to develop this book as a contribution to our profession.

Library of Congress Catalog Card Number: 94-067252
ISBN Catalog Number: 0-935989-61-7
NAEYC #145

Editor: Carol Copple; *Editorial assistance:* Beth Panitz; *Copyediting:* Betty Nylund Barr; *Production:* Penny Atkins; *Design:* Jack Zibulsky

Printed in the United States of America

Contents

Foreword

I N RECENT YEARS, especially since the passage of the Americans with Disabilities Act (ADA), early childhood educators and special educators have become more aware of the necessity of communicating and collaborating with one another. Now that all early childhood programs must be prepared to serve children with special needs, staff confront a host of new challenges and opportunities. Early childhood professionals are eager to learn how to best serve children with disabilities and how to create successful, inclusive programs that enhance the lives of all the children and families who participate.

Having become convinced through years of research and experience that including children with disabilities in mainstream settings benefits them and their peers, special educators advocated for legislation mandating inclusion. They are strongly committed to seeing it succeed. It is this commitment that stimulated co-editors Mark Wolery and Jan Wilbers and the other contributors to write this research monograph. They want to see children with special needs well served in early childhood settings, and they are convinced that research in special education provides information and strategies vital for effective inclusion.

We at NAEYC are pleased to publish this monograph, contributed by such an outstanding team of special education researchers. We may view some of the authors' teaching suggestions with reservation; however, we strongly support all of the fundamental points about inclusion and believe that early childhood educators should be familiar with the research-based educational implications described here. We are glad to have the opportunity to share with the early childhood field this thoughtful synthesis of an extensive and pertinent literature.

—*Carol Copple*
Editor

Preface

I N THE PAST FEW YEARS, the need for a monograph similar to this one has become increasingly apparent for several reasons:

• P.L. 101-336 (1990), the Americans with Disabilities Act, requires that equal access to all facilities and services be provided to individuals with disabilities, and it prohibits discriminating against them.

• Discussions appeared in the literature focusing on the relevance of developmentally appropriate practices (Bredekamp 1987) to the education of young children with developmental delays and disabilities (e.g., Carta et al. 1991; Johnson & Johnson 1992).

• Continued progress is being made on developing comprehensive, statewide service systems for infants and toddlers with disabilities and their families (U.S. Department of Education 1993).

• In the 1992–93 school year, all states had mandates in effect to provide free, appropriate public education to preschoolers (children 3 through 5 years of age) with disabilities (U.S. Department of Education 1993).

• The majority of early childhood programs of various types report enrolling at least one young child with developmental delays and disabilities (Wolery et al. 1993).

• New regulations were established for providing services to young children with disabilities in Head Start programs (Federal Register 1993).

• Many families of young children with disabilities continue to be supportive of and to request inclusive services for their young children with disabilities.

• Many, if not most, professionals in early childhood special education recommend providing services for young children with disabilities in inclusive settings.

Together, these events and forces suggest that a need exists to provide early childhood personnel with information about how to design and implement services for young children with disabilities in the context of programs designed and operated for young children without disabilities. However, the literature related to services for infants, toddlers, and preschoolers with developmental delays and disabilities and their families is extremely large. The relevant research and resulting implications for practice are of sufficient size and diversity that they cannot be described and explained adequately in a single volume of readable size. Thus, *Including Children with Special Needs in Early Childhood Programs* was designed as a foundational resource from which readers may begin to secure the information needed to develop defensible practices. In taking this tactic, we have three goals:

• to draw implications for practice from the existing research that will be useful in providing early childhood services to young children with developmental delays and disabilities in programs with their typically developing peers,

• to provide the citation of additional sources to assist personnel in improving their practices, and

• to emphasize that much remains to be learned about providing high-quality and effective services to young children with developmental delays and disabilities and their families.

The ultimate aim, of course, is that early childhood services will be improved for all young children, particularly services for families and young children who have special needs that compromise their learning, development, and well-being.

In chapter 1, historic and foundational information about including young children with developmental delays and disabilities is presented. In chapter 2, Donald Bailey summarizes themes and issues related to implementing family-centered services, and he draws implications from the relevant research for practice. In chapter 3, Mary Beth Bruder describes issues related to collaborating with members from various disciplines to develop defensible early childhood services. In chapters 4, 5, 6, and 7, information related to designing and implementing classroom-based services for young children with disabilities is described. Chapter 4 focuses on assessment issues, chapters 5 and 6 focus on intervention practices, and chapter 7 focuses on implementing those practices in classrooms. In chapter 8, Jane Atwater, Lois Orth-Lopes, Marleen Elliott, Judith Carta, and Ilene Schwartz describe issues related to planning and implementing services for helping children with disabilities and their families make the transition from one program (e.g., an early childhood program) to another (e.g., early elementary education). In chapter 9, summary statements are made and issues for future research are identified. The topics addressed in each chapter represent large bodies of research, and in fact, major texts could and have been written on the issues addressed by each chapter. Thus, this monograph is best viewed as an appetizer and the literature cited herein as the main course.

Across the chapters, several salient themes are presented; six of these deserve mention. *First*, there is an explicit assumption that young children with developmental delays and disabilities should be served in programs that also serve their typically developing peers—in part for logical reasons, but more importantly because it is responsible public policy that is supported by the research as a reasonable and defensible practice. *Second*, families of young children with special needs are key players in making decisions about how services are structured and provided and about the effects that the families desire from those services; thus, services for young children with developmental delays and disabilities cannot be provided meaningfully when they are provided without collaboration with the children's families—not as the recipients of services but as the central focus from which our efforts emanate. *Third,* early childhood programs for young children with special needs must be purposeful endeavors that are designed and implemented to improve the learning, development, and well-being of young children in specific and clearly articulated ways for each child. *Fourth,* defensible services for young children with special needs and their families are not the jurisdiction of professionals from any single discipline; rather, a group of individuals with differing types of expertise, in conjunction with families, should jointly plan, implement, adjust, and evaluate the services that are provided. *Fifth,* although practices should be informed by values, logic, and experience, each practice must be informed and based on sound research; fortunately, a considerable amount of relevant research has been and continues to be conducted. This research activity is appropriate and should be supported because much remains to be learned and put into practice. *Sixth,* services for young children with special needs and their families are evolving; this document is not the final word or comprehensive manual on practices but a snapshot of current practices. Although we hope that this document will be used to help implement defensible practices for young children with disabilities and their families in inclusive settings, we also hope that it will be a catalyst for the development and evaluation of "new and improved" practices.

— Mark Wolery
Allegheny-Singer Research Institute, Pittsburgh, Pennsylvania

— Jan S. Wilbers
Scott County Public Schools, Georgetown, Kentucky

Acknowledgments

M ANY PEOPLE ASSISTED in the development of this monograph, and they deserve our public acknowledgment. We are grateful to the contributors who wrote selected chapters: Jane B. Atwater; Donald B. Bailey, Jr.; Mary Beth Bruder; Judith J. Carta; Marleen Elliott; Lois Orth-Lopes; and Ilene S. Schwartz. Each of these individuals gave freely of their unique expertise to write summaries of the research and draw implications for practice. We appreciate their contributions greatly. The efforts and encouragement of Sue Bredekamp, Carol Copple, and Polly Greenberg of the National Association for the Education of Young Children were extremely instrumental in getting this project started and ensuring that it was completed. We are grateful for the opportunity they provided to us, and we appreciate their patience and understanding when we fell behind deadlines. We also are grateful for Betty Nylund Barr's careful copyediting of this document. We are particularly grateful to Sue Bredekamp for recognizing the need to address all children in efforts to improve early childhood practices and programs, for endeavoring to increase professional dialogue and knowledge pertaining to inclusive practices, and for initially conceptualizing this monograph. We appreciate her care and concern for young children. We also are grateful for the support provided by the administration of Allegheny-Singer Research Institute, particularly Leslie Shuttleworth, Trevor R.P. Price, and Robert T. Rubin; and we appreciate the assistance given by our colleagues and co-workers: Leslie Anthony, Jeffri Brookfield, Nicola Caldwell, Carl J. Dunst, Anneleisa Filla, Debbie S. Glass, Mary Horvath, Julie Katzenmeyer, Christine L. Salisbury, Erin Snyder, and Margaret G. Werts.

This project was supported, in part, by a cooperative agreement from the Early Education Program for Children with Disabilities of the U.S. Department of Education (Research Institute on Preschool Mainstreaming, Grant Number HO24K30001) to St. Peter's Child Development Centers, Inc., of Pittsburgh, Pennsylvania, through a subcontract to Allegheny-Singer Research Institute. However, the opinions expressed do not necessarily reflect the policy of the U.S. Department of Education, and no official endorsement should be inferred. Nonetheless, we appreciate the leadership provided by James Hamilton and Martha Bryant of the Early Education Program for Children with Disabilities.

Finally, we are grateful to our spouses, Ruth A. Wolery and D. Reed Wilbers, who were patient with us and provided substantial social support during the work on this project; and to Jessi, Jenny, and Josh Wilbers, who gave of their mother's time.

Chapter 1

Introduction to the Inclusion of Young Children with Special Needs in Early Childhood Programs

Mark Wolery and Jan S. Wilbers

RECENT LEGISLATION, including the Americans with Disabilities Act (P.L. 101-336), and literature pertaining to early childhood services indicate an increasing trend toward full inclusion of children with disabilities in all early childhood settings. Historical differences exist in the professional backgrounds and practices of individuals who serve young children with disabilities and those who serve children without disabilities; they often are educated through different college or university programs, belong to separate professional organizations, and follow different bodies of research. Yet all early childhood personnel have a similar purpose—providing experiences to enhance the development and well-being of young children. Although a complete merger of the practices of the two groups remains to be worked out, young children with and without disabilities are increasingly being served in the same programs.

For more than two decades, professionals have addressed the issue of serving children with and without disabilities together. The benefits and rationale for such programs have been described (Bricker 1978; Peck & Cooke 1983),

All children have special needs—each child, regardless of abilities and background, has unique needs and deserves special adult attention.

practices have emerged (Safford 1989; Allen 1992; Peck, Odom, & Bricker 1993), and model programs have been evaluated (Bricker & Bricker 1973; Rule et al. 1987; Templeman, Fredericks, & Udell 1989). These activities produced a considerable amount of knowledge; some of it is described in this monograph, yet much remains to be learned. This chapter addresses four goals: to describe (a) children who have special needs, (b) the benefits of and barriers to inclusion, (c) the historical and policy issues related to providing services to young children with special needs, and (d) the general goals for early childhood experiences.

Who are young children with special needs?

Various answers can be given for the question, Who are young children with special needs? Many individuals agree that all children have special needs—each child, regardless of abilities and background, has unique needs and deserves special adult attention. The term *special needs*, however, has come to mean children with disabilities or developmental delays.

Issues of terminology

In this monograph we interchangeably use the terms *children with . . .* or *children who have . . . special needs, disabilities,* and *developmental delays* to refer to a distinct subset of children from birth to age 8. These infants and young children are said to have special needs because their well-being, development, and learning are compromised if special and expertly designed attention is not given to their early education. In the past, other terms were used to describe this group, such as *exceptional children, handicapped children, special education children,* and many others. These terms are avoided because they are objectionable to families and others. Also, phrases such as *special needs children, disabled children,* or *delayed children* are not used. The placement of the adjective before the noun increases attention to their disabilities rather than to the fact that they are, first, *children,* and then, children who happen to have developmental delays or disabilities. A fundamental assumption of inclusion is that all children are children and that our practices should reflect that reality.

Children's needs

Children with special needs are similar in many respects to children without disabilities. All children share needs for food and shelter, for love and affection, for affiliation with others, for opportunities to play and learn, and for protection from the harsh realities of their environments. All children deserve freedom from violence, abuse, neglect, and suffering. All children deserve interactions and relationships with adults who are safe, predictable, responsive, and nurturing. All children deserve opportunities to interact with peers who are accepting, trustworthy, kind, and industrious. All children deserve early educational experiences that are stimulating, interesting, facilitative, and enjoyable.

Children with special needs, however, are different from children without disabilities; they have needs that children without disabilities do not have.

They need environments that are specifically organized and adjusted to minimize the effects of their disabilities and to promote learning of a broad range of skills. They need professionals who are competent in meeting the general needs of young children *and* are competent in promoting learning and use of skills important to the specific needs of children with disabilities. Also, they need personnel who value working cooperatively with families to meet family needs and to help families promote their child's development. (Wolery, Strain, & Bailey 1992, p. 95)

They also need professionals who are skilled in working with members of other disciplines (Bruder, this volume, chapter 3) and who value all young children, whatever their respective abilities. In this monograph we describe selected adult competencies and practices for meeting the special needs of children with developmental delays and disabilities. These practices are based, at varying levels, on the foundations of research, experience, and logic.

Classification of children with special needs

Children with disabilities can be classified in a number of ways. Perhaps the most relevant classification system deals with their eligibility for early intervention and special education services. To be eligible for such services under the Individuals with Disabilities Education Act (called *IDEA*—formerly the Education of the Handicapped Act), children can fit into any of 13 defined categories that identify the type of disability: deafness, dual-sensory impairments, hearing impairments, mental retardation, multiple handicaps, orthopedic impairments, other health impairments, serious emotional disturbance, specific learning disabilities, speech (language) impairments, visual impairments and blindness, traumatic brain injury, and autism. Because of the detrimental effects of early labeling, IDEA allows states to use the category "developmental delay" for young children with special needs. Each state has specific criteria and measurement procedures for determining children's eligibility for early intervention and special education services, including what constitutes developmental delay.

Other classification systems also exist. Many children will be diagnosed by their physicians as having specific conditions and/or syndromes. For example, children may be diagnosed as having cerebral palsy, spina bifida, muscular dystrophy, and many other conditions. Children with such diagnoses may be eligible for special education services under a category such as "orthopedic impairments." Literally

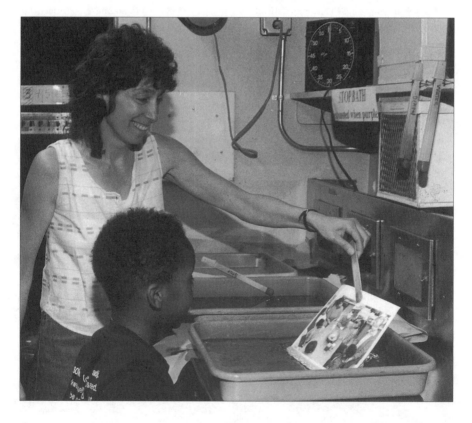

Children with disabilities are a highly diverse group of individuals, and their learning and development are influenced by many factors.

hundreds of different conditions can result in disabilities and/or developmental delays. Some conditions have a clear cause, but others do not; some conditions have a general prognosis, but others do not (McLaren & Bryson 1987). A number of environmental variables (for instance, poverty, physical and sexual abuse, exposure to toxins, diseases, and injuries) can put children at risk for developmental disabilities. Environmental and biological factors work together to increase the risk of children having developmental delays and disabilities (Baumeister, Kupstas, & Klindworth 1990; Crocker 1992).

What early childhood professionals should know and do about children's disorders

Educators, including special educators, cannot be expected to know about every potential condition and factor that can have negative effects on children's learning and development. However, early childhood professionals should recognize several things about children's disorders (these are described below), and they should be prepared to take specific actions.

Children with special needs are very different from one another. A great deal of variation is expected, given the diverse diagnoses and causes of the many different conditions. Children who have the same diagnosis or who are eligible for services under the same category may have very different abilities and needs. Nearly every condition can have effects that range from mild, to moderate, to severe. For example, two children may have mental retardation, one mild and the other severe. Despite the fact that they have the same diagnosis, the abilities of the child with mild mental retardation may be more similar to the abilities of children with communication disorders than to the abilities of children with severe retardation. Also, the effects of nearly every diagnosis are influenced by environmental factors, such as the nature of support that families receive and their available resources. For some conditions (such as visual and hearing impairments), the age of onset will influence the extent to which children's development is affected. Similarly, in most cases the age of diagnosis and subsequent intervention are important. In short, children with disabilities are a highly diverse group of individuals, and their learning and development are influenced by many factors.

The various disorders do not necessarily occur in isolation. Some children may have only a visual impairment, a hearing impairment, or a health condition. Other children may have a given disorder and a number of others. For example, some children with mental retardation also have hearing and orthopedic impairments, others have both hearing and visual impairments, and others have communication and behavioral disorders. Having one disability does not inoculate children against other disabilities, although intervention can result in the prevention and treatment of secondary disabilities (Pope 1992; Ramey & Ramey 1992).

A diagnosis rarely results in precise prescriptions for educational practices or precise prognoses. A great deal of research has been conducted to identify the differences of children with given diagnoses from the general population in the hope that a differential treatment will emerge. However, such a simple one-to-one mapping of treatment and diagnosis has not emerged. A diagnosis may suggest the need for certain broad categories of interventions. For example, children with communication disorders are likely to need the services of speech-language pathologists; however, so do children with hearing impairments, mental retardation, autism, and other disorders. The nature of the interventions are tied more directly to the child's current abilities, the influence of specific environmental factors and instructional strategies on their learning, and the resources and goals of their families. Thus, early childhood personnel should not assume that a given diagnosis requires a specific type of intervention. There are, of course, exceptions, such as certain seizure disorders that require selected medications, but these prescriptions are not made by early childhood staff.

The prognosis in most cases is influenced substantially by factors other than the diagnosed condition. These factors include the amount and quality of support given to the family, the quality of the intervention and educational programs the child experiences, the health of the child, the educational level and socioeconomic status of the family, and many other factors (Bailey, this volume, chapter 2). General prognoses can be made (for example, a child with a mild speech-language impairment may be expected to function at more advanced levels than a child with severe mental retardation, dual sensory impairments, and cerebral palsy), but precise predictions of how young children will function 10 to 20 years in the future are not reliable. This, of course, is true for children without disabilities as well. Many factors influence any child's continued learning, style of interacting and approach to life, and future health and happiness.

Identifying and knowing the cause of the disorder rarely results in precise educational practices. We frequently assume that understanding the cause of a condition will result in knowledge relevant to treatment, but this often is not the case with young children who have disabilities. Knowing that a given child's disorder was

Early childhood personnel are key persons in identifying children who may have developmental delays and disabilities.

genetically caused, was due to a chromosomal disorder, was a result of a high fever, or was due to meningitis rarely leads to specific practices in the classroom. Such information may be sought and needed by families for a variety of reasons; for example, knowing the probability that subsequent children would have a given genetic disorder is important to families in deciding whether to have more children. However, such information is rarely helpful to teams in planning early education programs. Rather, the child's current abilities and the goals and priorities of the family are more relevant in planning successful early childhood experiences.

Early childhood teachers should assist in identifying children who may have developmental delays and disabilities. Many young children with special needs are not identified as such prior to their contact with professionals. As a result, early childhood personnel are key persons in identifying children who may have developmental delays and disabilities. This identification can occur through informal observations of children, screening with developmental scales, and sensory (vision and hearing) screening (Meisels & Provence 1989; Wolery 1989; Meisels & Wasik 1990). Early childhood personnel must understand child development, the factors that influence it, and its general course during the early childhood years. Being aware of this information and carefully observing children from day to day can result in concerns about potential developmental delays and disorders. When such concerns arise, we should not assume that children will "outgrow" the problem because, in many cases, they will not; rather, we are responsible for securing assistance from other professionals. This should involve discussions with the family, consultation with related-service personnel (see Bruder, this volume, chapter 3), and referral to other experts. If the concerns are confirmed, then the child can receive the needed services. If, however, the concerns are not confirmed, then little harm is done, assuming the issue is treated sensitively with the family. Clearly, early childhood personnel are not responsible for making diagnoses, but they have useful information for professionals who diagnose children. Early childhood personnel should know the procedures for referring children to other professionals; the criteria used by their state for eligibility for early intervention and special education services; how to give useful information to other experts; and how to interact sensitively with families regarding these issues.

Early childhood personnel should learn about the conditions of children who are in their programs. Because many different disorders exist, it is impractical for early childhood personnel to have a working knowledge of each condition. However, if a child with a particular diagnosis is in an early childhood program, personnel in

If a child with a particular diagnosis is in an early childhood program, personnel in that program should learn all they can about the disorder.

that program should learn all they can about the disorder. A variety of sources of information are available. Most introductory special education texts (such as Fallen & Umansky 1985; Blackhurst & Berdine 1993; Haring & McCormick 1994) have general information on many conditions. Detailed textbooks also are available for each of the more common conditions, such as communication disorders, autism, mental retardation, sensory impairments, learning disabilities, and physical disabilities. Similarly, sources (such as Jones 1988, Blackman 1990, and Batshaw & Perret 1992) have information about many health and medical conditions. Besides using written material, early childhood personnel can obtain useful information from other professionals, such as special education and related-service personnel (see Bruder, this volume, chapter 3) in the local school district, the departments of special education at local colleges and universities, and individuals in state departments of education. Many parent and professional organizations also have useful information to supply. Early childhood staff should not overlook the information that family members can provide; many have a wealth of information about their child's disorder and about its effects on their child.

Benefits of and barriers to including children with disabilities in early childhood programs

A majority of the early childhood programs designed for typically developing children report that they enroll at least one child with a disability (Wolery, Holcombe, et al. 1993). Terms used to describe such services include *integration, mainstreaming, least restrictive environment,* and *inclusion.* Generally, *integration* is a broad term for describing any enrollment of children with and without disabilities in the same program (Odom & McEvoy 1988). *Mainstreaming* is used to describe the enrollment of children with disabilities in programs having a majority of children who are not disabled (Odom & McEvoy 1988). *Least restrictive environment* is a term used to describe a setting among other settings that is appropriate for the child and provides the most contact possible with nondisabled children. *Inclusion,* on the other hand, assumes that all children should be served in the same programs they would have attended if they did not have disabilities (e.g., in neighborhood programs); inclusion has an underlying philosophy that all children belong together (Salisbury 1991). In this monograph, the term *inclusion* is used in most cases.

Proposed benefits of preschool inclusion

In 1978, Bricker presented social-ethical arguments, educational-psychological rationale, and legal and legislative precedents for early childhood integration. She suggested that benefits existed for children with and without disabilities, for their families, and for their communities. Some of these benefits are listed in table 1.

Three general statements can be made about these proposed benefits. First, *the benefits of preschool inclusion are well known.* Many general early childhood educators (Wolery, Huffman, Brookfield, et al., n.d.) and faculty members who prepare them (Wolery, Huffman, Holcombe, et al., n.d.) list benefits of preschool inclusion. Further, they rank the benefits of inclusion in much the same way whether or not they enroll children with disabilities in their programs.

Second, *families of children with and without disabilities appear to be positively disposed toward preschool inclusion* (Lamorey & Bricker 1993). Many families of children with disabilities favor inclusion but are concerned about the adequacy of the curriculum for their children (Bailey & Winton 1987). Also, much remains to be learned about how to foster positive contacts between families with children who have and do not have disabilities.

Third, *many of the proposed benefits do not occur without purposeful and careful supports to promote them* (Fewell & Oelwein 1990; Lamorey & Bricker 1993). For example, many children with disabilities do not imitate their peers, but with instruction they learn to do so (Carr & Darcy 1990; Venn et al. 1993). Children with disabilities seem to benefit from inclusion, particularly in relation to social development and social skills (Buysse & Bailey 1993). However, many children with and without disabilities do not interact frequently unless supports are provided to encourage such exchanges (Odom & McEvoy 1988; Lamorey & Bricker 1993). Fortunately, a number of intervention strategies are available to promote both social interactions (Odom & Brown 1993) and communication (Notari & Cole 1993). Similarly, accurate views and positive attitudes do not necessarily result simply from integration; adults' behavior substantially influences children's attitude formation (Stoneman 1993). Thus, inclusion in and of itself will not guarantee that the proposed benefits will occur. The manner in which programs are implemented and operated influences the likelihood that benefits will be realized. Much of this monograph is devoted to describing how to ensure that those benefits occur.

Barriers to preschool inclusion

Despite the logical reasons for preschool inclusion, the existence of barriers to inclusion must also be recognized. Odom and McEvoy (1990) list five barriers: (a) lack of adequate training in general *and* special early education, (b) philosophic differences between the two disciplines, (c) lack of related services in many programs, (d) lack of monitoring systems, and (e) negative staff attitudes.

Personnel preparation. College and university training programs for general and special early educators often are segregated. This may lead to lack of skill on the part of both types of early educators. Faculty members who prepare general early childhood educators identified the lack of adequate preparation and consultation as a barrier to preschool inclusion more frequently than any other barrier (Wolery,

Table 1. Proposed Benefits of Preschool Inclusion

Recipient of benefit	Description of benefit
Children with disabilities	1. They are spared the effects of separate, segregated education—including the negative effects of labeling and negative attitudes fostered by lack of contact with them. 2. They are provided with competent models that allow them to learn new adaptive skills and/or learn when and how to use their existing skills through imitation. 3. They are provided with competent peers with whom to interact and thereby learn new social and/or communicative skills. 4. They are provided with realistic life experiences that prepare them to live in the community. 5. They are provided with opportunities to develop friendships with typically developing peers.
Children without disabilities	1. They are provided with opportunities to learn more realistic and accurate views about individuals with disabilities. 2. They are provided with opportunities to develop positive attitudes toward others who are different from themselves. 3. They are provided with opportunities to learn altruistic behaviors and when and how to use such behaviors. 4. They are provided with models of individuals who successfully achieve despite challenges.
Communities	1. They can conserve their early childhood resources by limiting the need for segregated, specialized programs. 2. They can conserve educational resources if children with disabilities who are mainstreamed at the preschool level continue in regular as compared to special education placements during the elementary school years.
Families of children with disabilities	1. They are able to learn about typical development. 2. They may feel less isolated from the remainder of their communities. 3. They may develop relationships with families of typically developing children who can provide them with meaningful support.
Families of children without disabilities	1. They may develop relationships with families who have children with disabilities and thereby make a contribution to them and their communities. 2. They will have opportunities to teach their children about individual differences and about accepting individuals who are different.

Children with disabilities seem to benefit from inclusion, particularly in relation to social development and social skills.

Huffman, Brookfield, et al., n.d.). General early educators list the lack of adequate preparation and consultation as a barrier second only to high child-to-staff ratios (Wolery, Huffman, Brookfield, et al., n.d.), and special early educators express many concerns about their preparation (Buysse & Wesley 1993). Good reasons exist for preparing general early childhood educators in the content of early childhood special education and for preparing special early childhood educators in the content of general early education (Odom & McEvoy 1990). Despite barriers to changing university training programs (Wolery, Brookfield, et al. 1993), some authors have recommended joint training programs (Burton et al. 1992; Miller 1992), and some models for joint training programs exist (Stayton & Miller 1993). However, research identifying the effects of joint training and successful practices in providing it remains to be done.

Training barriers, however, cannot be addressed adequately only by changing college or university training programs; staff development and in-service training programs are needed (Kontos & File 1993; Wolery, Martin, et al. n.d.). Klein and Sheehan (1987) identified some key components of staff development programs, including "(a) individual staff development rather than large group presentations, (b) active involvement in programs as opposed to passive listening, (c) demonstration of strategies and skills on-site with immediate feedback from a supervisor, and (d) a planned, integrated staff development program rather than isolated and unrelated training sessions" (p. 19). Training with these components often results in desirable changes in the trainees' behavior (Venn & Wolery 1992).

Philosophic differences. Although philosophic differences exist *within* general and special early education, some differences exist *between* the two fields. These differences arise from the diverse origins of the two fields, from their different purposes, and from their unique traditions; however, commonalities also exist. Several authors have recently discussed this issue (for example, Carta et al. 1991; Norris 1991; J. Johnson & Johnson 1992; Mallory 1992; Wolery, Strain, & Bailey 1992; Carta et al. 1993; K. Johnson & Johnson 1993; Wolery & Bredekamp n.d.). The differences may lie in areas for which complete data are not available and may reflect differences in emphasis rather than fundamental disagreements (Bredekamp 1993; McLean & Odom 1993).

Related services. As discussed by Bruder (this volume, chapter 3), young children with disabilities and their families often require services from a variety

Young children with disabilities and their families often require services from a variety of disciplines.

of disciplines. Odom and McEvoy (1990) questioned whether adequate related services are available in early childhood programs. Recent findings suggest that many programs that include preschoolers with disabilities do not employ—even on a part-time or consultant basis—members from disciplines directly related to the children's disabilities (Wolery, Venn, Schroeder, et al. 1994; Wolery, Venn, Holcombe, et al., n.d.). Providing adequate related services requires a team of individuals who collaborate with one another and with families, rather than a collection of professionals from different disciplines (Bruder, this volume, chapter 3).

Statewide monitoring systems. Because each state educational agency (state department of education or state department of public instruction) is responsible for providing free, appropriate educational services to children 3 through 5 years of age with disabilities, they must have mechanisms for monitoring those services. As a result, a number of policy issues have arisen, such as who can legitimately provide such services, where those services can occur, and what controls the state educational agency has over those services (Odom & McEvoy 1990). On such points, considerable confusion exists. Strategies have been developed to help local programs work through policy questions and issues (Smith & Rose 1993).

Negative staff attitudes. Negative staff attitudes, if translated into staff behavior, can be a barrier to nearly any innovation or practice. Despite some instances in which staff members clearly are opposed to inclusion, it appears that general early childhood educators as a group do not perceive negative staff attitudes as a major barrier to inclusion (Wolery, Huffman, Brookfield, et al., n.d.). On the contrary, it appears that many general educators are receptive to preschool inclusion but that they face substantial barriers in implementing it (e.g., high child-to-staff ratios, lack of adequate training, lack of adequate consultation from special educators and related services).

Other barriers. Besides those barriers already identified, obstacles to inclusion of children with special needs include the emphasis on academic achievement (and de-emphasis of social outcomes) in the educational reform movement, competition for shrinking fiscal resources, lack of flexibility in teachers' contracts, and lack of clear policy directives (Strain & Smith 1993).

Parents of children with disabilities have consistently been at the forefront of the movement to secure the civil rights of individuals with disabilities.

Historical and policy foundations of early childhood services for children with disabilities

The history of early childhood special education is relatively short. The first major legislative action specifically targeting young children with disabilities occurred in 1968. The first professional journals devoted exclusively to early childhood special education started publication in the past 15 years (i.e., *Journal of Early Intervention* [formerly the *Journal of the Division for Early Childhood*] in 1979, *Topics in Early Childhood Special Education* in 1981, and *Infants and Young Children* in 1988). The field has undergone tremendous growth and change, which has been influenced by broad societal forces, by shifting theoretical perspectives, and by litigation and legislation—primarily at the federal level. Although all of these forces interact to form our history, they are discussed separately in the following paragraphs.

Societal forces

The extent and nature of nearly all kinds of human services are influenced by the major forces that characterize society at selected points in history. In the past century, three broad societal forces have influenced the current status of early childhood special education.

Society's views of children. Although most families have always valued their children, the manner in which society has viewed children has changed dramatically during this century (Broman 1982; Bailey & Wolery 1984). For example, prior to the Fair Labor Standards Act in 1938, child labor was common. The early and middle part of this century was marked by tremendous growth in attention to young children in general. For example, many preschool laboratories were established (e.g., Clinic of Child Development at Yale, Bank Street College, Merrill-Palmer Institute, and the Child Study Institute at Columbia Teachers College), professional organizations of early educators were established (for example, the National Association for Nursery Education [NANE] in 1926—renamed the National Association for the Education of Young Children in 1964), and professional journals appeared (such as *Childhood Education* in 1924 and *Young Children,* originally called the *NANE Bulletin,* in 1944). This interest in young children set the stage for interest in young children with disabilities.

Society's changing views toward civil rights. As has been well documented in the mass media, many groups of individuals (such as racial minorities, women, and individuals with disabilities) were not accorded full participation in society nor equal access to public and private accommodations and services during much of this century. Through persistent litigation in the courts and civil rights legislation at the federal level, society slowly began to acknowledge the claims of these groups to full

participation in society. Individuals with disabilities, including young children with disabilities, constituted one group that benefited from this shift in society's views from exclusion and separation to inclusion and integration. Much of this occurred as a result of previous civil rights legislation and the advocacy efforts of families who had children with disabilities (Cutler 1993). Parents of children with disabilities have consistently been at the forefront of the movement to secure the civil rights of individuals with disabilities.

Society's changing views toward education. The tradition of public education in the United States has been strong for two centuries; however, changes have occurred in society's perceptions of the power of education to improve the national status and improve the lot of selected groups of citizens. The push to improve America's world standing through education was exemplified by the increased attention to education after the Soviet Union's launching of Sputnik. The use of education to improve the lot of certain groups of citizens is seen in the funding of Head Start. This faith in education to effect change has influenced the determination of who is entitled to public education. Recently, education has been the primary means for improving the lives of individuals with disabilities, and this commitment is illustrated in the following statement by Bricker (1970):

I wish to affirm my belief in the importance of the nervous system and to indicate a conviction that a host of events can do damage to it and to its functioning. However, only the failure of a perfectly valid, perfectly reliable, perfectly efficient program of training will convince me that the identification of the deficit is sufficient reason to stop trying to educate the child. (p. 20)

Theoretical perspectives

The treatment by society of individuals with disabilities often is based on society's collective views about the human condition (Lane 1979). Two major shifts in our understanding of human development have substantially influenced the current status of early education for young children with disabilities.

Influence of the environment on children's development. In the early and middle part of this century, children's development was often viewed as being influenced primarily by biological forces (i.e., the maturational perspective, as espoused by Gesell and his colleagues; Gesell et al. 1940). Intelligence, as measured by IQ tests, was viewed as fixed and unchangeable. However, two books and the evidence on which they were based caused individuals to place considerably more faith in the influence of the environment: Hunt's (1961) *Intelligence and Experience* and Bloom's (1964) *Stability and Change in Human Characteristics.* Similarly, competing perspectives were proposed for understanding children's development and learning. For example, Hunt and others popularized Piaget's view of children, and his works were translated to English (e.g., Piaget 1951, 1952). Similarly, Bijou and Baer (1961, 1965, 1978) wrote a series of books that articulated the behavioral perspective of child development. Concomitantly, a number of behavioral investigators published reports indicating that changes in environmental factors—such as reinforcement and other events following behavior (Ayllon 1963; Wolf, Risley, & Mees 1964; Risley 1968), teaching strategies (Baer, Peterson, & Sherman 1967), and interactional patterns (Harris, Wolf, & Baer 1964)—could substantially improve the lives of individuals with disabilities. This led to attempts to merge Piagetian and behavioral perspectives (Bricker & Bricker 1974; Dunst 1981) and laid the foundation of early childhood special education.

Influence of the ecological perspective. In the 1970s the influence of the environment on children's learning and development was well recognized, but much of the supporting research was conducted in laboratories and artificial contexts. This led Bronfenbrenner (1977) to conclude that our knowledge of children's development was based on "the strange behavior of children in strange situations with strange adults for the briefest possible periods of time" (p. 513). His analysis focused a substantial amount of attention on the ecologies in which children live and function and led to viewing families as systems within other systems. As a result, major changes occurred in how intervention programs interact with families (Dunst 1985; Bailey & Simeonsson 1988b; Dunst, Trivette, & Deal 1988; Bailey, this volume, chapter 2), and more recently in how early education classrooms are designed (Haring 1992; Peck 1993). This perspective, coupled with an abundance of evidence from applied, ecologically based behavioral research (cf. Strain et al. 1992), forms the current foundation for early childhood special education.

Litigation and legislation

The changing societal and theoretical forces are reflected in existing litigation and legislation. Much of this change was initiated through legal suits by families of children with disabilities and from the advocacy work of professional organizations such as the Council for Exceptional Children, Association of Retarded Citizens, American Association on Mental Retardation, and Association for Persons with Severe Handicaps. Much of the litigation was designed to secure the civil rights of individuals with disabilities, and in large part it mirrors the struggles of other disenfranchised groups.

The Americans with Disabilities Act is major civil rights legislation extending beyond educational issues to require that individuals with disabilities have equal access and reasonable accommodations to public and private services.

A number of major laws have influenced the current status of early childhood special education. A list of some of these laws is provided below, and more complete descriptions of their history and content can be found in Smith 1988, Turnbull 1990, and Garwood and Sheehan 1989. The laws exist, in large part, because of the diligent advocacy work of parents of children with disabilities. Seven acts deserve special note.

P.L. 90-538 (1968) established the Handicapped Children's Early Education Program (currently known as the Early Education Program for Children with Disabilities). This law authorized funds for the development, evaluation, and dissemination of model programs for serving infants and young children with disabilities. Programs funded from this act have been and continue to be a major force in developing knowledge about services for young children with disabilities and their families. This law and the action that resulted from it can legitimately be called the birth of early childhood special education.

P.L. 93-644 (1974) amended previous Head Start legislation and required that 10% of the children served by Head Start programs must be children with disabilities. This act established the first nationwide mainstreaming program for preschool children. Recently, the regulations governing the provision of services to young children with disabilities in Head Start have been revised (*Federal Register* 1993).

P.L. 94-142 (1975), the Education for all Handicapped Children Act, established a national policy related to the education of children with disabilities from ages 3 to 21. The major impact of this law was for children 6 years of age and older; nonetheless, its provisions have been central in shaping current early childhood special education. For example, this law formalized use of the Individualized Education Program (IEP) (discussed in chapter 4).

P.L. 98-199 (1983) authorized funds to help states plan and develop early intervention services for children from birth to age 5.

P.L. 99-457 (1986) effectively mandated the provisions of P.L. 94-142 for preschoolers (children ages 3 through 5) and provided incentives to states to serve infants and toddlers who had disabilities or were at risk for having disabilities (Garwood & Sheehan 1989). The framework specified in this law for serving infants and toddlers acknowledges the ecological perspective of services and requires an Individualized Family Service Plan (IFSP) (discussed in this volume, chapter 2).

P.L. 101-576 (1990) reauthorized the Education for all Handicapped Children Act (PL 94-142) and renamed it the Individuals with Disabilities Education Act (IDEA); it also established two new categories: autism and traumatic brain injury.

All preschool children, regardless of their disability, are entitled to free, appropriate public education.

P.L. 101-336 (1990), known as the Americans with Disabilities Act, is major civil rights legislation that extends beyond educational issues. Specifically, it requires that individuals with disabilities have equal access and reasonable accommodations to public and private services, including equal access to enrollment in early childhood facilities (U.S. Department of Education 1993). This act prohibits discrimination against individuals with disabilities because of their disability.

These laws and their subsequent amendments influence how early education is provided to young children with disabilities. The laws contain several important features.

• All preschool children (ages 3 through 5), regardless of their disability, are entitled to free, appropriate public education. No child can be excluded because of her or his disabling condition.

• Each preschool child with a disability must have an IEP or, if younger than 3 years of age, an IFSP.

• The procedures used to identify, classify, and place children in special early education programs must be nondiscriminatory—that is, the tests and measures must be used for the purpose for which they are intended and administered by adequately trained individuals, and all measures and assessment practices must be

free of bias. Also, appropriate prior notification and consent must be obtained from parents prior to the administration of such measures for classification, planning, and placement.

• Children must be placed in the least restrictive appropriate environment. This means that services must be provided to the extent possible with nondisabled children.

• Parents have a right to question and challenge any actions taken by the school in relation to their child's education.

• Parents have the right to be involved in planning and developing the state and local educational policies and in developing and implementing their child's IEP or IFSP.

This body of legislation has been a major force in shaping the field of early childhood special education. Certainly it has helped to provide the framework for specifying the goals of early childhood services for children with disabilities.

Goals of early childhood services for children with disabilities

The goals of early childhood services for children with disabilities can be identified on at least two levels: the goals that are generally applicable to nearly all young children with disabilities, and the goals that are applicable to individual children. A

Table 2. **General Goals of Early Education with Young Children Who Have Disabilities**

---

1. To support families in achieving their own goals

2. To promote children's engagement, independence, and mastery

3. To promote children's development in key domains

4. To build and support children's social competence

5. To promote children's generalized use of skills

6. To provide and prepare children for normalized life experiences

7. To prevent the emergence of future problems or disabilities

---

Source: From D.B. Bailey & M. Wolery, *Teaching infants and preschoolers with disabilities*, 2nd ed. (Columbus, OH: Merrill, 1992), 35.

Children with developmental delays who do not interact and communicate well with peers often develop behavior problems to get their needs met, but this can be prevented.

list of goals that are applicable to most young children with disabilities is presented in table 2. The goals that are applicable to individual children are derived from assessments of their current developmental functioning, their current patterns of responding, their intervention histories, and the demands of the environments in which they spend time (see Wolery, this volume, chapter 4). In addition, consideration is given to the demands of future environments (such as those to which they will transition) (Salisbury & Vincent 1990; Rosenkoetter, Hains, & Fowler 1994; Atwater et al., this volume, chapter 8) and the priorities and concerns of their families (Bailey, this volume, chapter 2). These goals, of course, are established through ongoing assessment using multiple measurement strategies, such as formal and informal observation, testing, and interviews with other people who know the child (Bailey & Wolery 1989; Benner 1992). Also, the goals are established through collaboration of a team of individuals, including family members and members from a number of disciplines (Rainforth, York, & Macdonald 1992; Bruder, this volume, chapter 3). The individual goals constitute the IFSP or IEP. Two general comments are relevant.

• Children's individual goals take precedence over general goals. The general goals in table 2 are desirable for nearly all children, including children with disabilities. In practice, however, greater emphasis will be placed on some of these goals for individual children with disabilities. Assuming that the individual goals are established by a team of competent individuals, including the child's family, then these goals have priority over the general goals.

• Children's early education experiences should be designed to meet the individualized goals (Bailey & Wolery 1992; DEC Task Force on Recommended Practices 1993). Goals for young children with disabilities are necessary for at least four reasons (Wolery, Strain, & Bailey 1992).

First, many young children with disabilities are dependent upon others. For example, children who do not feed themselves must be fed by someone else. There are few justifications for allowing children to remain dependent upon others when they can learn the skills to be more independent.

Second, the disabilities of many young children prevent them from learning efficiently on their own. For example, children with major communication problems will have difficulties interacting with their peers, and children who do not play with toys will be unable to learn from play. Little justification can be proposed for allowing them to continue in states that interfere with their learning and success.

Third, young children with disabilities develop more slowly than do their chronological agemates. If they continue in the slow paths of development, they will become progressively further behind and less similar to their peers. Little justification can be proposed for allowing this to occur.

Fourth, the disabilities of young children with developmental delays often results in secondary handicaps. For example, children who do not interact and communicate well with their peers often develop behavior problems to get their needs met. Little justification exists for allowing children to acquire secondary handicaps that will interfere with their development and learning.

As a result, securing early childhood services for children who have disabilities requires a focus on identified outcomes. In addition, the law (IDEA) requires that individualized goals be written for each child with disabilities.

It is important to note, however, that establishing goals does not mean that the early childhood experiences are sterile, are devoid of child-directed learning, rely solely on teacher-directed instruction, or are inflexible (Carta et al. 1991, 1993; Wolery, Strain, & Bailey 1992). Rather, it simply means that the early childhood experiences are planned and implemented to promote learning and use of important skills and patterns of interacting. In some cases the individualized goals can be met through the usual activities and interaction patterns that exist in high-quality early childhood programs (Bailey & McWilliam 1990; Bredekamp & Rosegrant 1992; Bricker & Cripe 1992). In other cases, adjustments will be needed to ensure that individualized goals are obtained. These adjustments, however, are often embedded within the context of usual activities and routines (Wolery & Fleming 1993); this issue is discussed in chapter 7.

Summary

Young children with developmental delays and disabilities are, first, children, and then, children who happen to have special needs. Their special needs require special attention to their early childhood services; however, this does not mean that they must be educated in separate, segregated programs. Rather, many young children with developmental delays and disabilities are served appropriately in programs with their typically developing peers. Many defensible rationales exist for providing early childhood services to children with and without disabilities in the same program. Barriers to such services may exist, but in a relatively short time span, a great deal of knowledge has been acquired about how to provide inclusive services. State and federal legislation and regulations govern how those services should be provided, and individualized goals must be established for each child with developmental delays and disabilities.

INCLUDING CHILDREN WITH SPECIAL NEEDS

Chapter 2

Working with Families of Children with Special Needs

Donald B. Bailey, Jr.

T HE ASSUMPTION THAT EARLY CHILDHOOD PROGRAMS ought to support families of young
children is deeply rooted in the history of child care services. In fact, the care of
children by someone other than the child's parents was born out of a need to assist
families who, for reasons of personal choice, finances, or court mandates, needed help
with childrearing for at least part of the day. Thus it should come as no surprise to
professionals in the early childhood field that family support is an integral part of
services for young children with disabilities. However, the history of early intervention, the legal requirements for family-centered services, and philosophical movements within the early intervention field create special considerations for early
childhood personnel who serve young children with disabilities.

This chapter provides a brief overview of the history and current status of the family
support mission of early childhood and early intervention programs. The rationale
for supporting families is presented, and current legal requirements are described.
The current status of family-centered practices and factors that serve as barriers to
their implementation are discussed. Finally, common concerns expressed by families are
described, and approaches that might be helpful in response to each are discussed.

Note: The author expresses appreciation to Virginia Buysse, P.J. McWilliam, and Robin McWilliam for
their helpful comments and suggestions on previous drafts of this paper.

Over the years families have taken an increasingly prominent role in the context of early intervention.

Family-centered practices

Today's movement toward family-centered practices can be understood more fully by tracing its historical, philosophical, and legal foundations.

Historical foundations

Whereas child care programs were initially established to support families, early intervention programs began with a different premise. Family support has always been advocated, but early intervention is more directly rooted in a fundamental mission of helping children who have or are at risk for a disability. Head Start, for example, was established to help break the cycle of poverty by providing a stimulating program of care as well as health and nutrition services to preschool-age children living in low-income environments. Although some evidence has been offered in support of the benefits of Head Start for families (e.g., Parker, Piotrkowski, & Peay 1987), most Head Start evaluations have focused on the benefits for children (e.g., Haskins 1989). Likewise, early intervention programs were established to provide early and intensive stimulation to children who were born with a disabling condition. The assumption underlying both of these efforts is the notion that early intervention can serve both a facilitative and a preventive function by enhancing learning and reducing or preventing school failure or developmental delays.

Over the years, however, families have taken an increasingly prominent role in the context of early intervention. Drawing on diverse theories emphasizing the ecology in which young children with disabilities live (Bronfenbrenner 1979; Garbarino 1990; Sameroff & Fiese 1990), professionals began to realize that working with families is an essential aspect of early intervention. Factors contributing to this realization included parent dissatisfaction with traditional relationships with professionals, federal and state legislation, research findings, and shifting philosophical and theoretical assumptions. Assumptions about families and the role of parents in early intervention have varied considerably through the years, and a wide variety of activities have been provided under the rubric of family services. Most services, however, fall into one of two broad categories: educational enhancement or family support.

Educational enhancement. A number of services have focused on enhancing the educational properties of the home environment. Educational enhancement activities are based on the well-founded assumption that the home environment shapes the child's cognitive, language, social, motor, and adaptive development. Forces at work in this environment include parent–child interactions, opportunities for exploration

The primary goal of family support services is to assist families as they cope and adapt to the challenges of having a child with a disability.

and stimulation, peer and sibling relationships, and contextual influences provided by neighborhoods. Although the importance of the home environment makes good intuitive sense, considerable research has been devoted to testing this assumption and documenting specific aspects of the home environment that are most likely to enhance development. A recent longitudinal study, for example, found that the overall amount of parental behavior directed toward the child, as well as the quality of verbal content associated with parenting, varied as a function of the family's social and economic status (providing evidence in support of early intervention for children living in poverty) and were strongly related to changes in the child's IQ over a 27-month period (providing evidence for the important role of parent behavior) (Hart & Risley 1992).

Educational enhancement activities typically have focused on providing educational experiences for parents to improve parenting skills. For example, a number of programs have been developed to improve the quality of interactions between children and their families, focusing primarily on helping parents read their children's cues and respond in a developmentally supportive fashion. The goal of these programs has been to provide parents with a set of general skills related to the amount, type, and quality of interactions with their children, in the belief that these skills would facilitate overall development. Other programs have taught parents how to implement teacher-designed curriculum activities and behavior management strategies. In the case of children with special needs, parents have been taught to carry out specialist-designed therapeutic activities in the home. The goal of these efforts has been to ensure that educational or therapeutic experiences that are designed and implemented by specialists are also applied in the home environment, facilitating the development and use of targeted skills.

Family support. A second type of family activity provided by early intervention programs is designed to help support the family in its efforts to raise a child with a disability. The assumption underlying family support programs is that families of children with disabilities face special challenges, ranging from personal reflections on the meaning of life events (for example, Why did this happen to me?) to functional challenges of trying to learn about and gain access to a wide array of services for themselves and their children. Thus the primary goal of family support services is not to teach skills related to child development (although this could emerge in the context of family support activities) but to assist families as they cope and adapt to the challenges of having a child with a disability.

Support services have varied, depending upon the assumed needs of families. Parent support groups were especially popular in the 1970s and 1980s, providing a context in which parents facing similar circumstances could meet each other;

discuss challenges, expectations, successes, and failures; and provide mutual support (Wandersman 1982). Other support services include providing information for parents prior to interdisciplinary team meetings, case management or service coordination (to help families gain access to services), information hotlines, respite care, resource-and-referral programs, parent-to-parent networks, and transition-planning services.

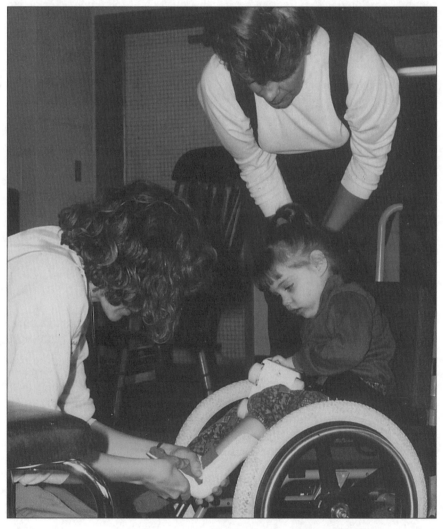

In practice, the educational enhancement and family support functions of early intervention often are not mutually exclusive. Teaching skills in handling behavior problems fulfills an educational as well as a family support goal. Likewise, a family support activity, such as a resource-and-referral program, may be needed because a family is having trouble locating a physical therapist who will teach them appropriate positioning or feeding techniques with their child. Regardless of the overlap, however, these functions (educational enhancement and family support) reflect the two primary reasons why early intervention programs have provided services for families of young children with disabilities.

Philosophical foundations

As early intervention programs have added family service components, professionals and parents have engaged in a wide-ranging series of discussions about the philosophical and value bases that underlie services to families. These discussions have led us to realize that family services are inevitably embedded within a framework of values and assumptions about families and a corresponding set of values and assumptions about professional roles and practices (Kaiser & Hemmeter 1989). With respect to assumptions about families, major changes have occurred over the past 20 years. Early assumptions essentially blamed parents for their child's disability. For example, at one time it was argued that autism was due to cold and insensitive maternal behavior; likewise, the problems of children living in poverty have often been ascribed to parental incompetence or lack of care. These early assumptions led to a view of early intervention as the vehicle by which inappropriate parenting styles could be altered on behalf of the child. Current assumptions, while recognizing cases of incompetent parenting, no longer "blame the victim." They focus more on individualizing services for families and on building early intervention efforts on the expressed needs and desires of family members.

A number of professionals and parents have written extensively in recent years about the role of families and early intervention programs (Dunst 1985; Bailey et al. 1986; Shelton, Jeppson, & Johnson 1987; Zigler & Black 1989). From these and other writings, several statements are offered here to summarize current thinking:

1. *Family support is a primary goal of any early intervention activity.* Thus any child care provider, early childhood teacher, special education teacher, therapist, physician, or any other professional working with young children with disabilities must recognize and assume this important professional role. Many people have suggested that this goal goes beyond helping families to "enabling and empowering" families so that they are not dependent upon professionals for decisions regarding the care and future of their children (Dunst, Trivette, & Deal 1988).

2. *Each family has its own culture and a unique set of strengths, values, skills, expectations, and service needs.* Although any professional who works with young children probably would agree with this statement, the implication—that services for families must be individualized—is not always carried through. In order for individualization to occur, professionals need to engage in an ongoing series of assessment activities (either formal or informal) that provide sufficient information to ensure that services are relevant to the individual family.

3. *Families have a right and a responsibility to play a primary role in determining the nature and extent of services provided for them and their child.* Historically, professionals have assumed a leadership role in determining the goals of intervention and the ways those goals would be achieved. However, research, legislation, and parent advocacy efforts have resulted in a significant role reversal in this respect. Early intervention is now viewed primarily as a consumer-driven enterprise, designed to be responsive to the needs and priorities of the consumers it serves— children with disabilities and their families. Two factors have contributed to this view. The first, brought about by family and advocacy movements, is a recognition of the basic rights of parents as consumers of services. The second factor, based on research and clinical experience, is a recognition of the likely failure of programs and services that are not consistent with family preferences and values (Bailey 1987).

4. *To provide appropriate services for families, a coordinated system of services must be in place.* One of the most frustrating aspects of being a parent of a child with a disability is the myriad of services, agencies, and professionals that are involved in one way or another in some aspect of early intervention services. A significant challenge for parents is to figure out who is in charge of what and how services can be obtained in the most efficient fashion possible. Current philosophy argues that it is the system's responsibility to make services easily accessible and understandable by families, and that professionals must work together in a cooperative fashion to provide appropriate and family-responsive services.

The following statement provides a concise summary of some major assumptions underlying family practices today:

Family-centered care is the focus of philosophy of care in which the pivotal role of the family is recognized and respected in the lives of children with special health needs. Within this philosophy is the idea that families should be supported in their natural care-giving and decision-making roles by building on their unique strengths as people and families. In this philosophy, patterns of living at home and in the community are promoted; parents and professionals are seen as

The legislation strongly encourages parent involvement in decision making and emphasizes that parents make the ultimate determination of goals and services to be provided.

equals in a partnership committed to the development of optimal quality in the delivery of all levels of health care. To achieve this, elements of family-centered care and community-based care must be carefully interwoven into a full and effective coordination of the care of all children with special health needs. (Brewer et al. 1989, p. 1055)

Not every professional would agree with all of the assumptions outlined above. Although the assumptions do reflect current thinking, they should certainly be tested and evaluated as professionals and parents experience new dimensions of services and new approaches to relationships between parents and professionals.

Legal and legislative foundations

A unique aspect of family services in early intervention is that in addition to having a strong philosophical support base, there are legal and legislative requirements with which all early childhood providers should be familiar. These requirements were originally established in 1986 in Public Law 99-457 and were updated and reinforced in the Individuals with Disabilities Education Act (IDEA 1990) and subsequent amendments.

Although early childhood care and education providers typically serve children along a full age continuum from birth to 8 years, it is important to realize that federal legislation (and, consequently, most state legislation) makes a major distinction between services for infants (children younger than 36 months of age) and services for preschoolers (children ages 36 months and older). In both age ranges the legislation strongly encourages parent involvement in decision making and emphasizes that parents make the ultimate determination of goals and services to be provided. However, the infant legislation goes much further in mandating that infant programs meet a number of specific requirements related to working with families. The five key provisions include the Individualized Family Service Plan; family involvement in child assessment; the assessment of family resources, priorities, and concerns; family involvement in team meetings and decision making; and the provision of service coordination.

Individualized Family Service Plan. Providers who have had experience working with young children with disabilities are probably familiar with the Individualized Education Program (IEP), a document describing children's skills and stating goals for services as well as strategies for achieving those goals. For children younger than 3, however, service providers must develop an Individualized Family Service Plan (IFSP), reflecting the increased emphasis on family services as an integral part of early intervention. The IFSP must include the following:

Programs need to have personnel who are trained in appropriate family assessment strategies.

1. a description of the child's present level of development in physical, cognitive, communication, socioemotional, and adaptive behavior;

2. a description of the family's resources, priorities, and concerns related to enhancing the development of the child;

3. major outcomes, criteria, procedures, and timelines for child and family goals;

4. a description of early intervention services necessary to meet child and family needs;

5. dates, intensity, and duration of services;

6. the name of a service coordinator who will help families gain access to needed services;

7. a transition plan to assist the child and her family in their move from infant and toddler services to preschool services; and

8. a description of the natural environments (e.g., homes, child care centers) in which early intervention services will be provided.

These requirements reflect a growing commitment to family-centered early intervention services in that they emphasize the importance of an individualized set of services to families based on each family's resources, priorities, and concerns. In doing so, they force professionals to rethink their roles and to include families as partners in the planning process.

Child assessment. The child assessment process must be comprehensive and multidisciplinary. Informed clinical opinion is explicitly acknowledged as an important source of information about children, reinforcing the information that parents and providers can bring to the assessment context. Recent amendments to the legislation specify that assessments are to be family directed, essentially stating that professional assessments must be responsive to the kind of information parents want from the assessment process. Issues related to team functioning and child assessment are described in chapters 3 and 4.

Family assessment. Through the IFSP, the federal legislation also requires that programs be able to assess the resources, priorities, and concerns of families. Although this process is voluntary on the part of families, it means that programs need to have personnel who are trained in appropriate family assessment strategies. Regulations state that such information must be obtained, at least in part, through a personal interview with key family members and that any reports of these assessments must include the family's own description of its resources, priorities, and concerns.

Team meetings. A team meeting must be held to plan the IFSP. With respect to family involvement, parents are viewed as primary team members, and they may invite other family members or an advocate to attend. The meetings must be held at times and settings convenient to the family and must be conducted in the family's native language.

Service coordination. Key to the effectiveness of an early intervention program is the provision of a service coordinator to help families and children receive all services they want and for which they are eligible, and appropriate procedures must be followed in making decisions about eligibility and services. Included in the service coordinator's responsibilities are coordinating assessments, facilitating the IFSP process, identifying service providers, monitoring service delivery, identifying advocacy services, coordinating with health providers, and facilitating the development of a transition plan.

The federal and state requirements emphasize the importance of families in the context of early intervention. Although the requirements place extra constraints on programs and sometimes seem to formalize the process in ways that we would not ordinarily choose, they establish a framework within which individualized services can be provided. Also, although these regulations are required only for children younger than 36 months of age, these practices likely are also important for older children.

Status and implementation of family-centered practices

To what extent are family-centered practices currently evident in early intervention programs? One could easily argue that early intervention programs already recognize the important roles that families play and that services are provided in accordance with this assumption. However, substantial data indicate that current practices fall short of expectations for family-centered services. Studies in early intervention settings, for example, have found that professionals focus their work primarily on children rather than on families (Mahoney, O'Sullivan, & Fors 1989; Mahoney & O'Sullivan 1990). In a survey designed to describe current practices in working with families, professionals reported only a moderate focus on families and perceived a significant discrepancy between typical and ideal practices with families (Bailey, Buysse, Edmonson, & Smith 1992). For example, when describing current practices with respect to parent participation in team meetings and decisions about child goals and services, professionals reported that while parents often are

Thorough preparation in working with families is infrequent for professionals in education, early childhood, and health.

encouraged to make suggestions about goals and services for their children, professionals still do most of the planning and decision making. Professionals reported that, ideally, parents and professionals should work together to form an intervention plan. Similar findings have emerged in research with nurses who work with chronically ill children in hospital settings. For example, Brown and Ritchie (1990) found that while nurses saw family-centered care as important, they often were not able to adhere to family-centered principles and spent most of their time working with and making decisions about sick children.

Why has the implementation of a family-centered approach been so difficult? Several salient factors have emerged in the research. Perhaps the most obvious factor is lack of training. Most education, early childhood, and allied health professionals have been well prepared to work with children. However, thorough preparation in working with families is less frequent for professionals in those disciplines. Bailey, Simeonsson, and colleagues (1990) found that the typical student in special education, physical therapy, occupational therapy, and speech and language pathology received only a few clock hours of training in working with families. Also, Mahoney and colleagues (Mahoney, O'Sullivan, & Fors 1989; Mahoney & O'Sullivan 1990) reported that service providers were more likely to rely on intuition than on formal training when trying to identify strategies for working with families. Furthermore, Bailey and colleagues (1991) found that early intervention professionals rated their skills in working with families significantly lower than they rated their skills in working with children. Thus it appears essential for college and university programs to begin including a stronger emphasis on family support in their training programs.

Interestingly, Bailey, Buysse, Edmondson, and Smith (1992) found that professionals were more likely to attribute the lack of family-centered services to factors other than inadequate university training. Lack of support and resources from the system was identified as a primary barrier, suggesting that administrative supports and resources (such as time and adequate staff) must be in place before professionals can adequately work with families. Another reason given by professionals for a limited family focus had to do with the families themselves. Professionals indicated that many families do not have the skills needed to participate as full team members and decision makers. Professionals also believed that many families were not interested in family services, preferring professionals to work only with the children instead. This finding may have revealed a deeply rooted concern among professionals that family-centered practices will result in detrimental effects on children, a conclusion supported by Brown and Ritchie's (1990) finding that nurses lacked trust in the ability of many families to care for their children or to make appropriate decisions about treatment options and Rushton's (1990) observation that professionals may view family-centered care as a threat to their authority. Bailey and

State and local agencies will need to plan inservice and continuing education activities designed to facilitate the movement toward family-centered services.

colleagues (1991) found that while professionals valued family roles, they had major concerns about how the family-centered model would be implemented and whether it would have negative consequences for children in need of educational and therapeutic services.

These factors suggest that the full implementation of family-centered practices in early childhood and early intervention programs is likely to be an extended and complex process. Community colleges, universities, and other institutions of higher learning must include more training and practical experiences so that graduates will have at least a basic set of competencies in working with families. This additional focus should also ensure that family support is recognized by all graduates as a key part of their professional identity, regardless of their specific discipline.

Although preservice training is important, the majority of individuals who will be working with young children over the next decade are already employed in the field. State and local agencies will need to plan inservice and continuing education activities designed to facilitate the movement toward family-centered services. The research described previously, however, indicates that this movement is complicated by an array of factors, including systems barriers, professional skills, and professionals' perceptions of their role and how it compares with appropriate roles for families. Ultimately, programs will need to recognize the complex systems involved in supporting children and families and engage in a range of ongoing activities that will provide and support family-centered services (Winton 1990). For example, Bailey, McWilliam, and colleagues (1992) have developed a model for change that involves an intensive internal analysis of current practices, followed by systematic identification of areas that need change and the establishment of concrete goals. The process includes all relevant team members as well as parents of children served by the team, all of whom are engaged in this process of reflection, analysis, and goal setting. Research and experiences in applying the model indicate that it can be a powerful mechanism for promoting change (Winton et al. 1992) and that involving parents in this process is key to its success (Bailey, Buysse, Smith, & Elam 1992).

Family resources, priorities, and concerns

To provide better support services for families of children with disabilities, early education and child care providers presumably need to understand the nature of needs most commonly experienced by these families. Recognition that it is important to identify common family concerns has led to many investigations of various aspects of family functioning, and a number of models of family support have been suggested in the literature.

A professional cannot make an "objective" assessment of family needs without considering how the family members view their needs.

All families have certain basic needs that must be fulfilled and functions that must be accomplished. Turnbull and colleagues (1984), for example, describe seven functions that must be achieved by every family: economic well-being, daily care, recreation, socialization, affection, self-definition, and educational/vocational preparation. Dunst (1990) argues that social support for families comprises multiple components, including relational support (social relationships), structural support (proximity of social networks), constitutional support (resources basic for health and well-being), and functional support (concrete aid and assistance). He also suggests that the extent to which a family member is satisfied with his or her support system is essential to understanding the effects of those supports.

Although many models of needs and resources have been suggested, almost all models acknowledge three related facts. *First,* families are likely to vary considerably in needs, resources, and priorities. *Second,* the family's perspective on needs, resources, and priorities is an essential component of any model. A professional cannot make an "objective" assessment of family needs without considering how the family members view their needs. Correspondingly, a resource is likely to be helpful only if the person receiving the aid *perceives* it to be helpful. *Finally,* all families have resources and strengths; thus any attempt to assess needs should be accompanied by a corresponding analysis of family resources.

The importance of an individualized understanding of families was emphasized in Public Law 99-457 by the requirement for a statement of family needs and strengths in the Individualized Family Service Plan. This requirement reflects the assumption that families vary with respect to needs and thus an individualized appraisal of needs is essential. The 1991 amendments (P.L. 102-119) changed this requirement to a statement of family resources, priorities, and concerns. Although the new wording maintains the emphasis on individualization, it reflects a concern among families of young children with disabilities that they not be viewed as "needy" but rather as having both resources and concerns. These discussions led us to develop definitions of family assessment and family needs to apply specifically in the context of early intervention:

Family assessment: the ongoing and interactive process by which professionals gather information in order to determine family priorities for goals and services

Family need: a family's expressed desire for services to be obtained or outcomes to be achieved

Family strength: the family's perception of resources that are at its disposal that could be used to meet family needs (Bailey 1991, p. 27)

These definitions suggest that a primary role of professionals is to seek to understand how families view their child and what kinds of services they would like from early childhood programs. The next logical question then concerns the outcomes likely to result from this process. What are the needs that families express

Parents of young children with disabilities are naturally concerned about what the future will be like for their child.

if asked to identify the kinds of services they would like from professionals? Although the answer will obviously be different for each family, research and clinical experience suggest several clusters that are likely to emerge as areas in which early childhood professionals need to be prepared to provide supportive services.

Information needs. One of the most frequent complaints of families is the lack of access to information about a variety of topics. Recent studies have identified several types of information most likely to be wanted by families (Bailey & Simeonsson 1988a; Bailey, Blasco, & Simeonsson 1992; Cooper & Allred 1992). In all three of these studies, the most frequently expressed need was for information about the availability of future services for their child. Parents of young children with disabilities are naturally concerned about what the future will be like for their child. Will she live independently? Will he have friends and be accepted by others? Will the schools provide the kind of services that she needs to be successful? Will he ever be able to marry and have a family? Who will care for her when we are too old to do so? Because such questions often are at the forefront of parental concerns, early childhood professionals should have a thorough working knowledge of services likely to be available in the near future. These expressed concerns also point to the importance of the transition from early intervention and preschool programs into public school programs and the special need for support at this time (see Atwater et al., this volume, chapter 8).

Educational enhancement activities are designed to improve the home as a learning environment.

Other frequently expressed information needs identified in the above-mentioned studies include needs for information about the child's disability, reading material about other families who have children with similar disabilities, and information about how to teach their child. All three of these studies found differences between needs expressed by mothers and those expressed by fathers. For example, fathers are more likely to want information about current services, presumably because mothers have traditionally been more involved with their child's educational planning and therefore are better informed about services (e.g., Bristol, Gallagher, & Schopler 1988). Collectively these findings suggest that parents view professionals as an important source for a wide range of information. This perception means that professionals must be available for information needs as they arise and either have this information or be able to gain access to it. This can be a challenge because parents want information that ranges from specific teaching techniques to broad-based community services. However, supplying this information is an important professional function. A particularly frustrating experience for families is trying to figure out who has the information they want.

It is unreasonable to assume that most early childhood educators will be able to provide families with all of the information they need; therefore, teachers must be aware of what they know and what they do not know. Lack of information on a given topic should not be viewed as professional incompetence but as an opportunity to assist families in finding a source that has the information. On the other hand, dispensing inaccurate information or not responding to families' information needs *is* unprofessional.

Parent training or education. Parents often want information about how to teach their child or manage his behavior. As described earlier in this chapter, educational enhancement activities are designed to improve the home as a learning environment. Educational enhancement activities typically focus on parents' behaviors in interacting with their children. For example, a parent could be taught to implement a teacher-designed curriculum activity at home, to conduct some therapeutic routines, or to change a particular style of interacting with her child. These activities are based on three primary assumptions. The first is that the home is a critical environment for facilitating development, an assumption that is readily justified.

The second assumption is that the extent to which families are involved in the education of their children may have a direct relationship to the effectiveness of intervention for children. Support for this relationship was provided recently in a study of early intervention with low-birthweight infants, in which researchers found that children's IQ scores at the end of treatment were strongly correlated with family involvement (Ramey et al. 1992).

The third assumption is that some parents may not adequately facilitate their child's development. Although this assumption is warranted in some cases, persons working with young children must recognize the negative consequences of communicating a message like this to parents. Parenting is a fundamental behavior that varies considerably across cultures and generations. Most parents perceive themselves to be the people who know their child the best. Educational enhancement activities can easily communicate the message that the professional does not perceive the parent to be a competent caregiver. Thus the first major guideline in providing and conducting educational enhancement activities is whenever possible, let those activities evolve from expressions of need or concern by parents rather than from an evaluation or judgment made by the professional. Of course, if the parent is virtually ignoring the child or otherwise acting in a way that is likely to harm the child, the professional has an obligation to advocate for the child's well-being.

Reviews of research on the effectiveness of involving parents as teachers have reached mixed conclusions. For example, Heinicke and colleagues (1988) reviewed 20 high-quality research studies and reported that 75% of them showed a successful outcome. On the other hand, White and colleagues (1992) reviewed 31 studies and concluded that "these studies do not provide compelling evidence that the inclusion in an early intervention program of this particular type of parent involvement results in benefits for participating children" (p. 110). The inconsistency in these findings suggests the need to consider the intent of educational enhancement activities and the way in which these activities are conducted. The findings also point out the challenges inherent in evaluating the effects of parent involvement.

Two studies are presented here as examples of the challenges. In the first study the authors taught mothers of preschool children with developmental delays to be more responsive and developmentally appropriate when interacting with their children (Tannock, Girolametto, & Siegel 1992). Nine group sessions and three home visits focused on turn taking, language modeling, and following the child's lead in conversations. The authors found that mothers who participated in the program used more language-modeling strategies and increased the number of conversations with their children. They were also more responsive to their children. However, although their children took more vocal turns, they did not show any improvements in communicative and linguistic abilities, as measured by developmental assessments.

In the second study, mothers of infants with developmental disabilities participated in six coaching sessions designed to provide feedback about overstimulation of children (Seifer, Clark, & Sameroff 1991). The mothers who received the coaching sessions were more responsive to their children and decreased the level of stimulation provided, as compared with mothers who did not participate in the coaching sessions. Also, the infants reduced their levels of fussiness and made greater gains on standardized developmental measures over a 10-month period.

Results of these and other studies (e.g., Alpert & Kaiser 1992) demonstrate that educational enhancement programs can influence parents' behavior and sometimes have demonstrable positive effects on children. Of critical importance is that families perceive the program to be something they need and that it will be useful for them. In addition, effective programs are likely to be individualized for each family, be provided at times and settings that are convenient and comfortable for families, include many practical examples and lots of opportunities for practice, and be flexible enough that parents can implement their program in ways that make sense to them. Also, professionals should make sure that educational enhancement activities are consistent with the values and interactional styles of the culture of each child served (Ogbu 1987; Lynch & Hanson 1992).

Family and social support. A third type of need families often express is for family and social support, or what Dunst (1990) describes as relational and structural support. Families receive social support from a variety of sources. Sometimes it comes from within the nuclear or extended family—from spouse, parents, in-laws, or siblings. Sometimes social support is provided by friends and neighbors or by closely affiliated groups, such as fellow members of churches or synagogues. Support can also be obtained through parents of other children with disabilities, from early childhood professionals who are good at listening and responding to concerns, or from specialists such as social workers, psychologists, family therapists, or psychiatrists. Research on social support indicates four important findings.

1. Different individuals prefer and seek out different forms of support. For example, it appears that mothers are much more likely to want opportunities to meet and interact with other families of children with disabilities than are fathers (Bailey, Blasco, & Simeonsson 1992; Cooper & Allred 1992).

2. When given a choice, most parents prefer informal rather than formal support systems. For example, parents would more likely look to friends, neighbors, family members, or acquaintances for child care help than they would a respite care agency.

3. A traditional support system that existed before the birth of a child with a disability can be a great help but also a source of frustration. For example, many parents, especially mothers, report that explaining their child's disability to friends, neighbors, and siblings can be very difficult for them.

Professionals should realize that almost every interaction they have with a parent or other family member will be evaluated by that family member on a continuum of how supportive it was.

4. Generally speaking, it is not the size of the support network that is so important but rather its quality. In other words, one good friend or a supportive spouse may be more important than a whole network of professionals and support groups.

How should professionals provide social support for families? This is a challenging question because most parents of children with disabilities—like most of us—do not turn to professionals for social support. We prefer to draw support from people we know, such as friends, a spouse, or family members. Two suggestions, however, may be useful. First, professionals should realize that almost every interaction they have with a parent or other family member will be evaluated by that family member on a continuum of how supportive it was. The best way to be supportive is to listen when parents talk and respond in a supportive and positive fashion. Many parents have complained that professionals are "just not listening" to what they have to say. Only the professional who has developed good listening skills and the ability to show that she or he has heard what parents say—through reflecting feelings and content as well as by asking supportive questions—is likely to be viewed as a helpful support (Winton & Bailey 1993). Professionals also should develop an awareness of available support services and, for those parents who want it, be prepared to offer information about parent support groups or professionals who could help provide specialized counseling.

Child care. A fourth need expressed by many families of children with disabilities is for an appropriate child care setting, which provides an important opportunity for early childhood professionals to support families. Families of children with disabilities often have difficulty finding a child care center or family child care home that is willing to accept their child. Because this problem can be a source of tremendous stress and frustration, child care professionals—including resource-and-referral agency personnel—can be a key resource in helping families find appropriate child care settings.

Research on family preferences indicates that making the decision about an early childhood setting is also stressful because families often are placed in a position of choosing between a self-contained program (one that serves only children with disabilities), with specially trained staff, and a regular child care setting (one that primarily serves normally developing children), with child care professionals who usually do not have extensive training in working with children with disabilities (Winton 1986; Bailey & Winton 1987). As parents and professionals evaluate this decision, at least three factors should be considered. First, the Individuals with

Disabilities Education Act states that children with disabilities must be placed in the most natural, or "least restrictive," environment possible. Second, the Americans with Disabilities Act requires that all public accommodations, including early childhood programs and family child care homes, must provide access to persons with disabilities (Surr 1992). Third, recent research indicates that integration, or mainstreaming, has clear benefits for children with disabilities (Buysse & Bailey 1993) as well as for the typically developing children who are being served in the setting (Peck, Carlson, & Helmstetter 1992).

Thus it is likely that families will want to spend considerable time evaluating an early childhood setting to see if it is appropriate for their child. An important family support activity is for early childhood professionals to demonstrate a willingness to serve children with disabilities and to help families as they make this decision. Families want assurances that early childhood professionals will work with them to make the necessary accommodations to ensure that the placement is successful. These accommodations may include providers' willingness to learn new techniques or procedures to ensure that the child with a disability receives safe and developmentally appropriate child care.

Community and financial services. A fifth category of needs expressed by parents relates to the community services that are available for families. For many families served by early intervention programs, financial needs are paramount; families may want assistance in obtaining basic resources, such as housing, food, clothing, transportation, or employment. If the family has a child with a special physical or medical disability, they may face considerable expense in securing specialized toys or equipment such as wheelchairs, braces, special glasses, or hearing aids. Other families may have difficulty gaining access to community resources that would be more readily available if their child did not have a disability. For example, finding an appropriate dentist can be a challenge when a child has a severe behavior disorder. A child with serious medical needs might limit a family's ability to attend church or enjoy a night out together.

Needs such as these are often challenging for professionals as well as parents. What is the appropriate role for early childhood professionals, who may not have the training or experience needed to help families meet community and financial needs? One area of support to be aware of is the service coordinator. Federal legislation for infants and toddlers requires that each family have a service coordinator available to assist them with a variety of concerns. The service coordinator's primary functions are to (1) coordinate the assessment and individualized planning activities needed to establish an Individualized Family Service Plan or an Individualized Education Plan, (2) help families gain access to the services to which they are entitled, and (3) be familiar with the various possibilities for payment for services and help families gain access to financial support when needed. Early childhood professionals should also be aware of the major service organizations in the communities in which families live. Key resources to know about include

• respite care agencies (which provide extended child care services—that may be overnight and could last several days—for families who need assistance),

• home health agencies (which provide in-home nursing and therapeutic services for children with disabilities),

Although most early childhood professionals should not be expected to be counselors, they should realize that families will often turn to them to discuss needs and concerns.

• parent groups (such as The ARC [formerly the Association for Retarded Citizens] and many other programs),

• special after-school or community programs designed to include young children with disabilities (offered through organizations such as public schools, city parks and recreation departments, and YMCAs), and

• key individuals in social services.

Finally, although most early childhood professionals should not be expected to be counselors, they should realize that families will often turn to them to discuss needs and concerns. In addition to providing information about existing services, professionals should also take the time to listen and respond to families in an appropriate fashion. Winton and Bailey (1993) describe a model of communicating with families, in which a major goal is for professionals to respond in ways that help families identify resources for themselves rather than relying exclusively on professional support. This approach is based on the assumption that early intervention programs should seek to "enable and empower" families to serve as advocates for themselves (Dunst, Trivette, & Deal 1988). For example, when parents express the need for overnight care for their child, rather than immediately suggesting an agency that could help, the professional may want to discuss the resources they have tried thus far and prompt them to explore options for using friends, neighbors, or other family members as resources. Because many families are not willing to leave their child with a stranger, immediately suggesting to them an agency that provides respite services may be viewed as an inappropriate suggestion. By taking the time to explore needs more thoroughly and responding in a facilitative fashion, professionals can help families see that they have the resources within themselves to address many of their concerns, thus the professional ultimately may build a more trusting and collaborative relationship between families and professionals.

Summary

As professionals continue to examine their roles and relationships with families, they will need to develop programs and services that respond to family resources, priorities, and concerns. Conducting research on the effectiveness of family support programs is a challenging task. One of the biggest challenges is identifying the outcomes that would be expected or hoped for as a result of family support activities. Broad goals could be established, such as improving parent teaching skills, reducing stress in families, or helping families become independent decision makers. But the

Family support programs must be individualized and based on parents' preferences for services.

ways in which these outcomes could be assessed are not readily agreed upon. Furthermore, because of the individualized nature of family support programs, a given set of outcomes may be appropriate for some families and inappropriate for others. Thus a variety of sources of information—such as research, accumulated experiences, and parent perceptions and behavior—must be used to make informed decisions about effective practices.

A major message that emerges from research and practice, as well as from the urging of parents, is that family support programs must be individualized and based on parents' preferences for services. This principle is reflected in federal legislation emphasizing the role of parents as decision makers. Research studies also provide evidence in support of family choices. Bailey and Blasco (1990), for example, asked parents to evaluate the usefulness of a survey of family needs and to describe how they would prefer that it be used in the context of early intervention. Most parents thought that the survey would be helpful but suggested that it only be offered as an opportunity that parents could choose to take advantage of if they wanted to do so. Parents also indicated that it was important to give family members options regarding how to share concerns because some would prefer a written survey whereas others might prefer conveying concerns through a conversation. Affleck and colleagues (1989) found that a support program for mothers whose children were leaving the neonatal intensive care unit was helpful only for mothers who thought they needed it. In fact, mothers who said they did not need the support program but got it anyway appeared to suffer some adverse consequences of the program, including a reduced feeling of competence and lowered feelings of control.

These studies suggest that intervention efforts must be responsive to parent priorities with respect to how information is gathered as well as whether and how services are provided. The way that decision making is approached is likely to have an impact on families, reinforcing or reducing their opinions of themselves as competent decision makers, depending upon professional attitudes and behaviors.

In conclusion, we offer the following suggestions for early childhood programs as tentative guidelines for family-centered practices:

1. A family focus should be central to the philosophy and practice of any program serving young children with disabilities. Accordingly, services to families should be a priority for program focus and activities.

2. Parents and professionals should collaborate in developing a program philosophy and a set of program practices that work for both parties. By involving families—who ultimately are the consumers of early childhood services—in the process of establishing policies and procedures, the chances of establishing a program that responds to family needs and priorities are enhanced.

3. Professionals should provide support and be responsive to parents who want to play major roles in decision making about child assessment activities, child services, and family supports. Families will be responsible for or want to support their children for the rest of their lives. One of the most important things we can do as service providers is to help families believe that they can cope with challenges and be successful in gaining needed resources and services.

4. Programs should have the means to gather information about the resources, priorities, and concerns of family members and should use that information to plan and provide individualized family services. Such information is essential if services are to meet the wide variety of needs likely to be expressed by families.

5. Programs should integrate services with other agencies and programs and work together to help ensure that families receive a coordinated set of easily accessible services. Parents frequently express frustration at the fragmentation of services and the lack of communication across agencies and programs. Collaboration can be difficult, but ultimately it will benefit the families being served as well as the programs engaged in service provision. (See chapter 3 for an in-depth discussion of collaboration.)

Chapter 3

Working with Members of Other Disciplines: Collaboration for Success

Mary Beth Bruder

KARA ATTENDS A HEAD START PROGRAM five mornings a week. In October Kara was referred to the special needs coordinator of the local Head Start program because of her behavior problems. Her parents agreed to have her tested by the local school district special education team. The special education team determined that Kara was not eligible for their preschool services but that she could receive speech and language services because of her articulation problems. The speech pathologist from the school district began to see Kara three mornings a week in a small room set aside for speech therapy at the Head Start program. The Head Start teacher did not know what went on in the speech room but hoped it was helping Kara's speech. Unfortunately, though, Kara's behavior in class kept getting worse, so the Head Start director asked the local mental health center to send a psychologist to the classroom to observe Kara. The psychologist asked the classroom teacher to provide a lot of data and suggested that she change her style of teaching. The teacher tried at first, but Kara's behavior did not improve, and the whole classroom routine was disrupted. The psychologist said that he could come to the classroom two hours a week to implement a behavior modification program, but he did not know if it would help. The Head Start staff (especially the teacher) now feel that Kara should be removed from Head Start and sent to a special education school because neither of the specialists have been able to help her. If the special education school will not take her, she will just have to stay at home.

Joley is 4 years old and has Down Syndrome. She has two younger brothers. Her mom, Mary, is single and works two jobs. Joley attends the Busy Bee Child Care Center for a total of seven hours a day. Her mom drops her off at 7:30 for breakfast. Joley spends the rest of the morning at the child care center. She is picked up by a bus at 11:30 to go to a preschool special education center (40 minutes away), where she attends a class every afternoon and receives special education and related services that include speech, occupational, and physical therapy. She returns to the child care center every day at 3:00 p.m. and stays until 6:00 p.m., when her grandmother picks her up. Joley does very well at the child care program, but the teachers think they should be doing more with her. They wish they knew what happened during the special education class and what all the special staff did to her. They also worry about all the transitions Joley has to make in one day. Joley's mother has also expressed concern about all the traveling her daughter has to do between the two programs.

When young children with disabilities are included in early childhood programs with children without disabilities, special education staff and early childhood staff share many of the same concerns. These concerns usually revolve around the appropriateness of the program for all of the enrolled children but most particularly for the children with disabilities. For such programs to be effective, early childhood providers and early childhood special educators clearly must work together with other professionals to plan, implement, and evaluate a program of supports and services.

The purpose of this chapter is to describe the types of professionals from various disciplines who traditionally have been involved with the provision of services to young children with disabilities; to describe strategies that facilitate collaboration with professionals across disciplines; and to provide recommendations for early childhood educators to use when implementing a service delivery model for children with disabilities that includes collaboration with professionals from other disciplines.

Professionals involved in the delivery of services to young children with disabilities

Special education legislation (the Individuals with Disabilities Education Act—IDEA) mandates a free and appropriate public education that includes special education and related services for all children (ages 3 to 21) with disabilities (or developmental delay, for children of preschool age). Special education is defined as "specially designed instruction, at no cost to the parent or guardians, to meet the unique needs of the child with a disability" (IDEA of 1990, Sec. 1401 [a] [16]) in accordance with an Individualized Education Plan (IEP). This instruction may be conducted in the classroom, in the home, in hospitals and institutions, and in other settings (such as community early childhood programs). As used in IDEA (1990), related services are defined as

transportation and such developmental, corrective, and other supportive services as required to assist a child with a disability to benefit from special education, including speech pathology and audiology, psychological services, physical and occupational therapy, recreation, including therapeutic recreation, early identification and assessment of disabilities in children, counseling services, including rehabilitative counseling, and medical services for diagnostic or evaluation purposes. The term also includes school health services, social work services in schools, and parent counseling and training. (Sec. 1401 [a] [17])

In addition, states must ensure that assistive technology devices or services, or both, are made available to a child with a disability if required as a part of the child's special education, related services, or supplementary aids and services (the terms used in this definition are defined on pp. 68–70). The legislation further states that the list of services is not exhaustive and that related services may include other "developmental, corrective, or supportive services as may be required to assist a child with a disability to benefit from special education" (IDEA of 1990, Sec. 1401 [a] [16]). Children participating in early intervention services (ages birth through 2) under Part H of IDEA are also eligible for a variety of services that are similar to the ones provided to preschool-age children.

Special education legislation (IDEA 1990) also defines who may provide special education and related services by requiring each state to ensure that such services are provided by "qualified personnel." A *qualified* person has been defined as a person who meets state-approved or recognized certification, licensing, registration, or other comparable requirements that apply to the area in which he or she is providing special education or related services. These requirements must be based on the highest state requirements applicable to the profession or discipline in which a person is providing special education or related services. Additionally, legislative regulations permit each state to determine specific occupational categories required to provide special education and related services and to revise or expand these categories as needed. These professions or disciplines need not be limited to traditional occupational categories. However, each state is required to provide information annually to the federal government on the availability of special education and related-service personnel, including audiologists; counselors; diagnostic and evaluation personnel; home-hospital teachers; interpreters for children with hearing impairments, including deafness; occupational therapists; physical education teachers; physical therapists; psychologists; teacher aides; recreation and therapeutic recreation specialists; vocational education teachers; work-study coor-

Young children with disabilities require the combined expertise of a number of professionals providing special education and related services.

dinators; and other instructional and noninstructional staff, such as administrators and supervisors.

Although there is no doubt that young children with disabilities require the combined expertise of a number of professionals providing special education and related services, the coordination of people and services is frequently overwhelming. For example, personnel having medical, therapeutic, educational/developmental, and social service expertise traditionally have been involved in the provision of services to young children with disabilities and their families. Each of these professionals may represent a different discipline and a different philosophical model of service delivery. In fact, each discipline has it own training sequence (some require undergraduate degrees, and others require graduate degrees) and licensing and/or certification requirements, most of which do not require specialization to work with young children (and their families) in particular. They tend to use different treatment modalities (e.g., occupational therapists may focus on sensori-integration techniques, and physical therapists may focus on functional movements using a neurodevelopmental approach). In addition, many disciplines have their own professional organization, and, unlike organizations focused on a limited age range (e.g., NAEYC), these organizations encompass the needs of people of all ages. Nonetheless, as services for young children with disabilities continue to grow, so, too, does the need for professionals in these disciplines.

An overview of the professional disciplines most typically involved in providing services for young children with disabilities and their families is presented in table 1. Descriptions of these disciplines include the primary mission and the major roles performed by professionals within the discipline. This information was developed by Bailey (1989c), with input from a representative group of members from each of the disciplines listed. As can be seen, some overlap exists in the missions and roles of the various disciplines included on table 1. In practice, the extent of this overlap may depend on the individual representing the discipline, as her clinical skills and belief system may have been further defined by her training program and work experiences.

As previously stated, the various professionals involved in providing special education and related services receive training specific to their discipline, and this training can affect the manner in which these services are provided. For example, some disciplines that provide related services have evolved from a medical orientation (e.g., therapies), and staff from these disciplines may be uncomfortable in early education classroom settings. These professionals may be used to providing hands-on direct services to a child in an isolated room rather than integrating the interventions into the child's educational setting. They may have never provided services to a child within a group situation (e.g., in an early childhood class), and as a result, they may not feel competent or confident doing so (Dunn 1991; Rainforth, York, & Macdonald 1992). However, the professional organizations for these disciplines have recently suggested to their members several alternatives to the medically influenced individual models most frequently used to provide therapy-based related services. The American Physical Therapy Association (1990), the American Occupational Therapy Association (1989), and the American Speech-Language-Hearing Association (1991) have recommended that therapists begin to provide educational-based related services by collaborating and consulting with other people within the educational setting of the child.

The situations described at the beginning of this chapter highlight some of the issues surrounding the provision of multiple services by multiple staff for the benefit of a child with developmental delays or disabilities. Each of the two situations involve well-intentioned staff from different disciplines striving to meet the developmental needs of a child within the context of a typical early childhood program. While the situations vary in a number of ways, each illustrates staff-related issues that have significant impact on both program functioning and child outcome. Chief among these issues is establishing effective strategies for staff from different disciplines and agencies to work together.

Research on working with other disciplines

Collaboration is a term used to describe a relationship between two or more persons, programs, or agencies. There is much confusion over the meaning of the term, especially with regard to the development of early childhood services (Kagan 1991). There can be many barriers to such collaborations, some of which are listed in table 2.

Kagan (1991) suggests that collaboration represents the culmination of a process that embodies a hierarchy of components, such as cooperation and coordination. Cooperation forms the base; it tends to exist without any defined structure. Coordination requires a commitment to smooth relationships among organizations. Both cooperative and coordinated models have been used extensively in efforts to improve programs for young children (Shenet 1982), yet rarely have they yielded an improved service model. This failure results because both cooperation and coordination allow separate agencies and staff to maintain their own autonomy as well as their own philosophy and service goals. Collaborative models evolve when the focus across programs and staff becomes the development of a joint solution to a service problem. Collaborations require that the involved agencies and staff agree on a

Table 1. Disciplines that Collaborate with Early Childhoo

Discipline	Primary mission	
Special education	To ensure that environments for infants and young children with disabilities (1) facilitate children's development of social, motor, communication, self-help, cognitive, and behavioral skills; and (2) enhance children's self-concept, sense of competence and control, and independence	
Psychology	To derive a comprehensive picture of child and family functioning, and to identify, implement, and/or evaluate psychological interventions	
Speech/ language pathology	To promote children's communication skills in the context of social interactions with peers and family members in school and in the community	
Occupational therapy	To promote children's emotional, physical, and social development through the use of purposeful activity, such as play and activities of daily living	
Social work	To support the family in its social context so that family members can provide the infant or preschooler an optimum environment for development	

Major roles

2. Plan educational interventions
3. Provide educational services
4. Implement consultants' recommendations
5. Assess family needs

7. Coordinate with other members of the interdisciplinary team
8. Evaluate program effectiveness
9. Advocate for children and families

---

1. Assess psychological/behavioral characteristics of children and their families
2. Identify psychological needs and resources
3. Plan and provide psychological/developmental interventions

4. Coordinate with other members of the interdisciplinary team
5. Consult with families or other professionals
6. Provide case management services, if needed
7. Design and implement evaluations of service effectiveness

---

1. Assess children's communication skills, both specifically and in the context of overall development
2. Screen children for communication problems
3. Recommend, plan, and/or implement individual or group interventions

4. Reassess children periodically
5. Coordinate assessments with families and other professionals
6. Consult with and/or train family members or other professionals
7. Evaluate intervention effectiveness
8. Refer to other programs or professionals

---

1. Assess children's developmental and functional performance in play, self-care, and interacting with the physical and social environment
2. Develop and implement occupational therapy interventions to enhance sensorimotor, cognitive, communication, physical, emotional, and adaptive skills
3. Work with families to enhance caregiving and family well-being

4. Design and develop adaptive equipment and seating to promote maximum functional ability and interaction with the environment
5. Coordinate with other members of the interdisciplinary team
6. Provide case management services
7. Provide services to prevent secondary physical or emotional problems

---

1. Assess the family's capacity to manage basic nurturant needs (e.g., food, shelter, protection, medical care)
2. Mobilize and link families to available supports (e.g., extended family, community groups, friends, churches, public agencies and programs); assess and build family strengths
3. Investigate allegations of abuse or neglect
4. Assess and provide services related to problems in family functioning (e.g., marital relations, parent–child interactions, child support)

5. Advocate for family rights and access to community services
6. Provide case management services, if needed
7. Coordinate with other members of the interdisciplinary team
8. Plan and implement family services, such as parent support groups, family therapy, marital counseling, or individual counseling
9. Evaluate the effectiveness of family services

51

Table 1 (continued)

Discipline	Primary mission	
Nutrition/ dietetics	To ensure that infants and preschoolers with disabilities achieve maximum nutritional status by facilitating (1) physical and mental growth and development; (2) enjoyment of food and eating within the social environment; (3) independence in feeding and eating; and (4) dietary treatment to compensate for metabolic disorders, nutrition-related health problems, or adverse drug-nutrient interactions	
Nursing	To diagnose and treat actual and potential human responses to illness; for infants and preschoolers with disabilities, this means (1) promoting the highest health and developmental status possible, and (2) helping families cope with changes in their lives resulting from the child's disabilities	
Audiology	To provide and coordinate services to children with auditory handicaps, including detection of the problem and management of any existing communication handicaps	
Medicine	To assist families in the promotion of optimal health, growth, and development for their infants and young children by providing health services	

Major roles

1. Assess nutritional status and quality of food intake
2. Work with caregivers to develop nutrition care plans
3. Provide caregivers with diet counseling and nutrition education
4. Assess family needs
5. Coordinate with other members of the interdisciplinary team
6. Refer families to relevant community services (e.g., food stamps, food pantry, or community kitchen; WIC program)
7. Conduct regular follow-up and evaluations of services

---

1. Implement medical plans to treat the underlying cause, or help parents implement the treatment plan
2. Work with parents to meet the basic needs of the child (e.g., health needs, daily care, feeding)
3. Recommend, plan, and/or implement interventions to improve the child's developmental status
4. Enhance the child's and the family's abilities to cope with the child's disabilities
5. Provide case management services, if needed
6. Refer to other programs or professionals

---

1. Assess pure tone air conduction thresholds, assess speech thresholds, and predict hearing loss from acoustic reflex, reflex-eliciting auditory tests, and communication handicap inventories
2. Conduct extended evaluation, including air conduction, speech thresholds, and word/sentence recognition tests
3. Conduct behavioral evaluation for sensorineural site that includes advanced acoustic reflex tests, tests of auditory adaptation, tests of frequency discrimination, and tests of intensity discrimination
4. Conduct auditory prosthetic evaluations, including such sound field tests as aided word/sentence recognition, warble tone thresholds, narrow-band noise thresholds, and comfortable and uncomfortable loudness levels while wearing an auditory prosthesis (e.g., hearing aid or assistive listening device)
5. Coordinate auditory (aural) rehabilitation, including orientation to auditory prosthesis, auditory training, and speech reading training

---

1. Assess health, growth, development, and deviation
2. Diagnose and treat health problems
3. Advocate for health and well-being of the child and the family
4. Provide referral and consultation to other agencies
5. Coordinate with other members of the interdisciplinary team
6. Provide education and support to families

The members on the collaborative team may vary according to the child's needs, but the family is always a team member.

common philosophy and service goal, which can only be achieved when joint agency and staff activities focus on building relationships. A number of additional components must be in place to ensure the success of a collaboration, including a commitment to collaboration as a viable service delivery model and the resources (usually time) needed to develop the model effectively.

Collaboration among the many service providers involved in the provision of services to children with disabilities has been supported through legislation for many years. The Individualized Education Plan (IEP) requires a collaborative team process for both planning and implementing services. The members of the team may vary according to the child's needs, but the family is always part of the team. Including a child with a disability within an early childhood program necessitates having a staff member from the program on the collaborative team.

Unfortunately, many training programs (both graduate and undergraduate) for professionals involved in providing services to young children with disabilities neglect to prepare students to participate on collaborative teams (Courtnage & Smith-Davis 1987; Bailey, Palsha, & Huntington 1990). As a result, collaboration by service providers from different disciplines remains a challenge, not unlike the situations described at the beginning of this chapter. The effectiveness of services provided by both specialized staff and early childhood program staff within an early childhood program depends upon the ability of both staffs to commit themselves to a collaborative model of service delivery.

While the necessity for collaborative service delivery models seems apparent, there is surprisingly little research on the process and outcomes of such models. Additionally, no research has been conducted on the various types of staffing patterns and their effectiveness for children with disabilities receiving special education and related services within early childhood programs. Most of the literature on collaborative service delivery across staff from different disciplines has focused on the school-age child with disabilities (e.g., Thousand & Villa 1990; Orelove & Sobsey 1991; Rainforth, York, & Macdonald 1992; Idol 1993). Recent contributions to the literature, however, have focused on the need to adopt models of collaboration to ensure effective service delivery across early childhood staff (e.g., Hanline 1990; Kagan 1991; Melaville & Blank 1991; File & Kontos 1992; Swan & Morgan 1992; Hanson & Widerstrom 1993). Two strategies that foster collaboration among staff are highlighted in this chapter: collaborative consultation and collaborative, transdisciplinary service delivery teams. These strategies are not mutually exclusive, and components of both strategies are frequently used in models of effective collaborative service delivery models. Both approaches require a commitment to the child with a disability as well as a commitment to joint service delivery. Of the two strategies, however, collaborative consultation is more easily accomplished within early childhood programs.

Table 2. Common Barriers to Interagency Collaboration

Competitiveness between agencies	Turf issues Lack of information about other agencies' function Political issues
Lack of organizational structure for coordination	Differing philosophies Distinct goals Haphazard team process Lack of facilitator Lack of monitoring and evaluation process Lack of planning Lack of power and authority to make and implement decisions
Technical factors	Resources: staff, time, budget Logistics: distance, geography
Personnel	Parochial interests Resistance to change Staff attitudes Lack of commitment to community needs Questionable administrative support Discipline-specific jargon and perspectives

Source: M.B. Bruder & T. Bologna, Collaboration and service coordination for effective early intervention. In W. Brown, S.K. Thurman, & L.F. Pearl, *Family-centered early intervention with infants & toddlers* (Baltimore: Paul H. Brookes, 1993), 109.

Collaborative consultation

A number of models for consultation have been used to provide services to children with disabilities (File & Kontos 1992). Generally speaking, consultation is the giving and taking of information between two or more people to (1) resolve a need, issue, or problem; and (2) improve the understanding that one or both individuals have of these issues and their ability to respond effectively to similar problems in the future (Gutkin & Curtis 1982). One person may be involved with different consultations with different staff. What is most important, however, is the relationship between the two key individuals involved in the consultation. When the consultation involves providing services to a young child with a disability, the child becomes the third person involved.

Consultation can be used to provide two types of services to a child with a disability: direct and indirect (Idol 1993). The consultant can provide direct educational and related services, such as assessment of and instruction in a child's deficit area (Idol, Paolucci-Whitcomb, & Nevin 1986). The consultant can also provide assistance to teachers who have children with disabilities in their classrooms as well as to the parents of these children (Idol 1993). Within an early childhood program that includes children with disabilities, it seems clear that both consultant functions are necessary.

As stated, most of the empirical basis for using consultation has evolved from research on a school-age population of children with disabilities. Although this scope is limited, the studies confirm that consultation is an effective strategy for service delivery (Medway 1982; Medway & Updyke 1985; Sibley 1986; Gresham & Kendall 1987; West & Idol 1987; Kratochwill, Sheridan, & VanSomeren 1988; Bergan &

It is important that the participants in the consultation together identify the need, issue, or problem.

Kratochwill 1990). In particular, consulting models of indirect service delivery in special education and related services has proven to be as effective as direct services provided in a pull-out (of the classroom) model when measures of children's achievement are compared (Miller & Sabatino 1978; Dunn 1990; Schulte, Osborne, & McKinney 1990). More important, however, teachers who called on consultants demonstrated positive changes in instructional techniques when using a consultant to meet a child's educational need (Meyers, Gelzheiser, & Yelich 1991). These outcomes have been replicated within early childhood settings (Peck, Killen, & Baugmart 1989; Dunn 1990; Hanline 1990).

Related research on consultation strategies has focused on the methods used during the process of problem solving (Tindal, Shinn, & Rodden-Nord 1990). Evidence suggests that both special educators and general educators prefer a collaborative model (Wenger 1979; Babcock & Pryzwansky 1983; Pryzwansky & White 1983) rather than an expert model. The collaborative model, derived from Tharp and Werzel 1969, has been defined as

an interactive process which enables people with diverse expertise to generate creative solutions to mutually defined problems. The major outcome of collaborative consultation is to provide comprehensive and effective programs for students with special needs within the most appropriate context, thereby enabling them to achieve maximum constructive interaction with their nonhandicapped peers. (Idol, Paolucci-Whitcomb, & Nevin 1986, p. 1)

Collaborative consultation encompasses a number of interpersonal competencies that cross discipline boundaries, including written and oral communication skills; personal characteristics, such as the ability to be caring, respectful, empathic, congruent and open; and collaborative problem solving skills (West & Cannon 1988). The last attribute, in particular, is crucial to the development of a relationship of parity between both (or all, if there are more than two) individuals involved in the consultation.

A number of principles have been identified as contributing to the successful implementation of collaborative consultation among professionals from different disciplines (Idol, Paolucci-Whitcomb, & Nevin 1986):

• *Mutual ownership of the process.* It is important that the participants in the consultation together identify the need, issue, or problem. They should accept mutual responsibility or ownership of the consulting process and subsequent outcomes. Each person must respect, recognize, and appreciate the others' expertise.

• *Recognition of individual differences in the change process.* All parties should be aware of the change process and the developmental stages of concern for change that have been identified (Hall & Loucks 1978). It is important that both recognize that people embrace change differently, at different rates and at different emotional levels.

> *All staff involved must demonstrate mutual respect for each other because each professional will benefit from the others' expertise.*

• *Use of reinforcement principles and practices to improve skills, knowledge, and attitudes.* When all of those involved in the consultation use effective teaching skills with each other and with the child with disabilities, positive outcomes accrue for all.

• *Use of data-based decision making.* The implementation of collaborative consultation strategies requires the adoption of a model of evaluation that measures the functional outcome of a child's behavior. The effects of each participant on the identified need, issue, or problem must be analyzed continuously to evaluate the effectiveness of the collaboration.

Consultation appears likely to become an increasingly prominent method of service delivery for early childhood special educators and related-service personnel (File & Kontos 1992). Many program models that include children with disabilities in community early childhood programs have supported this model (Bagnato, Kontos, & Neisworth 1987; Jones & Meisels 1987; Klein & Sheehan 1987; Kontos 1988; Bruder 1993). However, the strategy of collaborative consultation for service delivery by professionals from different disciplines cannot be advocated without noting the barriers. Staff from different agencies, who often have different philosophies of service, financial resources, and time constraints, may not understand and respect one another's professional frameworks and skills (Johnson, Pugach, & Hammitte 1988; Johnson & Pugach 1991). Sometimes staff from one agency or discipline perceive themselves to be more highly skilled than are staff from the other discipline (Carter 1989; Pugach & Johnson 1989). This often can happen in the context of a collaboration between an early childhood teacher and a special educator; the teacher may be less skilled than the special educator in intervention, although she is more skilled in many other aspects of working with young children. All staff involved need to acknowledge such existing barriers before beginning the collaboration. All staff involved must demonstrate mutual respect for each other because each professional will benefit from the others' expertise. This is the very core of a collaborative consultation relationship.

The first situation described at the beginning of this chapter is an example in which the adoption of a collaborative consultation process could benefit the staff and, most importantly, Kara. If such a strategy were used, the situation could be resolved in a positive manner, such as described below:

Before asking for Kara's removal from the Head Start program, the program director requested a meeting between the classroom teacher, the speech pathologist, the psychologist, and Kara's parents. At the meeting the group decided to try one more strategy to try to help Kara's behavior. The speech pathologist agreed to redistribute her time with Kara, although she expressed uncertainty about the chances of Kara learning better communication and language skills outside a distraction-free therapy environment. She began to spend time with Kara in the classroom twice a week and used her third day to meet with the teacher during lunchtime to help identify approaches the teacher could use to help Kara communicate her needs more effectively. The psychologist also agreed to come to the classroom twice a week to record the times when Kara's problematic behavior seemed to be worse. He met with the teacher and parents weekly to identify the events that led to the behavior episodes and the strategies that seemed to help Kara. He also demonstrated to both Kara's teacher and her parents techniques that seemed to be effective with Kara. For example, Kara was given a sticker chart, which was used by the teacher every time Kara appropriately communicated her needs. She was also given more verbal cues to prepare her for transitions, a particularly difficult time for her. After six weeks of consultation, Kara's behavior showed a big improvement, and the psychologist reduced his time investment to twice-a-month visits with the teacher. Kara's speech and language has improved, and the speech pathologist has learned to provide services within Kara's classroom activities, in group situations. The teacher also feels much more comfortable and effective in meeting Kara's needs.

Collaborative, transdisciplinary service delivery teams

The collective mission of individuals constituting a collaborative educational team is to design and implement programs in which individual children achieve their educational goals (Rainforth, York, & Macdonald 1992). Collaboration, in this instance, can be defined as a process of problem solving by team members (usually representing different disciplines), each of whom contributes his or her knowledge and skills equally (Vandercook & York 1990). Collaborative consultation is a component of an effective service delivery team. The added challenge is the development of collaboration between and among a group of individuals for a sustained length of time, during which multiple services and professionals are required by one child. Unfortunately, for a group of individuals to operate as a collaborative service delivery team requires much more than taking on the label of "team." A group of people become a team when their purpose and function stem from a common philosophy with shared goals (Maddux 1988). An overview of the differences between a group and a team are illustrated in table 3.

The types of teams that typically function in early intervention have been identified as multidisciplinary, interdisciplinary, and transdisciplinary. On a multidisciplinary team, the professionals represent their own discipline and provide isolated assessment and intervention services. This includes individual report writing, individual goal setting, and discipline-specific direct intervention with the child and/or family. There is minimal integration across disciplines, making it very difficult to develop coordinated, comprehensive programs for children and their families. On an interdisciplinary team, each of the professionals carries out specific disciplinary

Table 3. Groups Versus Teams

Groups	Teams
Members think that they are grouped together for administrative purposes only. Individuals work independently, sometimes at cross purposes with others.	Members recognize their interdependence and understand that both personal and team goals are best accomplished with mutual support. Time is not wasted struggling over "turf" or attempting personal gain at the expense of others.
Members tend to focus on themselves because they are not sufficiently involved in planning the unit's objectives. They approach their job simply as hired hands.	Members feel a sense of ownership for their jobs and the unit because they are committed to goals that they helped establish.
Members are told what to do rather than asked what the best approach would be. Suggestions are not encouraged.	Members contribute to the organization's success by applying their unique talent and knowledge to team objectives.
Members distrust the motives of colleagues because they do not understand the roles of other members. Expressions of opinion or disagreement are considered divisive and nonsupportive.	Members work in a climate of trust and are encouraged to openly express ideas, opinions, disagreements, and feelings. Questions are welcomed.
Members are so cautious about what they say that real understanding is not possible. Game playing may occur and communication traps be set to catch the unwary.	Members practice open and honest communication. They make an effort to understand each other's points of view.
Members may receive good training but are limited in applying it to the job by the supervisor or other group members.	Members are encouraged to develop skills and apply what they learn on the job. They receive the support of the team.
Members find themselves in conflict situations that they do not know how to resolve. Their supervisor may put off intervention until serious damage is done.	Members recognize that conflict is a normal aspect of human interaction, but they view such situations as an opportunity for new ideas and creativity. They work to resolve conflict quickly and constructively.
Members may or may not participate in decisions affecting the team. Conformity often appears more important than positive results.	Members participate in decisions affecting the team but understand that their leader must make a final ruling whenever the team cannot decide or when an emergency exists. Positive results, not conformity, are the goal.

Source: R.E. Maddux, *Team building: An exercise in leadership* (Los Altos, CA: Crisp Publications, 1988), 5.

A transdisciplinary approach requires the team members to share roles and systematically cross disciplinary boundaries.

assessments and interventions; however, there is a formal commitment to the sharing of information throughout the process of assessment, planning, and intervention. The transdisciplinary approach was originally conceived as a framework for professionals to share important information and skills with primary caregivers (Hutchinson 1978). This approach integrates a child's developmental needs across the major developmental domains. The transdisciplinary approach involves a greater degree of collaboration than other service delivery models and, for this reason, may be difficult to implement. However, it has been identified as the ideal approach to the design and delivery of services within a model for young children with disabilities receiving services in early childhood programs (McGonigel 1988; Hanson & Hanline 1989; Linder 1990).

A transdisciplinary approach requires the team members to share roles and systematically cross discipline boundaries. The primary purpose of this approach is to pool and integrate the expertise of team members so that more efficient and comprehensive assessment and intervention services may be provided. The communication style in this type of team involves continuous give-and-take between all members (especially with the parents) on a regular, planned basis. Professionals from different disciplines teach, learn, and work together to accomplish a common set of intervention goals for a child and her family. The role differentiation between disciplines is defined by the needs of the situation rather than by discipline-specific characteristics. Assessment, intervention, and evaluation are carried out jointly by designated members of the team. This teamwork usually results in a decrease in the number of professionals who interact with the child on a daily basis. Other characteristics of the transdisciplinary approach are joint team effort, joint staff development to ensure continuous skill development among members, and role release (Lyon & Lyon 1980; Noonan & Kilgo 1987; McCollum & Hughes 1988; Woodruff & McGonigel 1988).

Role release refers to a sharing and exchange of certain roles and responsibilities among team members (Orelove & Sobsey 1991). It specifically involves a "releasing" of some functions traditionally associated with a specific discipline. For example, the physical therapist may provide training and support to the early childhood teacher to enable her to do much of the hands-on interaction with a child. Likewise, the nurse may provide training to all team members to monitor a child's seizures. Effective implementation of the role release process requires adequate sharing of information and training. Team members must have a solid foundation in their own discipline, combined with an understanding of the roles and competencies of the other disciplines represented on the team.

In the transdisciplinary approach, the child's program is primarily implemented by a single person or a few persons, with ongoing assistance provided by team

The transdisciplinary strategy facilitates the delivery of appropriate interventions across developmental domains throughout the child's day, as opposed to having a specific speech group, fine motor group, gross motor group, and so forth.

members from the various disciplines (Orelove & Sobsey 1991). In most early childhood programs, the teacher and program assistants take on the primary service delivery role. At times this role may also be appropriately assumed by a special education teacher who provides services within the early childhood program on a regular basis. Related-service support staff, most commonly therapists, often serve as consultants to the teachers. In this way the child's therapy as well as other needs are integrated into the daily routine of the classroom. This strategy facilitates the delivery of appropriate interventions across developmental domains throughout the child's day, as opposed to having a specific speech group, fine motor group, gross motor group, and so forth. This does not mean that therapists stop providing direct services to children (Orelove & Sobsey 1991). For therapists to be effective, they need to maintain direct contact with the child with a disability. The provision of this team model should never be used as a strategy to justify the reduction of staff.

As with collaborative consultation strategies, there is a limited research base on the use of a collaborative team that uses a transdisciplinary approach with young children with disabilities attending early childhood programs. Various components of the transdisciplinary approach, however, have proven beneficial to both children with disabilities and staff. One important finding is that teachers, as well as parents and paraprofessionals, have been able to demonstrate competence and achieve subsequent positive outcomes for children by implementing practices taught to them by members of other disciplines (Albano 1983; McCollum & Stayton 1985). For example, teaching staff have been able to implement motor interventions taught to them by an occupational therapist (Inge & Snell 1985). Studies have shown that the integration of a child's developmental needs into an integrated intervention program using typical routines and activities resulted in increased skill acquisition for the children, as well (McCormick & Goldman 1979; Albano 1983; Campbell, McInerney, & Cooper 1984; Giangreco 1986). These studies, like the studies of collaborative consultation, focused primarily on school-age children.

Although collaborative, transdisciplinary service delivery teams appear simple in concept, implementation of this strategy can be difficult because of the differences between it and the more familiar, structured, discipline-specific team structures. Barriers to effective use of the strategy have been identified as philosophical and professional, interpersonal, and administrative (for a thorough discussion of these barriers, see Orelove & Sobsey 1991). In particular, the time commitment required to implement a collaborative team model effectively among all individuals may be difficult for some early childhood programs. Additionally, many special education and related-service staff may not have expertise or experience in a collaborative, transdisciplinary team approach, thus affecting the feasibility of such a strategy.

The team leader should foster a climate in which all members feel free to contribute their ideas.

One principle that can help facilitate the development of a collaborative service delivery team is use of an effective team process (Bailey 1984). Lowe and Herranen (1982) identified six stages of team development; these are outlined in table 4. Although teams will vary as to the applicability of these stages, it seems reasonable to suggest that team process will be affected differently at various points in time. Other components that have been identified to facilitate an effective team process (Dyer 1977; Shonk 1982; Starcevich & Stowell 1990) include

• *Team composition.* There is no rule for determining the appropriate number and type of staff who should be involved with a child who has a disability. The parent is always a member of the team, as is a staff member from the program in which the child receives services (e.g., early childhood teacher, child care provider).

• *Team goals.* Teams must devote time to jointly identifying and clearly defining goals and objectives. A truly effective team process can exist only when members share responsibility for accomplishing common goals.

• *Member roles.* The members of the team are unique individuals who may each have different skills, knowledge, and personalities. For teams to be effective, each individual must have a clear role and identified responsibilities. In addition to the typical discipline-specific roles, members may assume other roles related to team development, maintenance, and problem solving.

• *Team work style.* The team's work style will determine the team's development and overall effectiveness. Effective team decisions will result from the use of a systematic problem-solving process, which should occur during planned meetings. The team meeting should function as a vehicle for facilitating the completion of the team's tasks and the achievement of its goals. An agenda and a follow-up meeting record can ensure the efficient use of everyone's time.

• *Team leadership.* Team leaders must adapt their style to meet the diverse needs and styles of the individuals that are part of the team. The team leader should foster a climate in which all members feel free to contribute their ideas. In this atmosphere, the members can express differing viewpoints and solutions to problems. As a team matures, leadership of the team may rotate among members.

A collaborative service delivery team consisting of professionals from different disciplines can be an efficient and effective method for providing services to a child with disabilities within an early childhood program. The second situation described at the beginning of this chapter provides the opportunity to explore a solution that results in a collaborative team.

Table 4. Six-Stage Process of Team Development of Lowe and Herranen (1982)

Stage	Features
I. Becoming acquainted	Group structures are hierarchical. Leadership is autocratic. Interactions are polite and impersonal. Team productivity is low overall.
II. Trial-and-error	Team members begin to work together toward a common goal. Team members align themselves with one or two other team members. Factions sometimes occur. Role conflict and ambiguity arise.
III. Collective indecision	Team members attempt to avoid direct conflict and achieve equilibrium. The group has norm for accountability.
IV. Crisis	Team members realize the importance of their mission. Team members express emotion.
V. Resolution	Team members make an effort to work together as a team. Communication becomes more open. Team members share leadership, decision making, and responsibility.
VI. Team maintenance	The client's needs are the major driving force. Conflict management and client–team relationships are important.

Source: F. Orelove & M. Sobsey. *Educating children with multiple disabilities* (Baltimore: Paul H. Brookes, 1991). 17.

Regular meeting times should be established between the early childhood program staff and the special education staff for ongoing communication about the child's progress.

Joley's mother agreed with the child care staff to request a meeting with the staff at the special education center. At the meeting she asked if there was any way the special education staff could help the child care staff. The members of the special education staff agreed to consult with the child care staff on a weekly basis to help teach them intervention techniques to use with Joley to address all of her developmental needs. The process was hard in the beginning because schedules were difficult to coordinate. Before long, however, members from both programs felt comfortable with each other and began to jointly help each other problem solve to meet Joley's needs. After four months of this regular communication and teaching and learning from each other, the special education staff believed that they should stop taking Joley out of her natural environment every day because the child care staff was doing such a good job incorporating her individualized interventions and adaptations into their classroom routines. Certain members of the special education team increased their visits to see Joley at the child care center to make up for their lack of daily contact, and evaluations of her progress suggested that this change in intervention benefited her enormously.

Recommendations for practice

Much has been written about the many barriers that can influence the success of an inclusionary model of service delivery for young children with disabilities. Effective use of this model requires a commitment from everyone involved to work together for the benefit of the child. These collaborations require crossing both discipline and agency boundaries. In doing this it is important that staff adopt service delivery strategies, such as collaborative consultation and collaborative service delivery teams. A number of other strategies can be adopted by early childhood programs as they become more involved in collaborations among professionals and agencies for the benefit of a child with disabilities. These strategies are listed in table 5 and described below.

• *First,* the early childhood program staff can become informed about the type of special education and related-service personnel that are available to children in their program. A local public school or early intervention program should provide these resources.

• *Second,* if a child in the program is identified as needing special education and related services or is already receiving such services, the program staff should contact the special education staff involved in the provision of these services.

• *Third,* staff from the early childhood program should request a meeting with the special education and/or related-services personnel who will be, or who are, involved with the identified child. The purpose of the meeting should be to collaboratively discuss the child's developmental abilities and his needs and goals as observed by the early childhood program staff. If an Individualized Education Plan (IEP) or Individualized Family Service Plan (IFSP) has not yet been developed, the early childhood program staff should participate in the process to assist in determining collaborative service delivery goals and strategies (e.g., collaborative consultation and/or service delivery teams).

• *Fourth*, regular meeting times should be established between the early childhood program staff and the special education staff for ongoing communication about the child's progress. If the special education staff is providing services (either direct or indirect) to the child at the early childhood program site, times for regular contact should be established, either through consultation or team meetings. During these meetings, collaborative problem solving should be given priority, as should the continued integration of a child's developmental goals (across developmental domains or areas) into all classroom routines.

Table 5. Practices Recommended for Early Childhood Professionals to Enhance Collaborations across Disciplines

1. Identify the special education and related-service personnel available to children in your program.
2. Contact the staff involved with the child identified for, or receiving, special education and related services.
3. Request a meeting with the special education staff to develop/review the IEP.
4. Establish regular meeting times with all staff involved with the child.
5. Provide staff development opportunities.
6. Establish and maintain regular communication mechanisms.
7. Evaluate child, staff, and program status on a frequent basis.

• *Fifth*, time should be provided for the early childhood staff to learn new behaviors that are child-specific (e.g., intervention techniques) as well as collaborative (e.g., effective communication and negotiation skills). Time for staff development is a rare commodity within early childhood programs. Nevertheless, staff development is an extremely important component in the development of collaborative service delivery models for children with disabilities. The time commitment for staff development does not have to be extensive, but it should be regular and ongoing. For example, staff meetings could occur biweekly, and child-specific skill development could be targeted for two 15-minute periods a week (e.g., naptime), during which staff are rotated.

• *Sixth*, ongoing communication mechanisms (both formal and informal) should be established and maintained among everyone involved in a child's program.

• *Finally*, the child's progress within the early childhood program should be evaluated regularly and intervention strategies adapted as needed. This evaluation should involve the child's family, the early childhood staff, and staff from any other discipline involved in the provision of services.

Collaborative consultation and collaborative service delivery teams using a transdisciplinary approach are effective strategies that can enhance the ability of staff from different disciplines to work together. Either of these strategies, as well as components from both, may be used to facilitate the successful placement of a child with disabilities within an early childhood program. Both approaches require the acquisition of new skills and different roles for early childhood teachers, the most important being that of a collaborator with professionals from different disciplines.

The Individuals with Disabilities Education Act specifies that children with disabilities are entitled to special education and related services. The following section is a reprint of the law (IDEA 1990) describing exactly what falls into the category "related services."

Sec. 300.16 Related Services

(a) As used in this part, the term "related services" means transportation and such development, corrective, and other supportive services as are required to assist a child with a disability to benefit from special education, and includes speech pathology and audiology, psychological services, physical and occupational therapy, recreation, including therapeutic recreation, early identification and assessment of disabilities in children, counseling services, including rehabilitation counseling, and medical services for diagnostic or evaluation purposes. The term also includes school health services, social work services in schools, and parent counseling and training.

(b) The terms used in this definition are defined as follows:

(1) "Audiology" includes—

(i) Identification of children with hearing loss;

(ii) Determination of the range, nature, and degree of hearing loss, including referral for medical or other professional attention for the habilitation of hearing;

(iii) Provision of habilitative activities, such as language habilitation, auditory training, speech reading (lip-reading), hearing evaluation, and speech conservation;

(iv) Creation and administration of programs for prevention of hearing loss;

(v) Counseling and guidance of pupils, parents, and teachers regarding hearing loss; and

(vi) Determination of the child's need for group and individual amplification, selecting and fitting an appropriate aid, and evaluating the effectiveness of amplification.

(2) "Counseling services" means services provided by qualified social workers, psychologists, guidance counselors, or other qualified personnel.

(3) "Early identification and assessment of disabilities in children" means the implementation of a formal plan for identifying a disability as early as possible in a child's life.

(4) "Medical services" means services provided by a licensed physician to determine a child's medically related disability that results in the child's need for special education and related services.

(5) "Occupational therapy" includes—

(i) Improving, developing or restoring functions impaired or lost through illness, injury, or deprivation;

(ii) Improving ability to perform tasks for independent functioning when functions are impaired or lost; and

(iii) Preventing, through early intervention, initial or further impairment or loss of function.

(6) "Parent counseling and training" means assisting parents in understanding the special needs of their child and providing parents with information about child development.

(7) "Physical therapy" means services provided by a qualified physical therapist.

(8) "Psychological services" includes—

(i) Administering psychological and educational tests, and other assessment procedures;

(ii) Interpreting assessment results;

(iii) Obtaining, integrating, and interpreting information about child behavior and conditions relating to learning.

(iv) Consulting with other staff members in planning school programs to meet the special needs of children as indicated by psychological tests, interviews, and behavioral evaluations; and

(v) Planning and managing a program of psychological services, including psychological counseling for children and parents.

(9) "Recreation" includes—

(i) Assessment of leisure function;

(ii) Therapeutic recreation services;

(iii) Recreation programs in schools and community agencies; and

(iv) Leisure education.

(10) "Rehabilitation counseling services" means services provided by qualified personnel in individual or group sessions that focus specifically on career development, employment preparation, achieving independence, and integration in the workplace and community of a student with a disability. The term also includes vocational rehabilitation services provided to students with disabilities by vocational rehabilitation programs funded under the Rehabilitation Act of 1973, as amended.

Sec. 300.16 Related Services (continued)

(11) "School health services" means services provided by a qualified school nurse or other qualified person.

(12) "Social work services in schools" includes—

(i) Preparing a social or developmental history on a child with a disability;

(ii) Group and individual counseling with the child and family;

(iii) Working with those problems in a child's living situation (home, school, and community) that affect the child's adjustment in school; and

(iv) Mobilizing school and community resources to enable the child to learn as effectively as possible in his or her educational program.

(13) "Speech pathology" includes—

(i) Identification of children with speech or language impairments;

(ii) Diagnosis and appraisal of specific speech or language impairments;

(iii) Referral for medical or other professional attention necessary for the habilitation of speech or language impairments;

(iv) Provision of speech and language services for the habilitation or prevention of communicative impairments; and

(v) Counseling and guidance of parents, children, and teachers regarding speech and language impairments.

(14) "Transportation" includes—

(i) Travel to and from school and between schools;

(ii) Travel in and around school buildings; and

(iii) Specialized equipment (such as special or adapted buses, lifts, and ramps), if required to provide special transportation for a child with a disability.

Chapter 4

Assessing Children with Special Needs

Mark Wolery

YOUNG CHILDREN WITH DEVELOPMENTAL DELAYS AND DISABILITIES are often assessed for a variety of reasons. In this chapter, some foundational terms and concepts related to the assessment of young children are defined. The major reasons for assessing young children with special needs also are described. However, the majority of the chapter focuses on two purposes of assessment: deciding what to teach (instructional program planning assessment) and determining whether children are learning as expected (monitoring). The chapter concludes with a discussion of the relevance of the NAEYC and NAECS/SDE (1991) position statement on curriculum and assessment practices to young children with disabilities.

Definition of assessment and measurement strategies

The word *assessment* often stimulates images of children being tested. As used in this chapter, however, *assessment* has a broader meaning–specifically, assessment is the process of systematically gathering information about a child. This definition raises two questions: Why is the information being gathered? and, How is the information gathered (i.e., What are the specific measurement strategies?)?

Assessment activities should not occur unless the purpose is clear.

The first question is answered in more detail in the next section; however, the common reasons for assessing young children are to screen them for developmental delays and disabilities, to determine whether they should be given a specific diagnosis, to decide whether children are eligible for special services, to plan their instructional programs and placements, to monitor their progress, and to evaluate the effects of the early childhood services (Benner 1992). The information gathered for one of these purposes (e.g., screening) may *not* be useful for another (e.g., planning instructional programs); each purpose often requires different assessment activities. Early childhood personnel must clarify their purpose in gathering information and must understand which measurement strategies are appropriate for that purpose. Assessment activities should not occur unless the purpose is clear; we should have specific questions that determine which assessment activities occur.

The answer to the second question (How is the information gathered?) has filled many books. However, at the most basic level, three major types of assessment activities are used: interviews, observations, and tests. Each of these strategies can be used in a variety of ways, and each is often used to gather information about young children with special needs. The specific manner in which the strategies are used depends, of course, on the purpose of the assessment. These strategies are described briefly in this chapter, but their use with young children with special needs is described more fully elsewhere (Simeonsson 1986; Wachs & Sheehan 1988; Bailey & Wolery 1989; Bagnato, Neisworth, & Munson 1989; Bracken 1991b; Benner 1992; Nuttall, Romero, & Kalesnik 1992; Linder 1993; McLean, Bailey, & Wolery n.d.).

Interviews

Interviews involve asking others who have relevant information about their views and perceptions. Some interviews are quite structured, with the questions asked in specific ways and the interviewee given limited choices of specific responses. Other interviews are more open-ended and are designed to solicit detailed information about a given issue or broader information about an array of issues (Winton 1988). Between these two extremes are a number of interview formats that include a mix of both types of questions and responses. Depending upon the purpose of assessment, each of these formats is useful to early childhood personnel. For example, to understand a child's interests and needs, a teacher might ask the child's parents a few general questions about these issues. However, in screening the child for developmental delays, the professional may use a structured interview that has questions about each area of development; an example of such a scale is the *Developmental Profile II* (Alpern, Boll, & Shearer 1980).

The flexibility of direct observation makes it particularly useful to early childhood personnel.

Observation

Observation involves watching and listening to a person (or, in some cases, a child or a program) and making a record of what occurs. Some observational measures involve providing ratings of children (Achenbach & Edelbrock 1983) or programs (Harms & Clifford 1980) on predefined dimensions. Other observational systems involve counting and/or timing children's behavior in prescribed ways. Some of these may be quite simple, such as counting the number of soiled diapers in a day; others will be quite complex, such as counting and timing children's social initiations and responses (Odom & McConnell 1989). Systematic observation can be used as a primary assessment strategy, or it can be combined with other measures, such as interviews or direct tests (Wolery 1989c). Observations may occur in children's natural environments, such as their homes and classrooms, or in more contrived situations, usually for research or diagnostic purposes. The flexibility of direct observation makes it particularly useful to early childhood personnel. Observation can be used to assess how children usually function, how they interact with their peers, how they play, and how they respond to different things in their environment. Also, observation is particularly useful in monitoring children's progress over time in natural situations (Cooper 1980). Wolery (1989c) provides examples of various observation forms and systems for monitoring children's progress.

Testing

Testing is perhaps the most widely recognized strategy for gathering information, although it may be less useful than interviews and observations to early childhood personnel when assessing young children with disabilities. Testing is less useful because tests rarely include adaptations to accommodate to children's disabilities, often contain items or sequences of items that are not instructionally relevant, and frequently are administered in artificial situations rather than in natural contexts (Bailey & Wolery 1989).

Generally, tests can be divided into two broad categories: norm-referenced and criterion-referenced tests, many of which are curriculum referenced (Bailey & Brochin 1989). Norm-referenced tests, such as IQ tests and the most common achievement tests, answer the question, How did this child perform in comparison to the group on which the measure was normed? Such tests are often used in screening and in making diagnoses. For the scores from such tests to be useful, the tests must be administered as their developers specify. Criterion-referenced tests allow children's performance to be compared to specific criteria for each item. The question they answer is, How did this child do in relation to a specified level of performance or knowledge? Curriculum-referenced tests allow children's performance to be compared to the objectives of some curriculum. Some tests focus on narrow parts of children's development (cognitive functioning, for example), and others focus on multiple aspects of development (such as cognitive, linguistic, and social development) (Bagnato, Neisworth, & Munson 1989; Bracken 1991a). Some tests can be administered by early childhood personnel, but others must be administered only by specifically trained professionals, often psychologists.

In contrast to such formal tests, informal assessment situations can be developed by teachers and other early childhood personnel. To find out if a child can do a particular skill (e.g., is able to match a pattern of pegs in a peg board or count objects), the adult may construct a specific assessment situation designed to elicit that skill. Such informal teacher-contrived situations are often quite useful in planning instructional programs. For example, if the teacher wanted to know whether a child would use words to request more toys or food, the adult might observe the child for several days. Leaving less to chance, the adult may try giving the child only a small portion of his favorite juice at snack to see if the child will say "more" or "more juice" (or the adult may give the child only some parts of a toy to see if he requests additional ones). Such situations permit informal assessment of children's requesting skills in their natural environment.

Purposes of assessment

As already noted, young children with and without disabilities are assessed for a number of purposes (Benner 1992). The decisions to be made, the types of assessment, and relevant questions about those decisions are shown in table 1. In this section, each type of assessment is described and the roles of early childhood staff are identified.

Screening

Screening is an assessment conducted to decide whether the child should receive further, more in-depth assessment (Lichtenstein & Ireton 1991; Thurlow 1992). The question being asked during screening is, Should this child be referred for additional assessment, monitored, or released from further monitoring and assessment (Wolery 1989a)? Diagnoses cannot be made and instructional programs cannot be planned from screening procedures. Children are screened for many reasons, such as their physical and health status, exposure to toxic substances (e.g., lead poisoning), developmental progress (Wolery 1989a), and sensory functioning (visual and hearing screenings) (Fewell 1991; Shah & Boyden 1991). Health professionals often screen children's physical and health status and exposure to toxins. Early childhood staff and other team members, such as speech-language pathologists, often screen children for developmental delays and sensory function. The screening may be accomplished by using specific screening instruments (see Wolery 1989a and Cohn 1992 for descriptions of selected instruments) or by using systematic observation over time.

Table 1. Assessment Decisions, Assessment Types, and

Decision	Assessment type	
Determine whether to refer the child for additional assessment	Screening	
Determine whether the child has a developmental delay or disability	Diagnostic	
Determine whether the child is eligible for special services	Eligibility	
Determine what the child should be taught	Instructional program planning	
Determine where the child should receive services and what services are needed	Placement	
Determine whether the child is making adequate progress in learning important skills	Monitoring of instructional program	
Determine whether the desired outcomes were achieved	Program evaluation	

Source: M. Wolery, P.S. Strain, & D.B. Bailey, Reaching the potentials of children with special needs. In S. Bredekamp & T. Rosegrant (eds.), *Reaching potentials: Appropriate curriculum and assessment for young children*, Vol. 1. (Washington, DC: NAEYC, 1992), 92–111.

Relevant Questions

Relevant questions
Does developmental screening indicate potential for developmental delay or disability?
Does hearing or visual screening indicate potential sensory impairments or losses?
Does health screening and physical examination indicate need for medical attention?
Does a developmental delay or disability exist? If so, what is the nature and extent of the delay or disability?
Does the child meet the criteria specified by the state to receive specialized services?
What is the child's current level of developmental functioning?
What does the child need to be independent in the classroom, home, and community?
What are the effects of adaptations and assistance on child performance?
What usual patterns of responding and what relationships with environmental variables appear to influence child performance?
What does the child need?
Which of the possible placement options could best meet the child's needs?
Does the child need specialized services, such as speech/language therapy, physical therapy, occupational therapy, or dietary supervision?
What is the child's usual performance of important skills?
Is the child using important skills outside the classroom?
Did the child make expected progress?

Diagnostic assessment asks, Does this child have a certain disability/delay/condition? and, If so, what is its nature and how severe is it?

Diagnosis

Diagnostic assessments are designed to determine whether a child has a given disorder and, if so, to what extent. The questions being asked in diagnostic assessment are, Does this child have a certain disability/delay/condition? and, If so, what is its nature and how severe is it? There are two levels at which children are assessed for diagnostic purposes. The first involves medical diagnoses that are conducted by physicians and other health care professionals using a range of diagnostic procedures. The presence of a medical diagnosis may not be related to developmental functioning or the presence of a disability. For example, children may have a particular medical diagnosis, such as near-sightedness, that does not affect development in substantial ways and is not considered a disability.

At the second level, children undergo assessments for determining whether they have specific disabilities. Such diagnoses are conducted by a range of different professionals and often by a team of individuals. For example, physicians often make diagnoses related to orthopedic and visual disabilities, speech-language pathologists make diagnoses related to communicative disabilities, audiologists make diagnoses of hearing impairments, and psychologists play a major role in making diagnoses of mental retardation. The measures used for making specific diagnoses of disabilities vary considerably, depending upon the diagnosis in question. For example, a test of cognitive functioning is often required in diagnostic assessments for mental retardation, but such a measure is not required in assessments for blindness, hearing impairments, or physical disabilities. Early childhood personnel often provide relevant information about a child to various professionals or other team members who are conducting diagnostic assessments.

Eligibility for special services

Eligibility assessment is conducted to determine whether a child meets the criteria for receiving special services that are not available to the general public. The question being asked in eligibility assessment is, Does this child qualify at this time for a certain service? For early intervention and special education services, designated state agencies (e.g., State Departments of Public Instruction) are responsible within broad guidelines for determining the procedures and criteria for being eligible for such services. Generally, this determination involves a diagnosis of disability; however, states may use different procedures for making this determination, particularly for young children. Early childhood staff may provide information to other team members who are conducting such assessments and may, in some cases, assist in collecting the needed information.

Assessment for planning a child's instructional program should answer questions such as, What does the child need to learn to do to be more developmentally advanced or independent in his or her living situation?

Planning instructional programs

Instructional program planning assessment is the process of determining what skills are important for the child to learn, what supports exist and are needed for those skills, and the specific nature of the situations in which the child lives and spends time. This process should involve an assessment of what the child is able to do and what he does do, as well as the things the child cannot or does not do on a regular basis. The general questions being asked are, What can this child do independently?, What does the child do with supports and assistance?, What does the child need to learn to do to be more developmentally advanced or independent in his or her living situation?, and, What appears to "work" with this child? The procedures for conducting such assessments are described later in this chapter. In such assessments, early childhood personnel are intimately involved in collecting information, summarizing that information, making decisions about the collected information, and using that information (with other team members) to plan instructional programs.

Placement assessment

Placement assessment is the process of determining which setting from among the potential options is most appropriate for a child. The specific question being asked is, Given this child's abilities and needs and the family's goals and priorities, what situation (classroom or program) will be best for the child? This question implies that (a) the child's needs and abilities are known; (b) the family's goals, concerns, priorities, and resources are understood; and (c) information about potential early education placements is available. Placement assessment requires a thorough instructional program planning assessment (to identify the child's abilities and needs), discussions with the family, and an assessment of the adequacy of potential placements. Several procedures exist for assessing preschool environments (cf., Wachs 1988; Bailey 1989a; Benner 1992; Nordquist & Twardosz 1992). Although placement assessment usually is not done at a formal level, it needs to be given careful attention, particularly as more varied placements become available to young children with disabilities.

Emphasis should be placed on identifying an early childhood program that is most appropriate for the child and matches the concerns and priorities of the family (e.g., for child care during specific hours, location near their home or work). It is also important to consider how that program should be adjusted and adapted to increase the chances that the goals set for the child will be realized. The early childhood staff may play two roles in this type of assessment. First, for children who are not yet in

In monitoring, the questions being asked are, Is this child learning and using the skills that have been identified as important? and, What aspects of the child's program should be changed?

their program, they may gather and provide the team with information about their activities and program. Second, for children who are already in their program, they may provide the same information about the program and help to identify how it could be adjusted to allow children's individual goals to be met. Of course, early childhood staff often will be responsible for making and carrying out any adjustments to the classroom activities and routines.

Monitoring progress

Monitoring is the process of determining whether one or more children are developing and learning as expected, and if not, determining what should be changed to improve the likelihood that they will progress as desired. The questions being asked are, Is this child learning and using the skills that have been identified as important? and, What aspects of the child's program should be changed? The answers to these questions are best determined from ongoing assessment of children using direct observation and interviews of individuals (family members, therapists, etc.) who interact frequently with the child. This process allows the team to gather information about how well they have linked the assessment results to the curriculum and what adjustments are needed to make a more effective link.

Early childhood staff play several key roles in monitoring assessments. Together with other team members, they collect information through observation and other means. Typically, they also assist in making decisions about whether the curriculum is serving its designed purposes and participate in decisions about the changes that should be made. In many cases early childhood staff will be the individuals who make adjustments to the curriculum if changes are indicated.

Evaluating the effects of the program

Evaluating program effects is the process of determining whether children achieved the goals established by their early intervention teams and determining the extent to which the program contributed to that achievement. The questions asked may vary, depending upon the purpose of the evaluation study, but usually include, Did the child achieve the goals that were set? and, Can children's progress or lack of progress be attributed to the early childhood program? In most cases only the first question is asked. Children with disabilities often receive intensive assessments at the end of each year and are required to undergo reevaluation on a regular basis. The role of the early childhood staff often is to provide information about the child's progress to other team members.

Planning the child's instructional program

The focus of this section is on conducting assessments for planning instructional and intervention programs. The types of information needed from such assessments are described, and then issues related to developing Individualized Education Plans (IEPs) are discussed. (The requirements and process for developing the Individualized Family Service Plan [IFSP] were described in chapter 2.)

Needed information

To plan an effective early childhood program for a child with a disability, the program planning team (comprising family members, early childhood personnel, and other professionals) needs four broad types of information, including information about (a) children's abilities and needs, with particular attention given to the family's perspectives on those issues; (b) instructional practices that are likely to be effective with the child; (c) the child's environments outside the early childhood program; and (d) the organization and structure of the program in which the child is to be placed. Instructional program planning assessments are systematic ways of gathering the information in these four areas.

Understanding the child's abilities and needs. When conducting assessments for planning instructional/intervention programs, teams must get information on children's current developmental and adaptive abilities and on children's needs for additional developmental and adaptive skills. Children's *abilities* refers to their past developmental accomplishments and their skills and patterns of interacting with the social and physical world. Because meaningful intervention is based on children's current abilities, early childhood personnel need to understand clearly what children usually do, what they are capable of doing, and the situations (contexts) in which they use particular skills. Children's *needs* refers to the developmental skills that require elaboration, the next steps in the development of more complex skills, and the adaptive skills that would make them more independent and competent in their current environments. It is important to note that *developmental needs* does not refer only to mastering the next step in a sequence of development. Often children's developmental needs involve learning to apply skills in a variety of different contexts and learning multiple ways of doing the same thing. For example, learning to walk is an important developmental skill; however, learning to walk in different situations (e.g., on carpeted floors, on slick floors, on an incline, on a gravel driveway, on the uneven surface of a grassy play area) is just as critical as learning the next step in the sequence of physical development (e.g., learning to run, hop, or skip).

Children's adaptive needs can be specific to their living situation. An important question to ask is, In the home and any other environment in which the child consistently spends time, what skills would make him or her more independent and more thoroughly integrated? These skills may not be developmental skills and may not be needed by all other children; however, learning to do them may have many positive benefits for the individual child. In understanding children's current abilities and needs, it is also important to identify the supports that exist in children's environments for particular skills. For example, what adaptive equipment is needed, what modifications of materials are required, and what assistance is given by adults (family members, teachers, etc.)? Often, a goal of early intervention programs is to reduce the amount of assistance that is provided so that children become independent in doing important skills.

Information on a child's developmental and adaptive abilities and needs cannot be obtained quickly or easily. Gathering this information requires an ongoing process of observing the child in different situations and interacting with the child over time, as well as interviewing family members, previous caregivers and therapists, and other people who interact regularly with the child. Many programs use developmental scales (e.g., norm-referenced and/or criterion- and curriculum-referenced instruments) to obtain information on children's developmental abilities and needs (see Bagnato, Neisworth, & Munson 1989; Bailey & Wolery 1989; and Nuttall, Romero, & Kalesnik 1992 for descriptions of these developmental scales). These measures often are helpful in providing a broad, overall picture of children's development and in identifying general goals for intervention. However, developmental scales often do *not* contain sufficient information to be used alone in establishing the high-priority goals. The information from such scales must be supplemented with observations, interviews, and informal assessment situations.

Because of the complexity of development, we often need to consider children's abilities and needs in different areas, such as social, communication, physical, cognitive, and self-care skills. Within each area, a variety of assessment tools and procedures are available. It is beyond the scope of this chapter to describe these procedures; however, several resources for each area are shown in table 2.

The reason for identifying children's needs is to establish the focus of the instructional program. Identifying the focus often involves writing goals and objectives for particular types of skills that the team agrees are important for the child. These objectives are the desired outcomes resulting from the child's participation in the early childhood program.

INCLUDING CHILDREN WITH SPECIAL NEEDS

Table 2. Resources Related to Assessing Various Areas of Development

Area of development	Resource
Social development and social interactions and play	– Knoff (1992) – Linder (1993) – Odom & McConnell (1989) – Wolery & Bailey (1989)
Speech, language, and communication development	– Benner (1992) – Bryen & Gallagher (1991) – Miller (1981) – Roberts & Crais (1989) – Seymour & Wyatt (1992)
Physical/motor development	– Benner (1992) – Dunn (1992) – Smith (1989) – Weeks & Ewer-Jones (1991) – Williams (1991)
Cognitive development	– Bracken (1991a) – Gillespie-Silver & Scarpati (1992) – Gyurke (1991) – Kamphaus & Kaufman (1991) – Langley & Harris (1989) – Schnell & Workman-Daniels (1992)
Self-care (toileting, feeding, dressing) and adaptive skills	– Benner (1992) – Harrison (1991) – Wolery & Smith (1989)

When families are involved in the assessment activities, they are more likely to participate in decisions about using assessment information.

In most cases a thorough assessment results in many more goals than can possibly be addressed in a meaningful way. As a result, choices must be made about which goals are most important. The family's views are critical when making such choices. Their perspectives about which goals are most important should be emphasized in planning the early childhood program. Ideally, families will be involved in each part of the assessment process: planning the assessment, gathering information, determining whether the assessment information is consistent with their perspectives of the child's abilities, and making decisions based on the assessment information. When families are involved in the assessment activities, they are more likely to participate in decisions about using assessment information (Brickerhoff & Vincent 1986). The primary rationale for attending carefully to the perspectives and choices of families is that they have the primary responsibility for the child's well-being, for rearing the child, and thus for living with the results of the child's early education experiences. Families are not responsible for planning the early childhood curriculum, but they are in a very strong position to expect particular types of skills to be learned as a result of their child's participation in the program. When families express desires for particular goals, then teams must be responsive to those desires. If a given goal is unrealistic, then teams have a responsibility to provide an understandable rationale and explanation of why the goal is inappropriate.

Early childhood staff members are intimately involved in identifying children's abilities and needs. They should assist other team members in planning and scheduling activities. They will likely participate in collecting some of the information by doing interviews, making observations, or using informal and developmental assessments. They will participate in summarizing the information and drawing conclusions about the child's abilities and needs and thus about the goals that are developed.

Identifying effective instructional practices. Planning an instructional program involves identifying which goals are important, but it also involves identifying instructional practices that are likely to be effective with the child. Various instructional practices for children with disabilities are presented in chapters 5 and 6. When conducting the assessment, the team should attempt to identify several things. This information is needed to link the assessment activities with classroom practices (i.e., the curricular interventions).

• *First,* the team should get information about the child's preferences for and interests in various toys, materials, and activities. Such information is usually obtained from interviews with family members and observations of children in their natural environments, including the classroom. This information is useful

INCLUDING CHILDREN WITH SPECIAL NEEDS

Early childhood staff are likely to provide and/or collect information on children's preferences and interests.

in identifying which activities and materials are likely to be successful in promoting learning.

• *Second*, the team should obtain information about children's levels of engagement and the amount of adult support that is required to sustain their participation in activities (McWilliam & Bailey 1992). Such information is best obtained through direct observation of the child in several different activities over multiple days.

• *Third*, the team should collect information on the child's responsiveness to adults and to peers. The focus of this assessment should be on what types of adult and peer behaviors appear to result in sustained interaction and positive reactions from the child. Again, direct observation is a useful measurement strategy for obtaining this information.

• *Fourth*, the team should determine whether the child complies with adult requests. The issue of concern is whether the child follows instructions given individually and to groups of children. This will assist the team in understanding what supports will be needed to help the child participate in classroom activities.

• *Finally*, the team should gather information about whether the child imitates adults and other children, which is often assessed through informal, game-like tests in which the adult and peers model various behaviors.

When all of this information is collected and analyzed, the team should have a clear picture of how various strategies will work with the child. Also, the assessment gives them information about how the preschool program should be organized to promote children's learning and development.

Early childhood staff are likely to provide and/or collect information on children's preferences and interests. They typically supervise the classroom activities while other team members collect information on children's engagement. Early childhood staff also are likely to provide or collect information about children's responsiveness to adults and peers and about their compliance with classroom routines and adults' requests. They may conduct assessments of children's imitative abilities.

Identifying the child's environments. When developing effective programs for young children with disabilities, teams must address issues that extend beyond the early childhood program. The goal is to develop a plan that will maximize learning and development in all parts of the child's life and will facilitate the family's sense of well-being. Following the family's lead, the team should consider how the child functions in the home, in other settings where she consistently spends large amounts of time, and in community environments in which she regularly participates, such as the grocery store, the playground, or the religious meeting place. This analysis

Following the family's lead, the team should consider how the child functions in the home and in other settings where she or he consistently spends large amounts of time.

involves identifying those environments and identifying the family's concerns and priorities for the child in those situations.

A major means of getting this information is interviews with family members and possibly other adults, including child care providers. Family members may also be asked to help collect information in such settings. For example, if a family is concerned about promoting positive interactions between the child and his siblings, the team could help the family collect information about such interactions. The team could devise a method for counting the number of positive and negative interactions and for documenting the situations in which negative interactions are likely (Arndorfer et al. 1994). Some members of the team also may need to conduct observations in settings outside the early childhood program.

The role of early childhood staff in this component of intervention planning assessment is threefold. First, they may conduct interviews with family members to determine their perspectives of the child's abilities and needs, to identify their concerns and priorities, to secure their views of the child's preferences and interests, and to select contexts in which observations should occur. Second, they may provide information on how the child functions outside the classroom (e.g., during field trips). Third, they should participate in analyzing the collected information to identify activities in the classroom that can be used to help children function in more advanced and adaptive ways outside the classroom.

Understanding the structure and organization of preschool programs. As already noted, planning instructional programs involves assessing children, but teams also must assess the early childhood program. This part of the assessment is done to determine how the high-priority goals and objectives can be addressed in the context of the preschool program. Assessing the program is also done to determine what adaptations, if any, are needed in the program.

Several types of information are needed, including information on how the physical environment is arranged (e.g., how different classroom areas are organized), the materials available, and the number of children who are served in the class (Bailey 1989a). Program assessment also involves how children move from area to area, how children access materials, and what adaptive equipment is available and how it is used. This assessment also should focus on children's schedules within the classroom, for example, how much time is spent waiting, how much time is spent in free play, how much time is spent in group activities, and what rules govern how children spend their time (Bailey & Wolery 1992). The assessment also should focus on children's roles in various activities; for example, at meals, do children serve themselves family style, or do adults distribute the food for each

By law, each child with disabilities must have a written Individual-
ized Education Plan (IEP) or an Individualized Family Service Plan.

child? The assessment should address the adult roles in various activities (Fleming et al. 1991). Does the adult lead the activity, does the adult monitor the activity and respond to individual children, or does the adult primarily assume a collaborative role? This information is critical in linking the results of the assessment (i.e., goals that have been set) to the activities and routines of the classroom. Information on designing and adapting programs for children with disabilities is presented in chapters 5, 6, and 7.

The early childhood staff play a central role in this component of the assessment. They provide information on how the class is organized and operated. They participate with the team in making decisions about what adjustments are needed in the ongoing curriculum, and they carry out the agreed-upon adaptations.

The Individualized Education Plan (IEP)

As already noted, assessment activities are conducted to develop an appropriate instructional program for the child. Achieving this goal requires teams to integrate all of the information about children's abilities and needs, the family's goals and priorities, the information on the settings in which the child spends time, and the structure and organization of the preschool program (Wolery 1989c; Barnett & Carey 1991; Barnett, Carey, & Hall 1993). With typically developing children, early childhood personnel often do this at an informal level. However, with each child who has a disability, integrating this information and developing a plan is a team endeavor that has a formalized process. The early childhood staff are critical players in these decisions.

By law, each child with disabilities must have a written Individualized Education Plan (IEP) or an Individualized Family Service Plan (IFSP; see chapter 2), depending on the child's age. Developed by a team that includes the child's family, the IEP and IFSP are based on the assessment results and are formal documents required for the child to receive special education and related services. Each school district and state may have different formats for writing the IEP, but certain specific information must be included on all IEPs. The required information is listed in table 3.

Several points about the IEP development are pertinent.

• *First*, the IEP is required by law and regulation. Thus, early childhood professionals must be aware of the components of the IEP and of the regulations related to its development (Turnbull 1990).

• *Second*, the IEP is a team endeavor that includes the child's family. It is not a document developed solely by the early childhood staff or other professionals (e.g., speech-language pathologists, occupational therapists, physical therapists). It requires participation of all team members *including* the family.

• *Third*, the IEP is a tentative document—a plan that may require revision. No team can be expected to plan an IEP that will be 100% successful. Most IEPs require modification as they are implemented and as children make progress.

• *Fourth*, the IEP must be reviewed on a regular (at least yearly), formal basis. The team must meet to review the child's progress and to make adjustments in the plan. Often the assessment information is updated before the IEP is reviewed. Although a yearly review is required, in practice the IEP should be reviewed more frequently.

Table 3. Information Required on IEPs

1. A statement of the child's present levels of educational performance, including academic achievement, social adaptation, prevocational and vocational skills, psychomotor skills, and self-help skills.

2. A statement of annual goals which describes the educational performance to be achieved by the end of the school year under the child's Individualized Education Program.

3. A statement of short-term instructional objectives, which must be measurable intermediate steps between the present level of educational performance and the annual goals.

4. A statement of specific educational services needed by the child (determined without regard to the availability of services), including a description of

    a. all special education and related services which are needed to meet the unique needs of the child, including the type of physical education program in which the child will participate, and

    b. special instructional media and materials which are needed.

5. The date when those services will begin and length of time the services will be given.

6. A description of the extent to which the child will participate in regular education programs.

7. A justification of the type of educational placement that the child will have.

8. A list of the individuals who are responsible for implementation of the Individualized Education Program.

9. Objective criteria, evaluation procedures, and schedules of determining, on at least an annual basis, whether the short-term instructional objectives are being achieved. (*Federal Register,* 41[252], p. 5692)

The IEP should be a dynamic rather than a static document— it should evolve and change as the child grows older and makes progress.

- *Fifth*, the IEP should be a dynamic rather than a static document—it should evolve and change as the child grows older and makes progress. Ideally, the IEP should help shape how the early childhood program is structured and operated for the child with disabilities. It should guide what early childhood and related-service personnel do and should be consulted frequently; it should not be a document that is developed and then filed away and never used.

Monitoring children's progress

The assessment activities are not completed once an IEP or IFSP is developed. The effects on children's progress of the early childhood curriculum and of the adjustments made in the preschool program are assessed. The purposes of such assessment are twofold. First, children's progress is monitored to determine whether they are acquiring and using the skills identified in their goals and objectives. Second, their performance is analyzed to determine whether changes should be made in the curriculum. Four important decisions should be made related to monitoring: (a) who should conduct the monitoring assessments, (b) how often progress should be monitored, (c) what measurement strategies should be used, and (d) in what situations the monitoring should occur.

Any member of the intervention team can monitor children's progress. Often early childhood teachers do a major portion of the monitoring because of their regular and extensive contact with children, but other team members may monitor specific goals. For example, the speech-language pathologist may monitor children's communication goals. When this occurs, however, the team member should consult with early childhood staff to determine whether they concur with the conclusions of the therapist. Similarly, family members may give program personnel regular information about how children are doing on their goals at home and in the community.

A yearly review of the IEP is required, but more frequent monitoring is necessary (Wolery & Sainato n.d.). In practice, monitoring may occur on many levels. We often monitor children on almost a moment-by-moment basis and adjust our behaviors and activities accordingly. Formal monitoring that includes collection and recording of information about children's progress should occur regularly but will vary by objective. Some objectives will require daily monitoring, others weekly, and still others more periodic. Generally, more frequent monitoring is used when children are having difficulty acquiring or using a particular skill and less frequently when they are making steady progress (Bailey & Wolery 1992). The purpose of this more

Monitoring children's progress should occur within the ongoing natural interactions and activities of the day.

frequent monitoring is to determine what adjustments are needed in the activities or in the adult instructional behavior.

Monitoring children's progress should occur within the ongoing natural interactions and activities of the day. Thus, direct observation, anecdotal records, and teacher and family judgment are the primary means of collecting monitoring information. Rarely, if ever, should norm-, criterion-, or curriculum-referenced tests be used to monitor children's progress—such tests are too time consuming and often

are used outside natural contexts. Generally, early childhood personnel can conduct the monitoring activities while they also engage in their ongoing teaching behaviors and management of the program. Nonetheless, the early childhood staff may need to have a plan for when they will monitor each objective to ensure that it gets done.

NAEYC and NAECS/SDE recommendations about assessment practices

In the 1991 position statement by NAEYC and NAECS/SDE about curriculum and assessment, several recommendations concerning assessment for planning instructional programs were made. In this section these recommendations are listed and the relevance of each to the assessment of young children with disabilities is addressed. The statements presented in italics were taken verbatim from the position statement.

1. Curriculum and assessment are integrated throughout the program; assessment is congruent with and relevant to the goals, objectives, and content of the program (p. 32). As already described, instructional planning assessments for children with disabilities are designed to get information to plan the curriculum for the child and to identify the needed program adaptations. However, once the initial assessment activities are completed and the curriculum is being implemented, assessment activities continue to monitor the effects of the curriculum. This ongoing assessment often results in revisions of the conclusions from the initial assessment and revision of the practices used in the classroom. Thus, assessment and curriculum are highly interrelated for children with disabilities.

2. Assessment results in benefits to the child, such as needed adjustments in the curriculum or more individualized instruction and improvements in the program (p. 32). The primary purpose of the initial assessment with children who have disabilities is to develop the IEP or IFSP and to determine what initial adjustments are needed in the early childhood classroom. This, of course, is done for the child's benefit. Likewise, ongoing assessment (monitoring) is needed to revise the curriculum and maximize the benefits of the program for the child.

3. Children's development and learning in all the domains—physical, social, emotional, and cognitive—and their dispositions and feelings are informally and routinely assessed by teachers' observing children's activities and interactions, listening to them as they talk, and using children's constructive errors to understand their learning (p. 32). Few disabilities affect only single areas of development; thus,

Meaningful instructional programs are based on the usual behavior of children in the natural environment during ongoing routines.

children who have disabilities should be assessed in all the identified domains of development and in their linguistic and communication development. As recommended, ongoing observation and interaction with children is a rich source of information about children's skills and their progress.

4. *Assessment provides teachers with useful information to successfully fulfill their responsibilities: to support children's learning and development, to plan for individuals and groups, and to communicate with parents* (p. 32). Assessment activities with children who have disabilities should, as described in the first section of this chapter, be conducted for specific purposes. A primary purpose is to determine how best to support children's learning and development. Also, the assessment can provide personnel with information for communicating with parents about the child. At the same time, early childhood personnel should realize that families of children with disabilities are tremendous sources of information about how their child functions outside the classroom. Early childhood personnel should systematically solicit such information in direct and appropriate ways from families.

5. *Assessment involves regular and periodic observation of the child in a wide variety of circumstances that are representative of the child's behavior in the program over time* (p. 32). A complete and accurate picture of how young children with disabilities function can, in most cases, only be obtained when the early childhood personnel have multiple opportunities to observe the child in different situations. Some of these situations for young children with disabilities may occur outside classrooms, such as in homes and in the community. Also, the observations should be focused—they should be conducted to answer specific questions (e.g., How does the child interact with peers in various situations? How does the child communicate his or her needs in different situations? How long does the child play, and what types of play occur with different materials?).

6. *Assessment relies primarily on procedures that reflect the ongoing life of the classroom and typical activities of the children. Assessment avoids approaches that place children in artificial situations, impede the usual learning and developmental experiences in the classroom, or divert children from their natural learning processes* (p. 32). Meaningful instructional programs are based on the usual behavior of children in the natural environment during ongoing routines. Thus, the assessment activities designed to develop those instructional programs also should occur in children's natural environments, including their classrooms. When the purpose of the assessment is diagnosis, children with disabilities may be assessed in artificial contexts. However, because of the artificial nature of such contexts, the information gained may not be useful in planning instructional programs.

7. *Assessment relies on demonstrated performance during real, not contrived, activities, for example, real reading and writing activities rather than only skills testing* (p. 32). The objectives that are established for young children with disabilities should be written in such a way that they reflect children's *behavior in context.* Thus, the assessment and monitoring of those objectives also occurs in the natural environment. Very few skills should be assessed outside the context in which they are meaningful.

8. *Assessment utilizes an array of tools and a variety of processes including but not limited to collections of representative work by children (artwork, stories they write, tape recordings of their reading), records of systematic observations by teachers, records of conversations and interviews with children, teachers' summaries of children's progress as individuals and as groups* (p. 32). These measurement strategies, as mentioned earlier in the chapter, are relevant for young children with disabilities. In fact, meaningful assessments of children's abilities and needs cannot be completed without using an array of different assessment techniques.

9. *Assessment recognizes individual diversity of learners and allows for differences in styles and rates of learning. Assessment takes into consideration children's ability in English, their stage of language acquisition, and whether they have been given the time and opportunity to develop proficiency in their native language as well as in English* (pp. 32–33). The regulations regarding assessment of children with disabilities require measures to be used in a nondiscriminatory manner and in the child's native language. Although legitimate and fair, these requirements present multiple difficulties for diagnostic assessments. However, the assessment methods used for planning instructional programs allow personnel to account for variability in cultural and linguistic backgrounds. Relying on naturalistic observation (Barnett, Carey, & Hall 1993) and family informants—perhaps with linguistic and cultural mediators (Barrera 1993)—allows the early childhood team to be sensitive to cultural and linguistic differences (for additional information see Barona 1991 and Walton & Nuttall 1992).

10. *Assessment supports children's development and learning; it does **not** threaten children's psychological safety or feelings of self-esteem* (p. 33). Children's usual behavior in natural situations can easily be assessed without causing children stress because observation—done unobtrusively—is a primary data collection means. However, sometimes there is a need to determine what children are capable of doing but do not do on a regular basis. Because such assessment activities can usually be devised as game-like activities, there is little reason to threaten children's psychological safety or feelings of self-esteem.

Collaborating with the family in the assessment sets the stage for establishing trusting relationships between families and staff members.

---

11. *Assessment supports parents' relationships with their children and does not undermine parents' confidence in their children's or their own ability, nor does it devalue the language and culture of the family* (p. 33). Assessment of children with disabilities must be conducted with the realization that each child exists within the context of his or her family. Ideally, families will be involved in planning and scheduling the assessment activities and in making decisions on the information that is secured. Actions that communicate to families that their perspectives and views are valued assist in ensuring that the family's confidence is not undermined. The early childhood team must be sensitive to the family's desires about the extent of their involvement, to the manner in which information is communicated to families, and to the manner in which information is solicited from families. Also, professionals must be aware of how families interpret the information and of their feelings about it. Collaborating with the family in the assessment sets the stage for establishing trusting relationships between families and staff members.

12. *Assessment demonstrates children's overall strengths and progress, what children **can** do, not just their wrong answers or what they cannot do or do not know* (p. 33). Understanding what children are able to do is central to planning instruction for children with disabilities. It is the base from which instructional goals and objectives are established and the base from which instructional activities to address those goals are devised. Thus, as much emphasis is placed on understanding what children can do as on what they need to learn to do.

13. *Assessment is an essential component of the teacher's role. Since teachers can make maximal use of assessment results, the teacher is the **primary** assessor* (p. 33). Providing effective early childhood education to children with disabilities requires the early childhood staff to be continually assessing what they are doing, what effects it has on children, and what children are doing. Staff use the assessment information to improve and modify the program for children with disabilities. However, other team members and the families also may engage in assessment activities and may use the results of assessments. The extent to which the teacher is the primary assessor for children with disabilities will vary from child to child. For example, with some children, the speech-language pathologist may play a primary role in assessing the child; with other children, the physical or occupational therapist may take a primary role; however, the early childhood staff, because of their extensive contact with children, play important roles in gathering and sharing information.

14. *Assessment is a collaborative process involving children and teachers, teachers and parents, school and community. Information from parents about each child's experiences at home is used in planning instruction and evaluating children's learning.*

Good assessment encourages children to participate in self-evaluation.

Information obtained from assessment is shared with parents in language they can understand (p. 33). For children with disabilities, assessment is clearly a collaborative process among early childhood staff, family members, and the representatives of other relevant disciplines. This collaboration requires all members of the team to use language that each individual understands. Also, each team member may have unique information about the child for planning instruction and monitoring its effects.

15. *Assessment encourages children to participate in self-evaluation* (p. 33). On an informal basis, early childhood personnel may assist children with disabilities in being aware of their behavior and making judgments about it. An emerging literature exists on teaching children with disabilities self-management strategies, including self-evaluation procedures (Sainato et al. 1990; Higgins-Hains 1992; Sainato, Goldstein, & Strain 1992).

16. *Assessment addresses what children can do independently and what they can demonstrate with assistance, since the latter shows the direction of their growth* (p. 33). Understanding children's developmental and adaptive abilities also involves identifying behaviors they display with and without supports. Often the supports come in the form of adult assistance. Fading and removing that assistance is a major part of teaching young children with disabilities (Wolery, Ault, & Doyle 1992); this issue is discussed in chapter 6.

17. *Information about each child's growth, development, and learning is systematically collected and recorded at regular intervals. Information such as samples of children's work, descriptions of their performance, and anecdotal records is used for planning instruction and communicating with parents* (p. 33). Although an initial assessment must be conducted to develop the child's IEP or IFSP, this is only the beginning of assessment activities. As the curriculum is implemented, its effects are monitored using a variety of measurement strategies (e.g., interviews, teacher judgment, direct observation, rating scales). In addition to the formal review of IEPs and IFSPs on a regular basis, children's progress on individual objectives should be monitored on an ongoing basis (e.g., weekly).

18. *A regular process exists for periodic information sharing between teachers and parents about children's growth and development and performance. The method of reporting to parents does not rely on letter or numerical grades, but rather provides more meaningful, descriptive information in narrative form* (p. 33). The IEP and IFSP are useful mechanisms around which early childhood personnel, other team members, and families communicate. Regular contact and discussions of children's progress related to the high-priority goals are recommended. Such discussions rarely include grades; however, on occasion they may include numerical counts or timing of the behavior that occurs. For example, if a goal is to increase sharing, then the teacher might report to the family that she noted three instances of sharing on a given day.

Summary

Young children with disabilities are assessed for a number of reasons, including screening them for developmental delays and disabilities, diagnosing them, determining their eligibility for special services, planning their instructional programs and placements, monitoring their progress, and evaluating the effects of the early childhood programs. Children with disabilities are assessed through direct testing, direct observation, and interviews with relevant others. Early childhood personnel are intimately involved in assessing children to plan an appropriate curriculum and monitor the effects of that curriculum. The families of children with disabilities are involved in all steps of the assessment process, and they participate on the early intervention team. The team must develop and implement an individualized plan for each child with disabilities.

Chapter 5

Designing Inclusive Environments for Young Children with Special Needs

Mark Wolery

A S NOTED IN CHAPTER 1, young children with developmental delays and disabilities have needs that are similar to, and unique from, their peers who are free of disabilities. This statement holds two implications. First, many of the techniques and interactional styles that early childhood staff use with children who do not have disabilities are useful, relevant, and effective for young children with disabilities. Second, to address the unique needs of young children with disabilities, adaptations in classrooms and in adults' strategies and interactional patterns may be needed. This chapter describes some of those adaptations and how to implement them. The chapter has three major sections. It begins with a description of foundational assumptions for classroom practices with young children who have special needs. The second section presents an overview of several available instructional strategies. The third section discusses issues related to designing classrooms that include young children with disabilities.

The behavioral perspective, although often seen as stressing the impact of the environment, in fact proposes that learning occurs from dynamic interactions between children and their environments.

Foundational assumptions

Nine assumptions, based on research and experience, guide the development of classroom-based services for preschoolers with disabilities. These assumptions are described in this section.

Many factors influence children's learning and development. This statement, of course, applies to children with *and* without disabilities. These factors include such diverse things as their genetic endowment, their mothers' prenatal health, the circumstances and complications of birth, their subsequent health and biological status, the educational and financial status of their families, the supports and resources available to their families, their temperament, their previous and current patterns of interacting with the social and physical world, and the effects they have on their families and those around them. Thus, the important forces that affect children's learning and development include past and current health and biological factors, societal and familial factors, and learning history and patterns of interacting. These factors work together to influence what children have learned, how they learn, and how we can support their development.

Children's experiences (interactions) with the environment influence their learning and development. Most individuals readily recognize that our experiences influence what we do, how we perceive the world, and how and what we learn. The developmentally appropriate practice guidelines (Bredekamp 1987; NAEYC & NAECS/SDE 1991) and similar recommendations in early childhood special education (DEC Task Force on Recommended Practices 1993) were written to guide professionals in organizing and operating early childhood programs to influence children's experiences so that they will learn and develop to their maximum potential. Most notable theories of child development assume that child–environment interactions substantially influence learning and development. Piaget (1951, 1952, 1954) maintained that four forces influence children's cognitive development: their interactions with the physical world, their interactions with the social world, equilibration (the balance between assimilation and accommodation), and biological maturation. Vygotsky (1978) also recognized that children's interactions with the physical world were important, and he stressed the influence of adults and peers in mediating those interactions to cause certain types of learning. The behavioral perspective, although often seen as stressing the impact of the environment, in fact proposes that learning occurs from dynamic interactions between children and their environments (Bijou & Baer 1961, 1965, 1978).

Particularly beneficial are those child–environment interactions that are initiated and directed by children and in which they are highly engaged.

The fact that child–environment interactions influence the child's learning and development produces at least two conclusions. *Some experiences have positive benefits on children's development, and others have negative effects.* Thus, as professionals, we have a responsibility to maximize children's growth-promoting interactions *and* minimize impeding interactions. Also, *experiences that occur within and outside early childhood programs are important.* This conclusion emphasizes the need for early childhood personnel to communicate on a frequent and regular basis with families and others who care for the child.

Particularly beneficial are those child–environment interactions that are initiated and directed by children and in which they are highly engaged. As previously noted, some child–environment interactions are more likely to have positive benefits for children than are others. These interactions often are started by the child (i.e., child initiated) and are sustained by the child's interest and motivation (i.e., child directed). Researchers believe that such interactions are relevant and appropriate to children's ability levels and thus contribute positively to children's development. It is generally assumed that children will learn more and benefit more if they are actively engaged with the environment. Engagement can be defined as actively manipulating or interacting with objects, activities, or other people in developmentally appropriate ways. McWilliam and Bailey (1992) present a hierarchy of engagement and suggest that some types of engagement result in more learning than do others. As noted in chapter 1, one goal of early intervention is to promote children's engagement at complex and challenging levels.

Many desirable child–environment interactions can occur within inclusive programs. The potential benefits of inclusion are well documented (e.g., Bricker 1978; Odom & McEvoy 1988; Safford 1989; Peck, Odom, & Bricker 1993). These benefits (see chapter 1, table 1) extend to children with and without disabilities, their families, and their communities. However, it is likely to be the child–environment interactions within those programs, rather than the mere fact of inclusion, that cause those benefits to occur (Fewell & Oelwein 1991). In chapters 5 and 6, strategies are described for increasing the likelihood that the positive benefits will be realized from children's experiences in inclusive programs; guidelines for integrating those strategies in inclusive classrooms are provided in chapter 7.

Many desirable experiences for children with special needs can occur within programs following the developmentally appropriate practice guidelines. Since publication of the guidelines for developmentally appropriate practice

(Bredekamp 1987), authors have analyzed the relevance of the guidelines for young children with special needs and have compared the guidelines to practices in early childhood special education (Carta, Schwartz, et al. 1991; Norris 1991; J. Johnson & K. Johnson 1992; Mallory 1992; Wolery, Strain, & Bailey 1992; Bredekamp 1993; K. Johnson & J. Johnson 1993; Carta et al. 1993; McLean & Odom 1993). Two conclusions are warranted. First, the guidelines of developmentally appropriate practice are seen as good starting points for serving young children with special needs, and second, those guidelines may require adaptations or modifications to meet the needs of young children with disabilities. In other words, young children with disabilities may engage in many positive and desirable experiences when enrolled in developmentally appropriate programs. However, to be maximally beneficial, children's experiences will need to be facilitated using strategies and adult behaviors not described in the guidelines. This chapter and the next describe some of those adaptations.

Child–environment interactions must be considered when planning and implementing early childhood programs. A basic notion of developmentally appropriate practice is *individual appropriateness* (Bredekamp 1987). Similarly, early childhood special education is based on the assumption that early childhood programs must be individualized for young children with disabilities (Barnett & Carey 1992). When making decisions about individualizing programs for children with special needs, teams must understand children's interactions with their environments—the early childhood program and other environments (e.g., home) in which children spend time. As described in chapter 4, such knowledge is best obtained by observing children in those settings over time and by talking with other people who also observe and interact with the child. The nature of those interactions (e.g., how children approach tasks, how they stay with activities, and how the environment responds to them) are critical pieces of information needed to plan useful early childhood programs for children with disabilities.

A primary role of early childhood personnel is to influence the nature and effects of child–environment interactions. The roles of some professionals, such as pediatricians, nurses, and nutritionists, are to prevent events that may cause developmental problems through immunizations, appropriate diet, and so on, or to treat other problems through surgery, medications, and other medical interventions. Such interventions primarily influence children's health status and biology. The role of other professionals, such as social workers and psychologists, is to deal with broader ecological and social issues that involve the family. They focus primarily on the factors that indirectly influence children's interactions with the environment.

Early childhood personnel have multiple roles with respect to promoting children's well-being. We assist health care professionals in promoting children's health by ensuring that children get adequate nutrition, rest, and activity. We often deal with broader social issues through our contacts with and supports of families. However, a central role for early childhood personnel in many programs, especially classrooms, is to influence the interactions children have with toys, materials, activities, peers, and adults. That influence occurs, of course, for the child's benefit—to increase the probability that each child will have experiences that allow him to learn desirable things, to gain feelings of self-worth and mastery, to enjoy learning, and to become an adaptive and valuable citizen in his community. In chapters 5 and

Most interventions needed by young children with special needs should be implemented within the context of ongoing activities in high-quality early childhood programs.

6 we refer to our attempts to influence child–environment interactions as *interventions*—teaching strategies.

The child–environment interactions of children with disabilities are tremendously complex. Any knowledgeable early childhood specialist recognizes that children's development and interactions with the environment are complex. This complexity is magnified and made more difficult to understand when children have developmental delays and disabilities. Observing the complexity is one thing, but making sense of those observations and translating that information into meaningful early childhood programs are quite another. Because of this complexity—as described in chapter 3—a team of professionals is required for young children with special needs. The important point is that early childhood personnel should not be expected to know what is needed and how to do everything to ensure that children's experiences will produce desirable benefits. Much of this information must come from other members of the team, such as special educators, speech-language pathologists, physical therapists, and occupational therapists. In this chapter, some interventions are described for positively influencing children's experiences. Early childhood special educators should have a working knowledge of these interventions, and early childhood program personnel can easily learn to use and adapt them to their classrooms and children.

Most interventions needed by young children with special needs should be implemented within the context of ongoing activities in high-quality early childhood programs. This chapter and the next describe specialized interventions that have been developed primarily for young children with special needs, although many also are appropriate for young children without disabilities. As described in chapter 7, most of these interventions can be embedded within the usual activities of programs and within staff members' ongoing interactions with children.

In summary, although many factors influence children's development and learning, their interactions with the social and physical world are a primary force. Many desirable child–environment interactions can occur within inclusive programs that follow the developmentally appropriate practice guidelines; however, adaptations of those programs may be needed. Recognizing the need for and the nature of those adaptations must come from information about how children interact within their unique ecologies. Although early childhood personnel are responsible for influencing child–environment interactions, children's intervention teams should provide support and assistance in planning and using those strategies in the contexts of ongoing interactions and classroom activities.

Intervention strategies

The past 25 years of concentrated research and experience providing early childhood services to young children with disabilities has produced many strategies for influencing their experiences. Although we have learned a great deal, we still have much to learn.

Table 1 presents a list of different *types* of intervention strategies. As the list indicates, early childhood personnel have many strategies from which to choose. Of course, many of these strategies can be used in combination, but they are presented separately to illustrate the range of potential strategies and for discussion purposes. The strategies that involve structuring the early childhood environment are discussed in this chapter. Those strategies that focus more on adults' interactions with children and on teaching peers without disabilities to interact positively with children who have disabilities are described in chapter 6. Many of these strategies also are useful and appropriate for children who do not have disabilities.

No single strategy will be necessary and successful for all children in all situations. Using the different strategies listed in table 1 will result in different types of experiences for children. As previously noted, child-initiated interactions with the environment are highly valued because they allow children to be independent learners, to interact in creative and useful ways, and to acquire the skills of self-direction and control. However, for some children, other issues may also be important. It may be necessary for the child to acquire and/or use very specific skills or patterns of interacting with the environment. Identification of these skills, of course, comes from the assessment and from the IEP or IFSP that is developed for the child by the early intervention team (see chapter 4).

In figure 1, the continuum of strategies is listed, and the likelihood that each type of strategy will produce child-initiated interactions with the environment or specific, adult-targeted behaviors is illustrated. Strategies on the left side of the figure are likely to result in high levels of child-initiated behavior or learning and less control of the content of child–environment interactions (i.e., specific behavior); strategies on the right side are likely to result in high levels of specific, adult-targeted behavior or learning and more control of child–environment interactions. The two diagonal lines represent the likelihood that these different types of child-environment interactions are likely to occur when the respective strategies are used. The diagonal line that starts high on the left and moves lower represents the likelihood of child-initiated interactions with the environment; the diagonal line that starts high on the right and moves lower represents the likelihood of specific, adult-targeted behavior.

Table 1. Potential Intervention Strategies

Intervention strategies	Useful references
Structuring the physical space and providing toys and materials that promote play, engagement, and learning	— Bradley (1985) — McWilliam & Bailey (1992) — Musselwhite (1986) — Odom & Strain (1984) — Sainato & Carta (1992)
Structuring the social dimension of the environment to include models and proximity to peers and responsive, imitative adults to increase engagement, interaction, communication, and learning	— Bailey & Wolery (1992) — McWilliam & Bailey (1992) — Dunst et al. (1987) — Odom, McConnell, & McEvoy (1992b)
Using children's preferences for particular materials and activities to promote engagement and learning	— Mason et al. (1989) — Koegel, Dyer, & Bell (1987) — Dyer, Dunlap, & Winterling (1990)
Structuring routines using responsive adult behaviors, naturalistic time delay, and transition-based teaching to promote interaction, communication, and learning	— Halle, Baer, & Spradlin (1981) — Schwartz, Anderson, & Halle (1989) — Wolery, Doyle, et al. (1993)
Using structured play activities to promote interaction, communication, and learning	— DeKlyen & Odom (1989) — Musselwhite (1986) — Odom, McConnell, & McEvoy (1992b)
Using differential reinforcement, response shaping, behavioral momentum, and correspondence training to increase the complexity and duration of children's responses and engagement and to encourage appropriate behavior	— Baer (1990) — Cooper, Heron, & Heward (1987) — Paniagua (1990) — Wolery, Bailey, & Sugai (1988)
Using naturalistic/milieu teaching strategies (e.g., models, expansions, incidental teaching, mand-model procedure, naturalistic time delay) to promote communication and social skills	— Bailey & Wolery (1992) — Kaiser, Alpert, & Warren (1987) — Warren & Kaiser (1988) — Warren & Reichle (1992)
Using peer-mediated strategies (i.e., providing specific training to peers) to promote social and communicative behavior in children	— Goldstein & Wickstrom (1986) — Kohler & Strain (1990) — Odom, McConnell, & McEvoy (1992b) — Strain & Odom (1986)
Using response-prompting procedures (e.g., most-to-least prompting, graduated guidance, system of least prompts, simultaneous prompting, progressive time delay, constant time delay) to ensure acquisition and use of specific skills	— Billingsley & Romer (1983) — Wolery, Ault, & Doyle (1992) — Wolery, Bailey, & Sugai (1988) — Wolery, Holcombe, et al. (1992)

Note: These strategies and their application are discussed in chapter 6.

The past 25 years of concentrated research and experience providing early childhood services to young children with disabilities has produced many strategies for influencing their experiences.

All of these strategies are appropriate for some children, for developing some skills, in some situations, at some times. None of these strategies are necessarily appropriate for all children, for developing all skills, in all situations, at all times. However, some of these strategies can be used in combination with one another. The strategy or combination of strategies that should be used will depend on the child's current abilities and interactions with the environment, the skills and abilities that need to be promoted, and the situation (i.e., the activities, the schedule, the peers and adults present, etc.).

For example, if the goal is to increase the duration of a child's play, then structuring the physical space and making interesting and inviting toys available is appropriate. If the goal is to increase social play, then toys with high interactive potential would be selected and peer-mediated strategies might be used. If the goal is to increase a child's use of two- and three-word statements that describe an actor and an action, then the naturalistic teaching strategies may be needed. If the goal is to increase a child's compliance with adults' request to clean up an activity area, then some of the differential reinforcement strategies may be appropriate. If the goal is to teach the child to put on a coat, use a spoon, or name pictures or objects, then the prompting procedures may be most appropriate. The strategy must be selected based on the goal or outcome that is desired. Some strategies will be effective with certain outcomes but not with others.

Description of strategies

In this section, five types of strategies are described; these include (a) structuring the physical space of classrooms and using materials, (b) structuring the social dimensions of the classroom, (c) using children's preferences for materials and activities, (d) structuring routines, and (e) using structured play activities. The word *structure* is used here in a broad sense, meaning how the classroom is designed, organized, and operated. Structure refers to the decisions that are made by early childhood personnel in all classrooms—decisions about how the physical space is arranged, what materials are available, and how individuals within the class interact and go through the day. The word *structure* is *not* used to denote a rigid, sterile, teacher-directed environment. In fact, most of the developmentally appropriate practice guidelines that address how classrooms are organized and operated are applicable to designing inclusive classrooms (Bredekamp 1987; Bredekamp & Rosegrant 1992; Carta et al. 1993; McLean & Odom 1993).

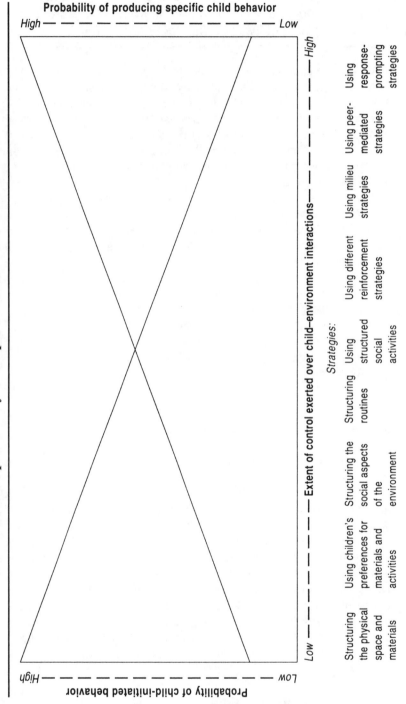

Figure 1. A proposed continuum of the extent to which various types of intervention strategies exert control in child–environment interactions by the amount of child-initiated behavior that will occur and the probability that specific child behavior will result

Physical space and materials

The general guidelines and considerations for designing classroom space for young children without disabilities are relevant for most preschoolers with special needs. For example, the space should be arranged to allow easy movement from area to area, the materials and areas should be stimulating and inviting, noisy areas should be separated from quiet areas, the areas and the materials within them should be safe, and adults should be able to scan the classroom visually from almost any vantage point in the room (McEvoy 1990).

Studies indicate that complex relationships exist between the amount of space and children's behavior. Too much space may mean more isolated behavior, and too little space (e.g., less than 20 square feet per child) may mean increases in negative interactions and aggression (Sainato & Carta 1992). However, other factors, such as the amount of materials available and the behaviors of adults, may also influence the effects of the space. Perhaps the most workable guideline is to arrange the classroom as seems appropriate and then make changes if the arrangement is not functioning as intended. For example, if particular areas seem crowded and have a high incidence of negative interactions, those areas should be made larger. If an area intended to promote cooperative play, such as the block area, seems to lend itself primarily to children playing on their own, reducing its size may promote more social play.

Some special considerations may be needed when children with disabilities are enrolled in a program (Bailey & Wolery 1992). For example, if a child has a severe visual impairment, then the space would have to maintain a predictable order, and the child would need to be oriented to that order. Changing the location of activity areas or the arrangement of materials within areas requires the teacher to orient the child with severe visual impairments to the change. If a child is in a wheelchair, then the areas must be arranged so that wheelchair access is possible. This may involve ensuring that sufficient space is provided for the child to get into different areas, as well as space within those areas for play to occur while the child is in the chair. Also, if a child requires large adaptive equipment, then the space has to be arranged so that the equipment will fit into the room. In most cases, specialists on the early intervention team can provide guidance on how to arrange the space for individual children.

As with space, most toys and materials that are appropriate for preschool children without disabilities are appropriate for young children with disabilities. Clearly, the toys should be safe, durable, responsive, and promote the types of play that are appropriate for the children involved (Musselwhite 1986). For example, realistic toys are often recommended for toddlers, while toys that stimulate imaginative play are appropriate for older preschoolers.

Most typically developing children play with toys and materials without being shown or told how, but some children with disabilities do not engage in such play spontaneously.

For young children with disabilities, several additional general guidelines can be proposed.

If necessary, assist children in learning to play with toys and materials. Most typically developing children play with a variety of toys and materials without anyone showing or telling them what to do. However, young children with disabilities may not spontaneously interact with or manipulate toys and materials. Because play is such an important medium for learning about the world and an important context for social interactions with peers (Bradley 1985), children who do not play with toys are at a considerable disadvantage. One goal for young children who do not play with toys is getting them to manipulate toys and materials. This may involve teaching basic movements associated with materials, such as banging, shaking, pushing, pulling, and otherwise manipulating toys. For such children, toys that "react" (make a noise or change visually) are recommended. Getting children to play with toys may also require physical assistance from adults in helping them learn to act on and manipulate toys (see chapter 6 for a discussion of prompts) (Bailey & Wolery 1984).

Another common goal is to help children play for more sustained periods of time. This is often accomplished by encouraging their play by playing beside them, responding to their manipulations of materials and toys with excitement, assisting them when needed, using toys that they prefer, and reinforcing longer periods of play (see chapter 6) (McWilliam & Bailey 1992).

Select toys and materials based on children's preferences and interests. As with typically developing children, children who have disabilities are more likely to play with toys they find interesting and appealing (Quiltich, Christopherson, & Risley 1977). Thus, teachers must observe children to determine what types of toys and materials they prefer. However, adults may need to take action to ensure that children sample the range of toys and materials that are available in the classroom. They may do so by showing children particular toys and materials as a group, introducing toys to children as they play, or suggesting that children play with particular toys or materials.

Provide toys and materials that encourage engagement, play, interaction, and learning. In part, the selection of materials and toys for children with disabilities should be done to promote learning and use of the skills specified on their IEP or IFSP goals. If a goal is to assist the child in sustaining his or her engagement with toys, then responsive toys should be used (Bambara et al. 1984). Another strategy to increase the amount of contact and engagement with toys is to rotate

For children who are learning to interact with peers and engage in social turns and conversational exchanges, toys that promote social interactions should be provided.

the availability of some toys and materials across different days or weeks (McGee et al. 1991).

Some toys or adaptations of toys appear to be related to particular types of behavior. For example, certain toys appear to result in more independent and isolated play, whereas others appear to result in a greater likelihood of social interactions with peers (Odom & Strain 1984). For children who are first learning to play with toys or whose toy play is not sustained, toys that promote independent use may be more appropriate. However, for children who are learning to interact with peers and engage in social turns and conversational exchanges, toys that promote social interactions should be provided in the presence of responsive peers. Among the toys and materials that are associated with a high degree of social interaction are dress-up clothes, balls, dishes, wagons, seesaws, blocks, dolls, trucks and cars, and many games. Among the toys that are less often played with interactively are puzzles, pull toys, paper and pencils, crayons, books, painting utensils, clay, and some constructive toys (e.g., Legos, Tinkertoys) (Odom & Strain 1984). However, it should be noted that some low–social-value toys can be used for promoting social interactions. For example, increases in social interactions are likely if two children

are working on a single puzzle; thus, how the toys and materials are used, as well as their basic properties, contributes to particular types of behavior.

Certain adaptations of toys and materials may result in communicative interactions with adults, which in turn can be used to promote language skills. Ostrosky and Kaiser (1991) recommend the following:

(a) providing interesting toys and materials,

(b) placing some toys out of reach but in sight to promote the likelihood of children requesting the materials,

(c) giving children "inadequate portions" of the toys to stimulate opportunities for requesting (e.g., giving a child some but not all of the pieces of a puzzle, giving a child a small portion of blocks),

(d) giving children choices about various toys,

(e) setting up situations that will require the children to request assistance (e.g., giving a child a container for which he cannot remove the lid), and

(f) creating situations that are silly, to give children opportunities to make comments.

Obviously, most of these strategies must be used when adults are available to be attentive and responsive to children's communicative attempts. Several instructional strategies can be used to expand and elaborate children's communicative skills when these material adaptations are employed (see Kaiser, Yoder, & Keetz 1992 and this volume, chapter 6).

Adapt toys and materials to promote attention, engagement, and play. Some children, because of physical limitations, are unable to manipulate toys in meaningful and playful ways. Play, however, remains an important goal for such children. An appropriate alternative for some children is to use adaptations that allow toys to be manipulated despite the children's limited movement abilities (Musselwhite 1986). A common adaptation is to use battery-operated toys and have children manipulate a variety of switches that will allow them to activate and deactivate the toys (Langley 1985; York, Nietupski, & Hamre-Nietupski 1985); another possibility is using computer-assisted toys and games (Horn, Hazel, & Hamlet 1991). When making such adaptations, consultation with a skilled speech-language pathologist and a physical or occupational therapist is recommended.

In summary, the guidelines for making decisions about space, materials, and toys for young children with disabilities are similar to those used when designing classroom environments for typically developing young children. However, special-

In most cases young children with and without disabilities do not engage in high levels of interaction with one another unless they are encouraged and supported in doing so.

ized arrangements and material use may be required for children with particular disabilities. In designing those adaptations, attention should be given to children's IEP or IFSP goals, and consultation should be sought from other members of the team.

Social dimensions of classrooms

The arrangement of the physical space and the availability of materials are important dimensions of early childhood classrooms, but the social dimensions of those settings also are critical issues to consider in designing inclusive classrooms for young children. *Social dimensions* refers to the behaviors and interactional styles of the adults and to the manner in which children are grouped and interact with one another.

Adult behavior. For children with and without disabilities, adults' behavior and interactional styles can promote or impede children's engagement in activities, their play with toys and materials, and the extent to which they benefit from participating in early childhood classrooms. Many of adults' roles in caring for and educating young typically developing children are appropriate with children with disabilities, including observing, responding, supporting, facilitating, and expanding children's play and engagement (Bredekamp & Rosegrant 1992). Several specific guidelines that are applicable for many young children with special needs are listed in table 2. In addition to these guidelines, the other strategies described in the remainder of this chapter and in chapter 6 are useful in promoting children's engagement, learning, and development.

Child dimensions and issues. Two rationales are often stated for including young children with disabilities in the same programs as their typically developing peers: to promote social and communicative interactions between the two groups and to provide children who have disabilities with peer models of appropriate and adaptive behavior (Peck & Cooke 1983). Although much remains to be learned about how to support social interactions and relationships between young children with and without disabilities (Odom, McConnell, & McEvoy 1992b) and about promoting children's imitation of appropriate peer models (Venn, Wolery, Werts, et al. 1993), some research addresses these issues and provides a basis for implications for designing classroom environments.

A substantial amount of research has addressed whether young children with and without disabilities actually interact with one another when they are placed in the same classroom. Two conclusions have been repeatedly supported. First, in most cases young children with and without disabilities do not engage in high levels of

Table 2. Guidelines for Promoting Elaboration of Children's Behavior

Author (Date)	— Recommended Strategies

Dunst et al. (1987)

- Be aware of and sensitive to the child's behavior and shifts in the child's behavior.
- Consider the child's behavior as purposeful (i.e., as an intent to interact with the physical or social environment).
- Respond contingently to the child's behavior and the assumed intent of that behavior.
- When a child is engaged in interactions with the environment, encourage him to continue that engagement.
- Provide models and set up situations that will present the child with the need and opportunity to engage in more complex and elaborate behavior.

Mahoney & Powell (1986)

- Engage in frequent play with the child.
- Observe the child's behavior, and manipulate objects and interactions that are similar to what the child is doing.
- Engage in short rather than long turns when interacting with the child.
- Wait for the child to initiate behavior or to respond to your initiations.
- Observe the child and imitate his or her behavior.
- Avoid using demands that produce the expectation that the child must display particular behaviors.
- Attempt to increase the duration of interactions by taking more turns and looking at or waiting expectantly for the child.
- Follow the child's lead in the pace of interactions.

Field (1982)

- Use simple, slow responses to the child's initiations.
- Promote imitation by imitating the child and responding to the child's approximations of imitation.
- Repeat the child's phrases and sounds (particularly if the child is an infant or a toddler).
- Observe the child, and wait silently for her initiations.
- Engage in reciprocal game playing.

MacDonald & Gillette (1988)

- Engage in game playing in predictable routines.
- Engage in taking turns with the child.
- Engage in waiting, then acting once, and then waiting and looking expectantly at the child.
- Imitate the child's actions and vocalizations.
- Observe the child, match your response to the child's, and then add an additional behavior.
- Play in a childlike way, and attempt to view the play as the child does.
- When interacting, be animated and engaging.
- Accept the child's responses to promote longer interactions.
- Display genuine emotions, such as affection.

interaction with one another unless they are encouraged and supported in doing so (Guralnick 1981; Odom & McEvoy 1988). Second, typically developing children appear to interact more readily and frequently with children who are similar to, rather than different from, themselves; the greater the difference in the children, the less likely are interactions (Guralnick 1981; Stoneman 1993). However, a number of factors influence and can modify the levels of social interaction (Bailey & Wolery 1992; McEvoy, Odom, & McConnell 1992). Similar findings exist regarding imitation of appropriate peer models. Young children with disabilities rarely engage in spontaneous imitation of their peers (Apolloni, Cooke, & Cooke 1977). However, a variety of strategies exist for promoting their imitation of typically developing children's behavior (Peck et al. 1978; Carr & Darcy 1990; Venn, Wolery, Werts, et al. 1993). From this research some general guidelines can be stated for structuring the social dimensions of preschool classrooms.

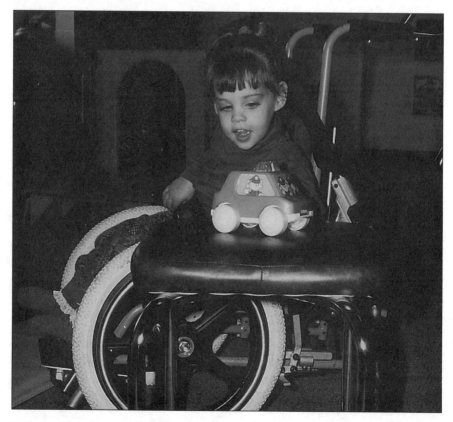

Generally, young children, including those with disabilities, are more likely to engage in social interactions and conversational exchanges when they are in small groups rather than large groups (Sainato & Carta 1992). This tendency suggests that whenever possible, inclusive classrooms should be structured in such a way that children spend large amounts of their time in small groups rather than in large groups.

The composition of the small groups also influences the amount and nature of engagement and interaction. Wolery, Anthony, and colleagues (n.d.) found that a young child with language delays who rarely interacted with her peers engaged in more frequent conversational exchanges when seated next to a loquacious peer during snack and meals, as compared to when she was seated next to children who talked infrequently. Other children who had disabilities, however, required specific teacher supports to increase their conversational exchanges. Additional research indicates that young children with disabilities are more likely to imitate peers who are more, rather than less, competent in completing experimental tasks (Peterson, Peterson, & Scriven 1977). Thus, in small groups, interaction and imitation may be more likely when the peers available to the child with disabilities are competent and skilled in the activities. Children are also more likely to play and interact with children of the same gender, but purposeful attempts to promote cross-gender interactions are successful without producing decreases in same-gender interactions (Sainato & Carta 1992). Thus, in inclusive classrooms teachers need to recognize that same-gender interactions are more likely but that cross-gender interactions should be promoted and encouraged as well.

Another important social dimension of early childhood classrooms is the age of peers. Some programs place only children of the same age in class together—same-age grouping—and others include children of different ages (e.g., 3 through 5 years of age) in the same class—mixed-age grouping. Generally, among typically developing children, the younger ones within mixed-age groupings appear to benefit, and older children appear to gain a slight benefit when they are in same-age classes. However, children with disabilities appear to benefit from being in mixed-age classes regardless of their age. The benefits occur in a number of dimensions, including general developmental progress and communication skills (Bailey, Burchinal, & McWilliam 1993; Blasco, Bailey, & Burchinal 1993; Bailey et al. 1993; Roberts, Burchinal, & Bailey n.d.). Mixed-age grouping may be more effective because it presents children with disabilities with behavioral models that are similar to but more advanced than their own behavior. Also, teachers in mixed-age classes may consistently provide activities and activity areas that are relevant to a broader range of child abilities than do teachers in same-age classes. Thus, if classrooms are roughly comparable in other respects, such as staff–child ratio, children with disabilities should be placed in mixed-age rather than same-age classes.

To summarize, the social dimension of the classroom is an important factor in promoting high-quality inclusion. The interactional styles that teachers use with typically developing children are often appropriate for young children with disabilities. However, careful attention should be given to the effects of adult behavior on children's engagement and their play. Social and communicative exchanges and peer imitation are more likely to occur when children with special needs are in small groups, when competent peers are in the group, when the group includes mixed ages, and when teachers encourage and support social exchanges and imitation.

Children's preferences

Like typically developing children, young children with disabilities have preferences for materials, playmates, and activities. Identifying those preferences and interests is important for children with and without disabilities. Usually preferences are identified by observing children during play and by asking others who know them well, such as family members. However, preferences may also be identified by systematically providing children with a range of choices and noting which materials, playmates, and activities they consistently select (Green et al. 1988). Of course, children's preferences may change over time (Mason et al. 1989); thus, identifying preferences is an ongoing task for early childhood personnel in inclusive programs.

When young children with disabilities are participating in preferred activities, they tend to show higher levels of engagement, be less resistant to adult interactions (Koegel, Dyer, & Bell 1987), and be less apt to engage in inappropriate behavior (Dyer, Dunlap, & Winterling 1990). For this reason, identifying and using activities and materials that children prefer is recommended. For children who have a restricted range of preferences, it may be important at times to encourage them to participate in activities that they would usually avoid or to play with toys or materials that they do not prefer. In such cases, making access to preferred activities and materials contingent upon having participated at some level in less preferred activities or having used less preferred materials and toys is also recommended (Jacobson, Bushell, & Risley 1969; Rowbury, Baer, & Baer 1976). At the same time, it is particularly important to encourage young children with disabilities to make choices and enhance their ability to do so. This is often accomplished by providing children with a defined range of choices and honoring their selections (Guess, Benson, & Siegel-Causey 1985; Kennedy & Haring 1993).

Expectations should be appropriate to the child's age and ability, but children should be encouraged to be as independent as possible.

Structuring routines

The routines that occur in classrooms, homes, and other contexts are regularly occurring events and often involve caring for basic needs, such as toileting, snack and meals, and napping. Others involve transitions from one location or activity to another, for example, arriving and departing from the classroom or going from play to cleanup time. Because routines occur on a regular basis and because they often involve adult assistance, they are opportune times for supporting children's communication, interaction, and learning. Routines that require more than a couple of minutes to complete (e.g., walking to a bus, diaper changing, snack) should involve interaction and communication (Venn & Wolery 1992).

Children with disabilities should complete routines as independently as possible (Bailey & Wolery 1992). For example, in family-style meals, children should participate in passing the dishes of food and serving themselves, and after eating, they should discard their napkins and used cups. When moving from one activity area to another, children should be encouraged to go to the new area without assistance; when putting on coats to go outside, they should be supported in putting on their own coats rather than having someone put their coats on them. Of course, such expectations should be appropriate to the child's age and ability, but children should be encouraged to be as independent as possible. In many routines and transitions, adult assistance is appropriate and necessary. However, to ensure that learning occurs during these routines, two strategies have been used: naturalistic time delay (Halle, Baer, & Spradlin 1981; Halle, Alpert, & Anderson 1984) and transition-based teaching (Werts et al. 1992; Wolery, Doyle, et al. 1993).

Naturalistic time delay, used primarily to increase children's communicative interactions and requests, involves (a) identifying times in routines when adults usually provide assistance, (b) delaying the assistance for a few seconds at those points in the routine and looking expectantly at the child, (c) providing a model if the child does not produce language, and (d) praising the child when language is forthcoming and allowing the routine to continue. This last step may involve providing the usual assistance. For example, naturalistic time delay could be used to assist children in requesting help. If an adult usually assists the child in zipping her coat, then during the routine of getting ready to go outdoors to play, the teacher would observe the child putting on her coat. When the child gets the coat on but does not have it zipped, the teacher might focus her attention on the child and look expectantly at her. The adult may then model, "Help, please," or some equivalent statement; allow the child to imitate; and then provide the assistance of zipping the coat. After a few times, the adult may not need to model the request but simply look expectantly at the child. This strategy is quite successful in increasing children's language initiations and in presenting adults opportunities to provide brief, nonintrusive language instruction (Schwartz, Anderson, & Halle 1989).

Transition-based teaching is similar to naturalistic time delay; however, the behaviors that are taught are not necessarily communicative responses. Transition-based teaching involves identifying skills that are important for the child to learn, such as naming particular objects or pictures. As the child begins to make the transition from one activity or area to another, the teacher gives the child an opportunity to respond. If the child is unsure of the correct response, a model or other prompt is provided. As soon as the child responds, the teacher praises her and the transition continues. This procedure requires just a few seconds at the beginning of each transition and often results in relatively rapid learning (Werts et al. 1992; Wolery, Doyle, et al. 1993). For example, as a child completes a puzzle and begins to move to another activity area, the teacher could say to her, "What's this color?" and point to a particular color on the puzzle. If the child responds, the teacher acknowledges the response and allows her to move on to the next area; if the child does not answer, the teacher says the color name, has her repeat it, and then allows the child to continue her transition. The primary difference between transition-based teaching and naturalistic time delay is that in transition-based teaching, the question asked of the child is not necessarily relevant to the transition as it is in naturalistic time delay.

Structured play activities

Certain types of behaviors are more likely to occur in some activities than in others. For example, more communicative exchanges and social interactions are likely to occur during low-structure activities such as snack or free play than during high-structure activities like circle time or language sessions (Kohl & Beckman 1984; Odom et al. 1990). However, some ways of structuring activities promote more interaction than others. Analyzing the amount of structure in a wide variety of play activities, DeKlyen and Odom (1989) found that increases in social interactions occurred for children with and without disabilities when the teacher provided certain kinds of structure to the activity. The structuring often occurred before the activity and involved the teacher setting rules, identifying an initial theme for the play, and identifying roles for the children. Although the play activities that were rated as high in structure resulted in more social interactions between children, there was no concomitant increase in teacher–child interactions during high-structure activities. Odom and colleagues (1988) provide detailed information on curricular activities that promote social interactions in integrated preschool classrooms.

A similar means of structuring activities is known as "affection training" or "friendship training" (McEvoy et al. 1988; McEvoy, Twardosz, & Bishop 1990). This type of structuring occurs when children are involved in teacher-led group activities, such as singing songs, doing finger plays, and playing games. Usually, at the beginning of the activity, the teacher provides a brief discussion of the value and importance of friends. During the group activity the games and songs are adapted to increase substantially the amount of physical contact and social interaction . This is promoted by changing the nature of the songs and games and by teacher encouragement. For example, in "friendship training" a song such as "Hokey Pokey" ("Put your right hand in, put your right hand out") could be adapted to "Put your right hand on your friend's head, put your right hand on your friend's back," and so forth. Such adaptations increase the amount of physical and social contact between children. While these activities produce increases in social interactions within the activity, they are also related to increases in social contacts during free play (Brown, Ragland, & Fox 1988; McEvoy et al. 1988). A manual that describes how to adapt typical songs and games is provided by Brown, Ragland, and Bishop (1989).

Summary

Many of the guidelines that teachers follow in designing the space, materials, activities, and social dimensions of the classroom for typically developing children are appropriate for designing inclusive classrooms. However, in some cases adaptations will be needed for individual children with special needs. The adaptations should be planned to promote learning and use of the skills identified in children's IEP or IFSP goals, and early childhood personnel should seek assistance from the early intervention team members in determining whether these adaptations are appropriate.

Chapter 6

Instructional Strategies for Teaching Young Children with Special Needs

Mark Wolery

Editor's Note: Some of the strategies the author describes in this chapter—and the very precise "specs" given for their use—may strike early childhood educators as highly technical or somewhat removed from the bustling, everyday world of the classroom. Certainly early childhood educators are well aware of the limits of behaviorism as the sole approach to children's learning and are wary of overreliance on rewards as a motivational technique. From this vantage point, some readers may have a negative first response to some of the techniques described in this chapter. Although we must be aware of the limitations and potential pitfalls of such methods, I urge readers to keep an open mind about them. The set of instructional techniques described in this chapter rests on the research of many investigators over many years; each procedure has proven its worth not only in the laboratory but in classrooms and other settings where children play and learn. Quite simply, these methods work. They are not for every situation, but when used appropriately, they often succeed where other methods fail. Research has also shown that most teachers and providers, with minimal instruction, are able to use these strategies effectively. As more and more early childhood programs begin to serve children with disabilities, we need to learn about these proven techniques and how they can help us to help children.

— C.C.

The concept of reinforcement has been misunderstood, misused, and abused by many educators, and many people have a "knee-jerk" reaction to its mention.

E ARLY CHILDHOOD PROFESSIONALS understand a great deal about how children learn and about how to support children's learning and development. Many of the practices that early childhood staff use to promote the engagement and learning of young children without disabilities serve as a useful foundation for including children with special needs. However, addressing the individual needs of young children with disabilities is a challenging task; fortunately, a variety of strategies have been effective in meeting the full range of their needs. These strategies occur on a continuum in terms of how much direct influence they have on children's experiences and the nature of their interactions with the environment. The strategies described in chapter 5 result in high levels of child-initiated interactions. In contrast, the strategies in this chapter are less oriented to encouraging child-initiated interactions, but they provide children with experiences that allow them to learn specific skills. When children's early intervention teams identify specific skills or patterns of behavior (responding to the social initiations of others, commenting on events around them, persistence, flexibility, etc.), the strategies described in this chapter are useful. These strategies are natural extensions of those described in chapter 5 and of those used by early childhood teachers on a daily basis. In fact, the strategies described in this chapter are often used in combination with those procedures.

From figure 1 in chapter 5, four types of procedures on the right side of the figure are described in this chapter: positive reinforcement, naturalistic procedures, peer-mediated strategies, and prompting techniques. Space limitations preclude a complete discussion, but the section at the end of this chapter (pp. 141–150) includes information on how to use selected strategies, and the interested reader should refer to the cited sources. Some technical language is used in this chapter. Unnecessary terms were avoided, but the strategy names were retained because they may be helpful in searching for additional information about them and in talking with special education colleagues.

Positive reinforcement

A large body of literature attests to the power of reinforcement to produce changes in the behavior of humans and other species (Cooper, Heron, & Heward 1987). Unfortunately, the concept has been misunderstood, misused, and abused by many educators, and many people have a "knee-jerk" reaction to its mention. In this section, reinforcement is defined and the justification for its appropriate use is presented. Procedures for identifying reinforcers for individual children, general rules for using reinforcers, and specialized uses are described. Three points, however, must be made to put this discussion in context.

The use of reinforcement does not reduce the necessity of providing early childhood classrooms that are full of inviting, interesting, fun, and meaningful activities.

First, the use of reinforcement with children who have disabilities—or with any child, for that matter—does not preclude or reduce the necessity of providing early childhood classrooms that are full of inviting, interesting, fun, and meaningful activities. Early childhood staff in inclusive classrooms must plan and use activities that capture children's attention, promote their engagement, are enjoyable to them, and are useful to them. Teachers also should use practices that are supportive of children. *Reinforcement procedures are used to supplement, not replace, such activities and practices.*

Second, excessive use of "external" reinforcement may be a sign that the early intervention team should evaluate what they are doing. If a child requires a great deal of praise, stickers, and adult attention to engage in a particular activity, the staff should determine whether the behaviors they are expecting of the child are important, whether the activity is necessary, and whether the activity can be adjusted to encourage more child-initiated engagement. For most children an excessive amount of such reinforcement is not needed or is needed for only brief periods of time. For example, some children may need a considerable amount of reinforcement when certain new activities are introduced, but after experiencing those activities, they may play and participate without external reinforcement. Similarly, when first learning a difficult but important skill, children may require more reinforcement, which is then reduced as they become more proficient. For some children, a lot of external reinforcement may be needed despite the early intervention team's efforts to plan interesting and enjoyable activities.

Third, reinforcement is simply a systematic way of supporting children's development and learning. Much of good teaching in early childhood classrooms involves encouraging children to try new things; supporting their engagement with toys, materials, and activities; facilitating their interactions with each other; and following their lead during play. When doing these things, we are often reinforcing children's behavior—perhaps unknowingly. With children who have disabilities, we may need to do this in a more purposeful and consistent manner. Using reinforcement should be viewed as an extension of what teachers already do rather than as a separate, new, or unusual style of interacting with children.

Definition of positive reinforcement

In technical language, "positive reinforcement is the contingent presentation of a stimulus following a response that results in an increase in the future occurrence of the response" (Wolery, Bailey, & Sugai 1988, p. 235). In nontechnical language this simply means that events that follow our behavior can influence whether we are likely to engage in the behavior again; if an event consistently follows a behavior *and* that behavior occurs more often, then we can say the behavior has been reinforced. When this occurs, we call the event that follows our behavior a "reinforcer." Everything we do is followed by other events—either we do something else, someone else does something, or the physical world reacts in specific ways. What we do happens in a stream or sequence of events and behavior; it does not occur in isolation from the world within and around us. For example, we move a cup to our mouth, and that act is followed by taking a sip, which is followed by swallowing and putting the cup down. Some of the events that occur in the stream of behavior have no influence on our behavior, others increase the likelihood that we will do it again, and others decrease the likelihood that we will do it again. *Positive reinforcement* is used to describe situations in which behavior is more likely to occur because of the events that follow it, and *reinforcer* is the name we give to those events.

Behavior–reinforcer relationships

Several well-documented facts about the relationship between behavior and reinforcing events are noteworthy.

• *Reinforcers can come from a variety of sources.* They may come from the effect the behavior has on the physical world, such as the reaction of toys when children use them. For example, a child who pounds with a toy hammer may be reinforced by the noise the hammer makes when it strikes an object, a young child playing at the water table may be reinforced by the sight and sound of the water from a cup pouring into the tub of water, and a child at the painting easel may be reinforced by the image that results when she moves a paintbrush across a piece of paper. Some reinforcers may come from the social environment, such as the reaction of peers and/or adults. For example, a child may repeat some "silly" behavior because of his peers' giggling reaction, and children may engage in cleanup because of adult approval. Still other reinforcers may come from within ourselves, such as a reduction in hunger or increased relaxation or excitement. For example, a child may ask you to push him on the swing because of the sensation he feels when swinging.

Two points are pertinent: many reinforcers may be operating and competing with each other simultaneously, and some reinforcers may be more powerful than others at a given time. The implication, of course, is that we need to understand which events are reinforcing to children and which reinforcers appear to have more influence than others. People often say that they tried reinforcement and it did not work. In many cases, a careful analysis of what happened indicates that they tried a weak reinforcer and it did not work as well as did more effective ones that

came from other sources. For example, praise may have been used, but it was less powerful than other events, such as the reaction of peers or the effects of the physical environment.

• *An event that is a reinforcer is most likely to increase those behaviors that it immediately follows.* The relationship is time-sensitive. In the stream of behavior that makes up our daily lives, the events that are reinforcing increase the behaviors they follow immediately, not behaviors that occurred several minutes previously. Thus, when we use reinforcers to support children's learning, we must ensure that the reinforcers occur immediately after the behavior we want to support. For example, if an important goal is to have a child play with toys near other children in a play area, then the reinforcement should be provided when the child is engaged in that play rather than later during snack, circle time, or at the end of the day.

• *Reinforcing events are more likely to increase the behaviors they follow if they occur every time the behavior occurs and only after the behavior.* In other words, using reinforcers is not magic; if a reinforcer follows a given behavior once or twice, it is not likely to cause a change in that behavior. It must happen consistently on several occasions. In fact, the behavior is likely to happen more often if the reinforcer

Reinforcers are an individual matter. For some children, rough-and-tumble play will be a reinforcer, but for other children it will not.

follows it each time. The implication for working with children is that we have to be vigilant in observing children, and then we must reinforce them each time the desired behavior happens. For example, if an important goal for a child is to share toys with his peers, then each instance of sharing should be reinforced. Of course, after the behavior happens often in desired situations, it will not need to be reinforced as often.

• *Events that are reinforcers at one point may not have the same effect later—the effectiveness of reinforcers can "wear off."* Repeated use of a reinforcer can cause it to lose its power. For example, when a child stacks several blocks and knocks them over and then rebuilds them and knocks them over again, it is likely that seeing and hearing the blocks fall is a reinforcer that is causing the child to build and knock over the blocks. However, after several building-and-knocking-over episodes, the reinforcing power of the sight and sound of the falling blocks is likely to dissipate. The implication is that repeatedly using a reinforcer may cause it to lose its influence. Thus, we need to use a variety of reinforcers, be careful not to overuse them, and recognize that a reinforcer that worked at one point in time may not work later.

• *Events that are reinforcers for some people will not work as reinforcers for other people—reinforcers are an individual matter.* For some children, rough-and-tumble play will be a reinforcer, but for other children it will not. Similarly, adult approval will be a powerful reinforcer for some children, but for other children, approval may have little reinforcing influence; unfortunately, for some children, disapproval may increase their behaviors more than will approval. The implication is that to use reinforcement we must know what events will work as reinforcers for each child. We cannot assume that what works for one child will necessarily work for another. Yet there are a substantial number of events that seem to have reinforcing effects on many children. For example, physical contact, freedom to do what one wants, opportunities to make choices, interesting sights and sounds, food, drink, and many other things are often, but not always, reinforcers for children and for adults.

• *Behaviors that are reinforced in one situation are most likely to be repeated in similar situations.* If a child is reinforced for a particular behavior in a specific situation, then the increase in the behavior will likely happen in that situation but may not generalize to other situations. For example, reinforcing a child several times over several days for cleaning up the block area will increase the likelihood that he will clean up the block area, but it might not change his cleanup behavior in the dramatic play area. The implication of this fact is that we should reinforce children for doing behaviors in situations where we want them to use those behaviors. Also, when we have reinforced children for engaging in a behavior in a given situation, the situation will begin to cue children that they should display that behavior in that situation. This is a desirable outcome because it means that learning has occurred and that less reinforcement will be needed in that situation.

• *Events that are reinforcing for a child can be given more influence if they are associated with more powerful reinforcers.* For example, if hugs are a strong reinforcer for a child but smiles and praise are not, then smiling and praising the child when hugging him will cause the smiles and praise to gain value as reinforcers. This concept is important because it means that the effectiveness of some reinforcers can be transferred to other events that are easier to use, are more socially acceptable, and are more likely to occur in the child's natural environment.

Justification for using reinforcement

Although there are many justifications for judicious use of reinforcers, perhaps the most important one is that reinforcement is operating and shaping children's behavior all the time. As children act on the world and the world reacts, some of their actions are reinforced. This reinforcement comes from the physical environment, from their peers, from the effects of the behaviors on how they feel, and from the adults in their world. We may not be aware that particular events are reinforcers, but our lack of awareness does not diminish their influence. If one accepts that reinforcement is occurring, then it follows logically that we should be aware of the events that are reinforcing and should use them to the benefit of children. Failure to recognize the power of naturally occurring reinforcers and failure to use reinforcers correctly may result in early educational experiences that promote dependence, lack of learning, antisocial behaviors, and other negative outcomes for young children.

Systematic and careful use of reinforcement can result in many positive benefits for children. It can allow them to learn patterns of interacting with the world that will enable them to be more independent learners, more efficient learners, more socially acceptable to their peers, less reliant on adults, easier to care for, and more developmentally competent (Cooper, Heron, & Heward 1987; Wolery, Bailey, & Sugai 1988; Barnett & Carey 1992). Reinforcement can help children use the skills they already have more frequently or in more desirable situations. It also can be used to teach them new skills and ways of interacting. Once children begin to do these things, they may find them pleasurable and interesting in their own right, and adults will no longer need to administer reinforcers for those skills.

The activities that children choose frequently are good candidates for reinforcers.

Procedures for identifying reinforcers

As previously noted, the events that are reinforcers can change with use and with the passage of time; they also may differ from one child to the next. Thus, early childhood personnel must decide what works as reinforcers for each child. Four useful strategies for identifying reinforcers are listed in table 1 below (Bailey & Wolery 1992). With many children, adults can try consequences that are frequently reinforcers for other children, such as a variety of forms of adult approval (e.g., hugs, praise, pats on the back, tickles), adult responsiveness, and allowing children to have particular toys or participate in preferred activities after a given behavior has occurred. Another tactic is to ask family members about what the child likes and does frequently. However, consequences that work with most children and families' suggestions may not work as reinforcers. To test the effectiveness of a possible reinforcer, adults should count the incidents of the behavior they want to increase in a specific situation for three or four days and then use the reinforcer for three or four days and continue to count the behavior. If the behavior increases, then it is likely that the consequence that was tried is in fact a reinforcer.

Another tactic is to observe children and note what they do and with which toys and materials they play when they have choices. The activities that children choose frequently are good candidates for reinforcers. Also, things that children frequently seek, ask for, or try to get may serve as reinforcers. In the occasional situation in which none of these tactics result in identifying effective reinforcers, the adults may want to conduct reinforcer preference tests. These tests involve providing children with choices of many different potential reinforcers in a variety of different

---

Table 1. Tactics for Identifying Reinforcers

• Try out things that often are reinforcers for children, such as adult approval, adult responsiveness, toys, and activities.

• Ask family members and other people who know the child about activities, materials, toys, foods, and so forth that the child likes and about things the child frequently does.

• Watch children for a few days, and try to identify the things that appear to capture their attention, behaviors that they display a lot, and materials that they use when they have choices.

• Provide children with choices from among a variety of toys, foods, and sensory stimuli, and identify the ones that the child frequently chooses.

Because reinforcers increase the behaviors they follow, not necessarily the behaviors we want to increase, we should ensure that the reinforcer comes immediately after the behavior that is being supported.

combinations (Mason et al. 1989). Those things that the child consistently chooses are likely to work as reinforcers (for additional information, see Cooper, Heron, & Heward 1987; Green et al. 1988; Wolery, Bailey, & Sugai 1988; and Mason et al. 1989).

Rules for using reinforcers

Identifying reinforcers is important, but it is only the first step; to be effective, the reinforcers must be used correctly and appropriately. Several general rules exist for using reinforcers correctly.

• *Use the reinforcer immediately after the behavior you want to increase.* Reinforcers increase the behaviors they follow, not necessarily the behaviors we want to increase. The adult must be attentive to the child and ensure that the reinforcer comes immediately after the behavior that is being supported.

• *Use the reinforcer every time the behavior occurs.* When the adults are *initially* trying to get a behavior to occur more often or to get it to occur in a specific situation, the behavior should be reinforced every time it occurs. The adult must be able to identify the behavior easily and use the reinforcer consistently. Later, when the behavior occurs when and where it should, less reinforcement should be given.

• *Use a variety of reinforcers when possible.* Because the effects of many reinforcers will dissipate when they are used frequently, it is wise to use several different reinforcers for each child. By using several different reinforcers, the effectiveness of a single reinforcer will "wear off" less quickly.

• *Use natural reinforcers when possible.* For many children, several reinforcers (e.g., food, drink, favorite toys and activities, physical contact, approval) will be identified as likely to be effective. Whenever possible, the more natural reinforcers—such as adult responsiveness or the opportunity to play with peers—should be used rather than food and drink, stickers, and other tangible reinforcers.

• *Pair less natural reinforcers with more natural events.* For many children, having interesting toys and activities available will be sufficient to ensure that they engage in activities. Ideally, we want children to rely on natural interest and motivation to participate and learn. With some children, however, this will not be sufficient, at least initially. As a result, adults should use reinforcers with such children and may even decide to try tangible ones (such as food or drink) to ensure that they begin to engage in the activities or interactions that will be valuable to them. However, when these less natural reinforcers are used, the adult should simultaneously use praise, toys, special activities, and choices after the behavior occurs. Using the strong reinforcer and the weaker reinforcer or neutral events together will help transfer the power of

Natural reinforcers are those that occur as a result of children's interactions with their physical and social environment and their participation in ongoing activities.

the stronger reinforcer to those that are initially weaker. Over time, the child's behavior will be maintained through natural reinforcers and intrinsic motivation.

• *As children begin to display the behaviors at desirable levels, give the reinforcer less frequently.* Initially, reinforcers should be used each time the behavior occurs, but as the child consistently displays the behavior, the adults should begin to use the reinforcers less frequently. The goal is to decrease the amount of external reinforcement needed while ensuring that behavior continues to occur. This outcome can be accomplished if the external reinforcer is used with more natural ones and if the adults are careful to decrease gradually the amount of reinforcement they use.

• *Ensure that high levels of natural reinforcement are available to children.* Natural reinforcers are those that occur as a result of children's interactions with their physical and social environment and their participation in ongoing activities. Strategies to maximize the effect of natural reinforcers include providing choices of activities and materials, providing novel materials and activities, rotating the availability of materials and activities across days or weeks, and reading cues and following the child's lead. Such tactics increase the chances that the activities and materials that support children's learning are naturally reinforcing to them.

Specialized uses of reinforcement

From research and practice, a number of specialized uses of reinforcers have been developed. Three of these are described in this section.

Differential reinforcement. As already stated, when a reinforcer consistently follows a given behavior, the child will perform the behavior more often. However, to promote development and learning, we do not want more behavior; we want children to use behaviors at appropriate times in meaningful ways. Almost any behavior can be adaptive and beneficial or can be maladaptive and harmful, depending on the situation in which the behavior occurs. For example, at a ball game it is acceptable to cheer and yell—particularly when the home team does something exciting; however, that behavior would be inappropriate at a solemn memorial service. Highly adapted individuals engage in many behaviors, but they use them in situations when they are needed, useful, and purposeful. Much of our task involves helping children learn *when* to do particular things. Differential reinforcement is an effective strategy in teaching children to use particular skills in specific situations.

Previously we stated that if a child were reinforced for cleaning up the block area for several days, he may learn to clean up the block area and keep doing it even when reinforcement is given infrequently, but he may not clean up the dramatic play area. This development of situation-specific behavior results from differential reinforcement, that is, reinforcement of a behavior in a specific context and not in other contexts. In the case of cleaning up areas of the room, the implication of this principle is simply to extend reinforcement to all areas where the child should clean up. According to the principle of differential reinforcement, if a behavior is appropriate only in a given context (or set of contexts), it should be reinforced in those contexts and not in others.

Correspondence training. Correspondence training involves reinforcing a "correspondence" between what children *say* and what they *do* (Baer 1990). It is used primarily for promoting children's use of skills that they have in their repertoire but do not use often enough or do not use in certain situations where they should

(McEvoy, Odom, & McConnell 1992). Although several different types of correspondence training exist (Paniagua 1990), two types are common. First, children are asked what they are going to do, reinforcement is provided, and then they are given an opportunity to do it. For example, if the teacher wanted a child to play in a particular way (e.g., without throwing the toys), he might ask her how she was going to play with the toys, reinforce her statements, and then provide her with a chance to play. Sometimes simply reinforcing children's statements about their intentions is sufficient to help them use the skill.

Another way of using correspondence training is to reinforce children for matching what they do with what they say they will do. For example, if the teacher wanted a child to play in a particular area for a few minutes, the teacher might ask him where he was going to play, provide him with an opportunity to play there, and then provide reinforcement after several minutes *only* if he played in that area. In this application of correspondence training, reinforcement is not given if children fail to do what they said they would.

Correspondence training has several distinct advantages. It is relatively easy to use; it does not require extensive training for the adult. It can be used easily in many different classroom activities. Adults can use the procedure as they help children plan their day or small periods of the day; it may help children learn to regulate and manage their own behavior. The procedure can be used to promote transfer of skills learned in one situation to another appropriate situation. For example, if a child has learned to share during snack time, then the teacher could use the procedure to promote sharing during free play.

Behavioral momentum. The primary application of behavioral momentum has been with children who do not consistently follow adult requests (Mace et al. 1988; Mace et al. 1990), although it can be used for other skills (Davis & Brady 1993). Children are reinforced for behaviors they readily display and then are immediately asked to engage in a behavior they are less likely to do. For example, if a child often does not clean up his play area, the teacher could use behavioral momentum. Before asking the child to clean up a play area, the teacher would go to the child and say, "Give me five," and reinforce the child when he did; then say, "Touch your nose," and reinforce the child when he did; and then say, "Touch my nose," and reinforce the child when he did. Each of these requests (or similar ones) would be delivered in rapid succession, and each would result in enthusiastic praise for compliance. At this point the teacher might say, "It's time to clean up; please put the toys away."

This procedure has resulted in compliance in a number of different contexts with various types of children. To use this strategy, the teacher must begin the behaviors that are fun for children to do, move through them quickly, and reinforce each; the

130

These procedures emphasize attention to whether a consequence is really a reinforcer for the child, as well as systematic application of each aspect.

idea is to keep the ball rolling. The advantages of behavioral momentum are obvious: it is easy to use, can be implemented in many different situations, and frequently reduces children's noncompliance.

With each of these specialized uses of reinforcement (differential reinforcement, correspondence training, and behavioral momentum), some similar factors will influence their effectiveness. First, in each case the event used as a reinforcer (such as a chance to read with the teacher, praise, or other consequence) must actually be a reinforcer for the child (i.e., must increase the preceding behaviors). Second, reinforcement should be used regularly and consistently. Using it one day, then not using it for a couple of days, and then using it again will increase the likelihood that it will *not* work. Third, the reinforcer should be given immediately after the desired behavior occurs, should be implemented only for that behavior, and should be accompanied by adult encouragement and other natural reinforcers. In many ways these procedures are similar to what early childhood personnel already do. What these procedures emphasize and require is attention to whether a consequence is really a reinforcer for the child, as well as systematic application of each aspect.

Naturalistic (milieu) strategies

Naturalistic teaching strategies involve brief interactions between children and adults, provide children with opportunities to learn new skills or practice existing ones, and result in access to natural reinforcers (Halle, Alpert, & Anderson 1984). The purpose of naturalistic strategies is to promote children's communication development (Kaiser, Alpert, & Warren 1987; Warren & Kaiser 1988). The procedures have been effective with children who have many different disabilities and who have a full range of language needs—including children with limited communication skills (e.g., they are at a one-word stage)—and those who have substantial language skills but are at risk for communication delays. The strategies initially were designed to promote transfer of skills from therapy sessions to free play and low-structure activities (Hart & Risley 1968; Rogers-Warren & Warren 1980), but they also often are used to teach new communication skills (Warren, McQuarter, & Rogers-Warren 1984).

Variations of naturalistic strategies are models and expansions, naturalistic time delay (see chapter 5), the mand-model procedure, and incidental teaching (Kaiser, Yoder, & Keetz 1992). These variations share certain elements. Information on using them is found in the cited sources and on pages 141 through 145. Naturalistic strategies have the following characteristics in common.

The interaction must be responsive to children's verbalizations, thus providing them with opportunities to use more complex language in natural and relevant situations.

• *Naturalistic strategies are used during ongoing activities and interactions*, thus their name, *naturalistic strategies*. They are used most often during low-structure activities, but many teachers use them throughout the day—at any time when communication is appropriate. For example, the strategies can be used at snack time as children talk with one another and with their teachers, during free play as children and adults play in various areas, during in-class transitions, in the course of art and fine motor activities as children interact with materials, and at any other time when interactions between children and adults are possible.

• *Naturalistic strategies involve repeated use of brief interactions between children and adults.* Because they are used in ongoing activities, these strategies involve brief interactions (a few seconds) between children and adults. For example, a goal for a child with limited communication skills may be to use single words to identify objects in his environment, such as different toys and other common objects (e.g., cup, spoon, etc.). While the teachers and child are rolling a ball back and forth, the teacher might roll the ball to the child and when the child gets it say, "Ball." If the child imitates the verbalization, the teacher responds positively and uses the word in a statement, "Yes, you got the ball" or "Big ball" or some similar statement that uses the word *ball*. As they continue playing with the ball, the adult may repeat this sequence several times.

• *Naturalistic strategies are responsive to children's behavior.* These strategies are used when children initiate interactions with adults or when children are focused on an activity or material but are open to adult interaction. For example, if a child often uses only single words to make requests for help or for materials, the teacher might use such opportunities to help the child learn more elaborate language. If the child says, "Paint?" when wanting to paint, the teacher may say, "Tell me more" or "What about 'paint'?" If the child responds by saying, "I want to paint," the teacher might say, "That sounds fun; let's paint," and immediately help the child get the needed materials. If, however, the child does not respond, the teacher would model a more elaborate statement (e.g., "Say, 'I want to paint.'") and let the child imitate, and then the teacher would help him get the materials for painting. The interaction must be responsive to children's verbalizations, thus providing them with opportunities to use more complex language in natural and relevant situations.

• *Naturalistic strategies involve giving children feedback and naturally occurring consequences.* An important feature of these procedures is that they honor the intentions of children's language. This is done by expanding what children have said *and* by responding to the content of their statements. Expanding children's language involves using their speech in more complex ways. If a child sees a peer fall down and says, "Fall down," the teacher could respond by saying, "Yes, Hoi fell down." Or if the child asks the teacher to read a book, the teacher may use the occasion to have the child practice more elaborate language to identify the book he wants read, but the teacher also would read the book to the child. The strategies are effective because children have opportunities to use more complex language, hear models of that language, *and* gain something from using language—their communicative intentions are addressed.

• *Naturalistic strategies require purposeful planning on the part of adults.* To use these procedures, the adult must tune in to children's communication goals and must be observant of children's behavior. Because the procedures are used when children initiate communication with adults and when children are open to adult interaction, teachers often arrange the classroom to increase the chances of having opportunities to use the procedures. For example, teachers may have some preferred materials on a "must ask shelf," give children limited portions of materials, or provide materials that are likely to produce comments.

These strategies have many positive features. They are effective with a wide range of children who have many different communication goals. They are easily used in ongoing activities and are natural extensions of adults' interactions with children. Variations of the strategies (see the section at the end of this chapter) can be used together. Many different types of early childhood teachers have learned to use them and have found them beneficial (Mudd & Wolery 1987; Warren & Gazdag 1990; Warren 1992). Parents also have learned to use them and report that they facilitate children's communication skills (Alpert & Kaiser 1992; Kaiser et al. 1994).

Peer-mediated strategies

Peer-mediated strategies involve using peers to promote learning in other children (Kohler & Strain 1990; McEvoy, Odom, & McConnell 1992). These strategies have been used to promote social interaction skills (Odom et al. 1985) as well as to facilitate communication exchanges and skills (Goldstein & Gallagher 1992). A variety of peer-mediated strategies exist, but they share some common elements: (a) the peers (usually typically developing children) are taught specific ways of engaging their less competent peers in social or communicative exchanges, (b) the peers are taught to persist in securing those social and communicative exchanges, (c) children with disabilities and their peers are given regular opportunities to play together and to use the skills, and (d) the teacher provides the children with support and reinforcement for playing together and for using the interactive behaviors.

The children who are chosen as peers in peer-mediated strategies should be selected carefully (McEvoy, Odom, & McConnell 1992). Usually they are selected because they tend to be highly social, have few negative interactions with other children, and are cooperative with the adults in the classroom. These children are taught the desired interactive skills in small groups and in short sessions (e.g., 10 minutes). These sessions often include a rationale for the training (learning how to make friends, helping other children be friends, etc.), verbal description of the skills, models of the skills, role playing, and reinforcement for practicing the skills (Strain & Odom 1986). The way that the rationale is conveyed and, indeed, the skills to be learned would vary with the age of the children. After receiving the training, the peers and the less competent child or children often are encouraged to play with one another in specific areas of the classroom. Although the teacher does not directly

INCLUDING CHILDREN WITH SPECIAL NEEDS

In reinforcing children for playing with classmates with disabilities, take care not to convey the idea that this is a disagreeable chore.

participate or assist in the play, the teacher should observe the play and give the peers feedback and encouragement for engaging in the social and communicative exchanges (McEvoy, Odom, & McConnell 1992). These procedures have been effective in promoting social and communicative interactions between children with typical development and children with a variety of disabilities.

Peer-mediated strategies may be used to increase the frequency of social interactions that a child with disabilities has with her peers. The adult would select three or four children who have good play skills, are social, and rarely have negative interactions with one another or with the child with disabilities. For three or four days the teacher would work with these children (see Strain & Odom 1986 for training scripts). She would tell them how to initiate interactions (e.g., by giving the child a toy, asking the child to play with them, or suggesting a play theme), role play these skills with peers, have them role play the skills with one another, and reinforce them for practicing the skills in the training sessions. Although many young typically developing children can use these skills with responsive and social classmates, the training is designed to help them use these skills with less responsive children and to persist in using these skills. After the peers could use these skills well and persist in using them, the teacher would have them and the child with disabilities play in short sessions (e.g., 10 to 15 minutes each) in a defined area of the classroom (e.g., dramatic play area, block area). Before the play episodes she would remind the peers to use the skills they had learned. The teacher would observe the play sessions and, if necessary, encourage the children to interact and play together. After the sessions the teacher should acknowledge or otherwise reinforce the children for playing, taking care not to convey the idea that this is a disagreeable chore ("I notice that you and Brian were having fun playing with the blocks"). (See chapter 8 for a discussion of activities designed to promote good feelings among children with disabilities and their peers.)

Prompting strategies

The usefulness of prompting strategies in teaching children new skills is supported in a large research literature (Demchack 1990; Wolery, Ault, & Doyle 1992). Although variations among prompting procedures exist, all of these strategies have three common elements: the procedures are used to help children learn a skill, the prompts (teacher help) are removed systematically as the child acquires the skill, and the procedures employ differential reinforcement. In this section, prompts are defined and described, general guidelines for using them are explained, and the advantages of these procedures are listed. Specific information on how to use prompting procedures is presented on pages 146 through 150.

Description of prompts

Prompts are help given by someone to assist another person in using specific skills (Wolery, Bailey, & Sugai 1988). Usually, prompts are given *before or as* a child attempts a skill. Prompts usually are given by adults, but peers also can use them (e.g., Venn, Wolery, Fleming, et al. 1993). Prompts may be classified in many ways; five common categories are verbal, gestural, model, physical, and pictorial.

Verbal prompts are statements by adults that help children acquire a particular skill. For example, when a child is intent on putting together a puzzle but is having trouble getting a particular piece to fit, the adult might say, "Maybe you should turn it and try it that way." This simple statement may be sufficient to help the child place the piece. Several types of verbal prompts exist, but each involves the adult saying something to help the child accomplish the behavior.

Gestural prompts are movements by adults that cue children to engage in behaviors. For example, if a child is learning to put a tape in a tape recorder but is having trouble getting the recorder open, the teacher might point toward the eject button. This pointing is a gestural prompt that may help the child learn to push the eject button to open the tape recorder.

Model prompts involve having the teacher perform the behavior that the child is learning to do; sometimes models are verbal (the teacher says something), and sometimes the models are motor behavior (the teacher does something). For example, if a child is in the process of learning her classmates' names and she wants to invite another child to play, the teacher might model (say) the name for her. If the child is learning to tie his shoes, the teacher might have him watch her tie her own shoes. Models are particularly useful prompts because children who imitate get a lot of information about how to do a particular skill from observing a model. Model prompts can be used with groups of children, and they come naturally to adults trying to help children learn new skills.

Physical prompts involve the adult touching the child and helping him or her engage in a behavior. In some instances, a mere nudge or touch might be enough to cue a child. For example, a child may need no more than a touch or slight pressure to his hand as it rests on the computer mouse to remind him to use the mouse to perform a function. In other cases, the adult may need to guide the child physically through an entire sequence of behavior. When a child with mental retardation is first

Use prompts that are effective but provide the least amount of help necessary.

learning to feed herself with a spoon, for instance, the adult may put his hand over the child's hand, help the child grasp the spoon, dip it in the food, and bring it to her mouth.

Pictorial prompts, also called *two-dimensional prompts,* are pictures of events that provide children with information about how to carry out particular actions or sequences of actions. For example, classroom cookbooks often use pictures to tell children what materials and utensils they need, what they should do first, and what they should do next; the pictures provide information (help) in doing the skill.

Guidelines for using prompts

Several guidelines are important in using prompts, and these are discussed below (Wolery, Bailey, & Sugai 1988; Wolery, Ault, & Doyle 1992).

• *Use prompts that are effective but provide the least amount of help necessary.* The purpose of using prompts is to give children information and help about how to perform the behaviors they are learning. Thus, only prompts that actually help children perform the behavior should be used. For example, using a model prompt with a child who does not imitate would not be effective. Sometimes teachers combine prompts such as verbal and model prompts (e.g., showing children how to put on their coats while describing how to do it). Such combinations are natural teacher behaviors and may provide more information to children than using only one type of prompt. However, to promote children's independence, teachers should provide only the amount and types of prompts that are necessary. If using a model or gestural prompt would give the child enough information to perform the behavior, then a physical prompt would be inappropriate.

• *Use prompts before or as children perform the skills they are learning.* Prompts can be thought of as bridges to help children move from being unable to perform useful skills to doing them independently; thus, timing the use of prompts is important. In most instances the prompts should be used either just before children are expected to perform the behavior or while they are doing it. This is done for two reasons: first, to provide children with the information they need, and second, to reduce the possibility of failure. For example, if a child is learning to pour from a pitcher to a cup, providing help as the child pours (e.g., using a verbal prompt to cue her that the cup is getting full) is better than waiting until a spill occurs. Using prompts before or while children are engaged in behaviors is not necessarily a natural way of interacting with children; a more natural reaction is to provide help only after children try and fail. However, when a skill is important, there is little

*The prompts that are used to assist children in learning skills must
be withdrawn as the learning progresses.*

justification for making children fail before they get help. Thus, in nearly all cases,
it is better to provide children with assistance before they experience failure.

• *Use prompts only when children's attention is engaged.* To be useful, teachers' help
in the form of prompts should only be given when children are attending to the
teacher or the task at hand. If children are not receptive to the prompts, then that
assistance will probably not be useful. Thus, teachers need to pay close attention to
children in order to know when and how much help should be provided.

• *Use prompts in a supportive and instructive manner.* Prompts should be supportive and conducive to learning. For example, if an adult is using a model prompt to
show a child how to tie his shoes, the adult should make the motions slowly so that
the child can observe them easily. Also, it will be more instructive if the child and the
adult are side by side rather than across from one another; the motions of the adult's
model will be identical to the motions that the child needs to imitate. Whenever using
physical prompts, the teacher should administer them in a supportive and
careful manner to be sure that the child is not hurt. Also, the adult should stand
or sit behind the child when using physical prompts to ensure that the movements are natural and smooth.

• *Provide reinforcement for children's behavior even when prompts are used.*
Although we want to reinforce independent and self-directed behavior, reinforcement should be given for performing the skill even when prompts are used. Such
reinforcement assists children in learning when to do the behavior and supports
their attempts in learning to perform the skill. The rules for using reinforcement,
discussed previously in this chapter, should be followed. As children learn to do the
skills without prompts, the reinforcement should be given less frequently.

• *Withdraw the prompts as children learn to perform the skills being taught.* For the
skills they learn to be useful, children must be able to perform them without help
(without prompts). Thus, the prompts that are used to assist children in learning the
skills must be withdrawn as their learning progresses. Several different strategies
exist for removing the prompts, including providing progressively less help over
time, completing withdrawing the help after several occasions of prompting, and
delaying the prompts and using them only when needed. The various prompting
procedures differ primarily in how the prompts are removed. Some of those procedures result in more rapid removal of prompts than others, but all of them have
some systematic way to withdraw the prompts so that children can perform the
behaviors without assistance.

• *Consult with the early intervention team before using physical prompts with
children who have physical disabilities.* Although often useful in providing children

with the type of information they need to perform certain skills, physical prompts with children who have physical disabilities (e.g., cerebral palsy) should be used only under the guidance of the child's physical or occupational therapist. Some physical prompts with such children may be counterproductive; however, with appropriate guidance from a therapist, physical prompts may be quite helpful.

Advantages of prompting procedures

Using prompts has several advantages. When used appropriately they effectively promote learning. Thus, when early intervention teams believe that a specific skill is important for a child to learn, the prompting procedures should be used. These procedures provide children with the help they need to learn, and then systematically withdraw that help so that children can be independent; as a result, children experience success rather than failure. Also, these procedures often result in frequent positive reinforcement, which produces positive interactions between children and adults. Finally, when teachers learn to use the procedures, they can apply them with many different children, with different skills, and in different contexts.

Summary

Many of the practices that teachers use for supporting the development and learning of children without disabilities are useful for children with disabilities. However, early childhood personnel should also be skilled in using additional instructional strategies. They should know how to identify and use reinforcers in the context of their ongoing interactions with children and in ongoing classroom activities.

Three specialized uses of reinforcement were described in this chapter: differential reinforcement, correspondence training, and behavioral momentum. Although these strategies require systematic use, they can be incorporated easily into classroom activities. In addition, teachers can use the naturalistic teaching strategies, which are useful in promoting children's communication skills. The naturalistic strategies require systematic use but are easily integrated in most classrooms because they are brief exchanges that are responsive to children's behavior and their communicative attempts. These strategies tend to be natural extensions of adults' usual interactions with children. Still other useful strategies include peer-mediated and prompting procedures. These strategies also require systematic use and can be implemented during ongoing classroom activities.

Four Teaching Strategies to Use with Young Children with Disabilities

The purpose of this section is to provide the reader with more detailed information on how to use four strategies that are effective in working with children with disabilities. Two of the described instructional strategies are naturalistic teaching procedures, and two are prompting procedures. The four strategies were selected because of their substantial research base *and* their usefulness to early childhood personnel who teach young children with disabilities. Other naturalistic and prompting procedures are available and are described in the sources cited throughout this chapter. Each strategy's uses, a brief description, steps for using the strategy, a short example, and special considerations are provided.

NATURALISTIC STRATEGIES

Mand-model procedure

Applications

The mand-model procedure is a naturalistic strategy for promoting children's skills in communication. It is used to facilitate transfer of skills from therapy sessions to classroom activities (Rogers-Warren & Warren 1980) and to teach new language skills (Warren, McQuarter, & Rogers-Warren 1984). The mand-model procedure can be used with children who have all types of disabilities and with a wide range of communication goals. It is especially useful with children who infrequently initiate interactions with adults.

Description

The mand-model procedure involves brief interactions between adults and children. During these exchanges the adult asks a question or makes a statement that gives the child an opportunity to use the behaviors from his or her communication goals. The adult also provides models of those behaviors. This procedure uses a specific type of adult verbalization: mands, which are non-yes/no questions or statements that require a specific response. The adult selects questions or statements related to the child's focus of play and asks several during each play session.

Steps for using the strategy

1. Identify the communication goals that are relevant for the child.

2. Identify times and low-structure activities in which the procedure will be used.

3. Ensure that the identified activity includes toys and materials that are likely to result in high levels of child engagement and play.

4. Allow or help the child to play with the toys and materials.

5. Play alongside the child, following his lead and being responsive to his communicative initiations.

6. When the child is playing but is receptive to adult interaction, do the following:
    a. Ask a question that is related to the child's focus of attention and that will give her a chance to use the behaviors related to her communication goals.
    b. After asking the question, look expectantly at the child for a response.
    c. If the child uses a communication behavior that is a goal, affirm her statement by expanding it (using her words in a more advanced way) and responding to the content of the statement. Continue the interaction or allow the child to continue playing.

d. If the child does not use the desired communicative behavior, provide a model of the behavior and look expectantly at her, indicating that you want her to imitate your statement. If the child imitates it, affirm her statement by expanding it and responding to its content. Continue the interaction or allow the child to continue playing.

7. Repeat steps 5 and 6 several times during the activity.

Example of use

A goal for Jamal is to use three-word statements that include an actor, an action, and an object (so as to communicate more effectively than one- or two-word verbalizations allow). The early intervention team has identified the block area that includes toy trucks, people, animals, and blocks as the area in which to use the procedure. This area was selected because Jamal readily plays there with high levels of engagement.

When Jamal is in the area, the teacher plays alongside him and observes what he is doing. He puts a toy man in one of the trucks and starts moving it down a block road. The teacher uses this as an opportunity to ask the question (mand); she says, "What's the man doing?" She then looks expectantly at Jamal and gives him three to four seconds to answer. If he answers, "Man driving truck," she may expand it by saying, "I hope the man's driving the truck carefully," and she continues with the play. If Jamal does not answer, she provides a model (i.e., "Say, 'Man's driving the truck'") and looks expectantly for him to imitate the statement. Over the course of the next few minutes, the teacher repeats this sequence using different questions that are related to the nature of Jamal's play, each time providing him with an opportunity to use a statement that has an actor, an action, and an object.

Special considerations

The mand-model procedure can be combined with other naturalistic strategies, such as the incidental teaching procedure, models and expansions, and naturalistic time delay.

Incidental teaching

Applications

The incidental teaching procedure is a naturalistic strategy for promoting children's communication skills. It has been used to promote transfer of skills learned in therapy sessions to classroom activities (Hart & Risley 1968) and to teach new language skills (Hart & Risley 1975, 1980). It can be used with children who have a variety of disabilities and is useful with a broad range of communication goals (Kaiser, Yoder, & Keetz 1992).

Description

The incidental teaching strategy involves brief interactions between adults and children that are started *when the child initiates to the adult*. The adult uses those initiations as an opportunity to request more elaborate language from the child and to model more elaborate language. This procedure can be used any time the child initiates to an adult, but it is often used in low-structure situations in which such initiations are likely.

Steps for using the strategy

1. Identify the communication goals that are relevant for the child.

2. Identify times, activities, and routines in which the procedure will be used.

3. Adapt the activity and arrange the environment to encourage frequent child initiations by presenting novel or new materials, placing some preferred toys in view but out of reach (a must-ask shelf), providing some materials for which the child may need help (paint containers with lids on them), and providing materials with missing parts (a puzzle without some pieces).

4. Be available to children, and wait for their initiations.

5. When a child initiates an interaction with you, you should do the following:

   a. Focus on the child, decide whether to use this initiation as a teaching opportunity, and be sure that you understand the purpose of the child's initiation.

   b. Ask for more elaborate language from the child by saying, "Tell me more," "Use words," "What about ___?" or a similar statement that would be understood by the child.

   c. Wait a few seconds for the child to produce a more elaborate or complex statement; while waiting, look expectantly at the child.

d. If the child uses more elaborate language, praise him, expand his statement, and respond to the content of what he has asked (e.g., if he asked for more materials, help him get them; if he asked for help, provide it).

e. If the child does not produce a more elaborate statement, provide a model of a more complex statement and look expectantly at him, indicating to him to imitate it. When he imitates it, respond to the content of the statement.

6. Repeat steps 4 and 5 throughout the day.

Example of use

A communication goal for Leah is to use descriptive words in her statements. The early intervention team has decided to use the procedure whenever Leah initiates a request to any adult in the classroom. However, they also adapted and arranged the classroom to increase the chances of Leah's initiation (see step 3 on p. 144).

During free play the teacher ensures that he is available to Leah. Leah approaches him and says, "Read me a book." The teacher focuses on Leah, decides to use this as a teaching opportunity, and says, "Which book do you want?" This statement sets the stage for Leah to describe a book. If she uses a statement that includes a descriptive word (e.g., "The *owl* book," "The *big* book"), the teacher expands her statement (e.g., "Oh, yes, let's read the *Owl at Home* book"), gets the book, and reads it to her. If she does not answer with a statement that includes a descriptive word, the teacher models a statement (e.g., "Would you like the owl book or the sleepy bear book?"), waits for her to indicate a response with a descriptive word, and then gets the book and reads it to her.

When Leah is in the dramatic play area, she says, "I want that hat," and points to a hat on the "must-ask shelf." The teacher says, "Tell me about the hat," and looks eagerly at Leah. If she says, "The feather hat," "The police hat," or any other statement with a descriptive term, the teacher gets the hat for her. If she does not use a descriptive term, he models a statement with a descriptive word and gives it to her after she imitates his statement.

Special considerations

The incidental teaching procedure can be combined with other naturalistic strategies, such as the mand-model procedure, models and expansions, and naturalistic time delay. Ideally, the procedure would be used throughout the day for any appropriate child initiation.

PROMPTING STRATEGIES

Graduated guidance

Applications

The graduated guidance procedure is a prompting strategy for teaching children skills that involve sequences of behaviors. It has been used to teach a variety of skills, such as self-dressing, spoon and fork use, hand washing, and other skills that involve several separate steps (Foxx & Azrin 1973; Bailey & Wolery 1984). Graduated guidance can be used with children who have a variety of different disabilities.

Description

In the graduated guidance procedure, the teacher provides the type and amount of help needed by the child to complete the skill being taught. The adult provides and then immediately withdraws the amount of prompting needed for the child to do the skill.

Steps for using the strategy

1. Identify the skill to be taught and the steps involved in performing the skill. Some skills require certain steps to be completed before other steps; for example, when eating with a spoon, the child must grasp the spoon, dip it into the food, lift the spoon from the bowl, move the spoon to the mouth, and so on. Other skills do not necessarily require each step to be completed before the next; for example, when one is dressing, the pants could be put on first, then the shirt, socks, and shoes, but the order could vary in many different ways.

2. Identify the times and activity in which the skill will be taught.

3. When the child is in the situation in which the skill will be taught, the teacher should

   a. Provide only the amount of help the child will need to start the skill, and then immediately withdraw that help as she begins performing the skill.

   b. If the child stops, immediately provide the amount and type of help needed to get her started again, then withdraw the help as she begins to perform the skill.

c. If the child starts to make an incorrect movement, interrupt it and provide the amount of help needed to get her moving in the correct direction, then immediately withdraw the help.

d. Provide verbal encouragement to the child as the skill is being completed, and reinforce her at the end of the sequence.

Example of use

A major goal for Carlos is to have him become a vital part of the class. In his class, the teacher uses a "snack helper" to assist her in preparing for snack time. The helper puts a cup and napkin on the table in front of each chair. Because the children view this role as a privilege, the early intervention team decides that learning to do it would benefit Carlos.

When it is Carlos's turn to be snack helper, the teacher gives him the napkins and says, "Put one by each chair." As Carlos walks toward the table, the teacher follows him, and when he gets to the first chair, she watches to see if he will place one napkin in front of the chair. He does, and then he stands there watching the other children play. When the teacher nudges his shoulder lightly and points to the next chair, he starts to put all the napkins down, so she stops that movement and helps him put one napkin in front of the chair. He moves to the next chair and puts a napkin down. The teacher says, "What a good helper you are," and waits for him to put another napkin at the next chair. As he completes distributing the napkins and cups, she follows him, providing prompts as needed and withdrawing them immediately as he continues setting the table.

Special considerations

The graduated guidance procedure requires the teacher to make moment-by-moment decisions about whether to provide and withdraw assistance. Failure to withdraw the prompts quickly can slow the child's learning of the skill. When using physical prompts, the teacher should be careful to not hold the child too tightly or make movements that would startle or hurt the child. Physical prompts with children who have physical disabilities should be used only under the guidance of a physical or occupational therapist.

Constant time delay

Applications

The constant time delay procedure is a prompting strategy for teaching children a wide range of skills, including those that involve a sequence of steps and single-behavior skills (Wolery, Ault, & Doyle 1992; Wolery, Holcombe, et al. 1992). It has been used with children who have a wide variety of disabilities. Constant time delay can be used in individual or in small-group instruction (Cybriwsky, Wolery, & Gast 1990) or dispersed throughout an activity or the day (Chiara et al. 1993).

Description

The constant time delay procedure can use almost any prompt, but models are most common. During initial instruction the adult gives the prompt before the child is expected to do the behavior. In subsequent instruction the adult gives the child an opportunity to perform the behavior and waits for the child's response; the prompt is given three to five seconds later if the child does not respond correctly.

Steps for using the strategy

1. Identify the skill to be taught.

2. Assess whether the child will wait a few seconds when he does not know what to do. (The rule for the child is "If I know, I respond; if I don't know, I wait for help.") If the child initially does not wait but acts immediately whether or not he knows what to do, then the teacher should teach him to wait.

3. Identify the times and activities in which the instruction will occur.

4. Identify what will cue the child to perform. Depending upon the skill being taught, the teacher or the natural environment may cue the child.

5. *Initial instruction:* When the child is in the situation in which the skill will be taught, the teacher should do the following:

   a. Ensure that the child knows it is time to use the skill, and immediately provide the prompt to ensure that he will perform the skill correctly.

b. When the child uses the skill correctly, provide reinforcement.

c. Repeat steps *a* and *b* several times, basing the number of times upon the difficulty of the skill and how quickly the child learns. The more difficult the skill and the slower the child's learning, the greater the number of times steps *a* and *b* are done.

6. *Subsequent instruction:* When the child is in the situation in which the skill is being taught, the teacher should do the following:

a. Ensure that the child knows it is time to use the skill, and wait three to five seconds for him to perform the skill or to start doing it.

b. If the child performs the skill correctly, reinforce him.

c. If the child waits for assistance, give the prompt after three to five seconds. If he responds correctly after the prompt, reinforce him.

d. If the child responds incorrectly, do not prompt and do not reinforce him.

Example of use

A goal for Latric is to name colors. The rationale for this goal is that her peers use the color words and she has asked about them. Also, to fit in, she sometimes uses the color words but does so incorrectly. When this happens, her peers look at her strangely and occasionally make negative comments. The team has decided to teach her to name the colors within the context of art activities and at other times during the day when she is working with materials that are distinctly colored.

When the children are at the art table or painting easel, the teacher intersperses five or six opportunities for Latric to name the selected colors. During the initial instruction, he sees her painting with yellow paint, comments on how beautiful her picture is, and then says, "Latric, what color is this? Yellow." She repeats, "Yellow," and the teacher says, "That's right, and you are painting such a pretty yellow house." A couple minutes later she is using the blue paint. He says, "Latric, what color is this? Blue." She repeats it, and he praises her, comments on her picture, and encourages her to continue painting. This sequence would be repeated several times during each activity for three or four days. After these three or four days, the teacher again sees Latric painting with the yellow paint and says, "What color is this?" He waits three to five seconds for her to answer. If she says, "Yellow," he praises her and comments on her picture. If she does not answer, he models the color name and praises her imitation of the model.

Special considerations

In using the constant time delay procedure, the adult systematically varies the timing of the prompt: during initial instruction the prompt is given before the child can respond; during subsequent instruction the prompt is delayed for three to five seconds. Although the exact timing of the prompt during subsequent instruction can vary, giving the prompt each time it should be given is critical (Holcombe, Wolery, & Snyder 1994).

Chapter 7

Implementing Instruction for Young Children with Special Needs in Early Childhood Classrooms

Mark Wolery

As NOTED IN CHAPTER 3, a team of individuals, including family members, is responsible for planning the early childhood experiences of young children with developmental delays and disabilities. The early intervention team conducts assessments to identify the child's abilities and needs, as well as relevant dimensions of the environments in which children spend time (chapter 4). They design the classroom to promote play, engagement, and learning (chapter 5), and they use systematic instructional procedures to teach valued skills (chapter 6). Another important function of the team is to determine how to implement instruction in the context of the existing classroom activities and routines. In this chapter, the process of adapting the classroom is described, and specific guidelines are proposed to help teams make such adaptations (for additional information, see Safford 1989, Bailey & Wolery 1992, Barnett & Carey 1992, and Bricker & Cripe 1992).

Organize assessment information on the child and the program

To make the adaptations that will enable young children with special needs to benefit from early childhood programs, teams must have information about the child *and* about the program. The types of information that teams need and sample questions are listed in table 1. In short, teams must know the child's abilities (what the child can do) and the child's needs (what the child should learn). They also need to know in what environments the child spends time and how those environments are organized, including the schedules of activities and routines, how activities are organized, and how the adults in those environments interact with children. If the team does not understand these dimensions of the relevant environments, including the classroom, there is little hope of making adaptations that can promote positive experiences for children with special needs.

Use purposeful interactions and activities

Because child–environment interactions are critical to promoting children's development and learning, and because all interactions potentially facilitate or impede children's development and learning, all activities and adult–child interactions should be analyzed to determine their effects on children. The benefits that children receive from participating in early childhood programs are tied to how well each part of the child's day is planned. However, *planned* does not mean that adults are directing children's interactions at all times; such arrangements would not promote independence and initiative. Rather, it means that the team realizes that every interaction and activity should be done for a purpose; the team is able to describe that purpose and organizes the child's opportunities for interaction so that those purposes will be met. The primary purposes, of course, are derived from the goals established by the team on the child's Individualized Family Service Plan (IFSP) or the Individualized Education Plan (IEP).

Table 1. Information Needed to Plan Programs for Young Children with Disabilities

Type of information needed   [Sample questions]

Goals for the child

— What is the child's current level of developmental functioning in communication, social, physical, cognitive, and self-care areas?
— What does the child need to be independent in the classroom, home, and community?
— What are the effects of adaptations and assistance on child performance?
— What usual patterns of responding and what relationships with environmental variables appear to influence child performance?
— What are the child's most important behaviors, skills, abilities, and patterns of responding?

Child's environments

— In what environments (home, classroom, etc.) does the child spend time?
— How much time is spent in each environment?
— Who cares for and interacts with the child in those environments?

Physical dimensions/organization of environment

— What materials and toys are in each environment?
— How are those toys and materials organized and placed about the room?
— Can the child access all areas and materials and, if so, how?
— How much space is available, and how many children and adults are in it?
— What adaptations of equipment and materials are needed?

Temporal dimensions/organization of routines

— What is the child's typical daily schedule (from awakening to bedtime)?
— How are activities within the classroom sequenced?
— How long do activities last?
— What routines (e.g., meals, toileting) happen every day?

Adults' usual roles in activities

— For each part of the day, what do adults do in relation to the child?
— When do adults observe children, interact with them, and take care of organizational tasks (prepare materials)?
— When, if ever, do adults lead activities?
— How do adults interact with children (e.g., direct a child, respond to a child)?
— What types of verbal interactions (e.g., questions, commands, comments) do adults use, and when?

Activity structures

— How is each activity in the classroom organized?
— How does the child get into and out of each activity?
— How does the child know what is expected in each activity?
— What is the child expected to do in each activity?
— How are expectations communicated to the child?

Too much "helping" by adults (or peers) keeps children from learning to be independent and from practicing the skills they need for independence.

Use the principles of independence and participation

Much of preparing high-quality early childhood programs for young children with special needs involves establishing a balance between ensuring that they do things on their own (without help) and ensuring that they are not left out because they cannot do something. The principle of independence suggests that children should be encouraged and allowed to do as much as possible for themselves. The activities and routines of the classroom and of other environments should be designed to help children be independent and become progressively more independent. With many children, doing things for them is often easier and quicker than letting them do these things themselves. However, such "helping" by adults (or peers) keeps children from learning to be independent and practicing the skills they need for independence. On the other hand, adults must be supportive of children's efforts, making decisions about when to give help based on the child's current skills, the child's efforts to be independent, age-appropriate expectations, and, of course, safety.

The principle of participation suggests that children should be a part of all activities and that appropriate adaptations should be made when independence is not possible or is unlikely. Sometimes children's disabilities keep them from being able to participate in some activity independently, or the activity requires a more advanced developmental level than a child has currently achieved. In such cases, adults should adapt the activity so that the child with disabilities can be involved, can participate as a member of the class, and is not left out of the activity. Some guidelines for making such adaptations are presented in table 2.

Promote skills and goals from multiple domains simultaneously

The early childhood curriculum and children's development are often thought of as having distinct areas, such as cognitive, communication, socioemotional, physical, and self-care, but, of course, each of these areas overlaps with the others. Many, if not most, skills include some components that are drawn from more than one of these areas. Many classroom centers or activities are thought to promote skills in particular areas, and, in part, they do; but many of these activity centers and activities can be useful for promoting learning in multiple domains. For example, the block center is often described as promoting logical-mathematical reasoning; as

Table 2. Guidelines for Using Partial Participation

Step	Description
1. Complete an inventory of a nondisabled person performing the skill.	Observe a nondisabled individual completing the target skill or activity in the designated environment, and record the needed behaviors and their sequence.
2. Complete an inventory of the target child performing the skill.	Observe the child performing the target skill or activity in the designated environment, and record all behaviors that are performed independently and those that are not performed independently.
3. Identify the behaviors that the child can be expected to learn independently.	Meet with relevant persons, such as the child's family and therapists, to determine which skills the child can be expected to learn to do independently. Make a list of these skills.
4. Identify the behaviors that the child cannot be expected to perform independently.	Meet with relevant persons to determine which skills the child is unlikely to learn over a long period of time. Make a list of these skills.
5. Generate a set of potential adaptations that would allow participation.	Identify adaptations that could be used to allow the child to participate in the activity.
6. Complete an inventory using the identified adaptation(s).	Attempt to use the adaptation of the skill or activity in the designated environment. Data should be collected on the extent to which the adaptation is successful in promoting participation.
7. Decide which adaptation will be used.	Over several opportunities, use the adaptations, and retain the most successful one.
8. Identify skills that will likely be acquired using individualized adaptations.	Identify the behaviors that are likely to be acquired if the adaptation is used. Employ systematic attempts to teach those skills.

Source: Adapted from D. Baumgart, L. Brown, I. Pumpian, J. Nisbet, A. Ford, M. Sweet, R. Messina, & J. Schroeder, "Principle of Partial Participation and Individualized Adaptations in Educational Programs for Severely Handicapped Students," *Journal of the Association for the Severely Handicapped* 7 (2) (1982): 17–22.

early childhood educators know, it also can provide opportunities for children to practice social interaction and communication skills as children talk with one another and share blocks or build a block construction together.

This guideline suggests that we should promote skills from multiple domains (cognitive, social, communication, physical, and self-care) within each activity and each activity center. This suggestion is based on the assumption that children learn skills best when they need these skills during natural child–environment interactions. For example, a painting activity may be a time for expressing how one feels and for exercising creativity, but if a child needs a color that a peer is using, this is also a good time to practice requesting, sharing, and negotiating ownership of possessions. To capture these natural opportunities to promote children's development and provide opportunities to practice and expand acquired skills, early childhood personnel must keep in mind that each activity has multiple purposes. Of course, the purposes that are emphasized depend on the benefits that the team believes are important for the child (i.e., the high-priority goals from the child's IEP or IFSP). Adults must be observant of children and events so that they can take advantage of each opportunity to promote more positive and facilitating experiences. To ensure that each activity promotes multiple skills across different areas, adults should analyze how classroom centers are designed, how adults in the program interact with children, and how activities are sequenced and operated.

Distribute teaching and learning opportunities for each goal throughout the day

As previously discussed, each activity and area of the classroom should have multiple purposes; the reverse side of that coin is that each goal should be addressed multiple times throughout the day (Bricker & Cripe 1992). If an important goal is to promote a child's conversational turns with peers, then the adults in a program should promote his involvement in conversations several times during the day. Opportunities for conversation occur at snack time, during free play, after reading a story, and during arrival and departure times. Although support for each goal should occur naturally when the need and opportunity arise, adults should try to promote each skill or goal at multiple times throughout the day. Having answers to the assessment questions listed in table 1 is necessary for implementing this guideline.

Use an activity/routine-by-skill matrix to schedule instruction

An activity/routine-by-skill matrix is a relatively simple device that is useful in planning children's days, checking the planning to ensure that important goals are being addressed, and monitoring whether adults are implementing the program as planned (Bricker & Cripe 1992). The activity/routine-by-skill matrix is a snapshot of the child's day. The steps for completing such a matrix are shown in table 3. When the team is trying to determine how all of the child's goals can be addressed in the existing activities of the classroom, this matrix will provide a way of seeing the

---

Table 3. Guidelines for Using an Activity/Routine-By-Skill Matrix

---

1. Down the left-hand column of the matrix, list the events (activities, etc.) in which the child will participate during the day. The events should be listed in the order in which they occur daily.

2. Below each listing in the left-hand column of the matrix, list the location of each event. The listing should include the entire day. The purpose is to provide instruction in all relevant locations.

3. Also in the left-hand column of the matrix, list the time that each activity will start and its expected duration each day.

4. Also in the left-hand column of the matrix, list the name of the adult who is responsible for implementing the instruction; if peers also are used, then they should be listed here as well.

5. Across the top of the matrix, list all of the skills that have been identified for instruction. Each column should include one behavior.

6. In the cells of the matrix, list the materials and specialized instructional strategies that will be used. If a skill is not addressed during a given event or time, then that cell should be left blank.

7. Check the matrix to ensure that skills will be taught by different adults using a variety of materials and settings to facilitate generalization.

Source: Adapted from E. Helmstetter & D. Guess, Applications of the individualized curriculum sequencing model to learners with severe sensory impairments. In *Innovative program design for individuals with dual sensory impairments*, eds. L. Goetz, D. Guess, & K. Stremel-Campbell (Baltimore: Paul H. Brookes, 1987), 260–66.

The best instruction occurs in context, that is, when the skill is needed by the child.

entire day at once. The matrix should be developed early in the planning stages for the classroom and then should be checked and adjusted periodically as the school year progresses.

Implement instruction in ongoing activities and routines

This guideline assumes that the best instruction occurs in context, that is, when the skill is needed by the child. It also assumes, however, that the usual organization and operation of most programs and the usual adult–child interactions are not adequate to address all of the learning needs of children with disabilities. Stated another way, the usual classroom practices may have to be adapted to ensure that children's goals are accomplished and that the benefits from early education are realized. In this section, several specific suggestions are provided for making these adaptations. These adjustments should be planned carefully, used systematically, and implemented consistently. They should not be used on some days and then not used again for several subsequent days; rather, the adjustments should become routine changes in how activities are implemented.

Embed instruction into existing activities and routines

Most programs follow some schedule of activities and routines each day. Predictability in activity schedules is highly desired—given, of course, that variety exists in what happens within those activities. Often many of the instructional strategies described in chapters 5 and 6 can be inserted into the usual activities without changing the activities a great deal (Wolery, Werts, & Holcombe 1994). When embedding instruction, adults must find times when the skills being taught are appropriate for the activity, determine whether they can implement the instructional procedure in that activity while accomplishing their other tasks and responsibilities, and select a strategy that will be effective.

For example, Venn, Wolery, Werts, and colleagues (1993) wrote about three young boys with disabilities who were not imitating their peers and needed to learn to do so. Because children engage in many different behaviors during art activities, this time was seen as ideal for the children with disabilities to develop certain skills by imitating their peers. Also during art time, the teacher who supervised the children spent time observing them, and she would interact with each child from time to time.

158

As a result, the teacher had several opportunities during the activity in which she had a few seconds (5 to 15) to implement an instructional procedure. A time delay procedure (see pp. 141–150) was used to teach the children with disabilities to imitate their peers. When one of the children with disabilities was in the art area with his peers, the teacher would wait for an appropriate time to embed the instruction. As a peer did his artwork, the teacher looked at the child with disabilities and said, "Jerrod, see what Brian is doing? You do it." She then immediately assisted the child with disabilities in doing what the peer had just done (e.g., dipping a paintbrush into the paint, pinching the end of a roll of clay). After providing the assistance, the teacher resumed observing the activity and interacting with children as needed. She waited a while and then used an

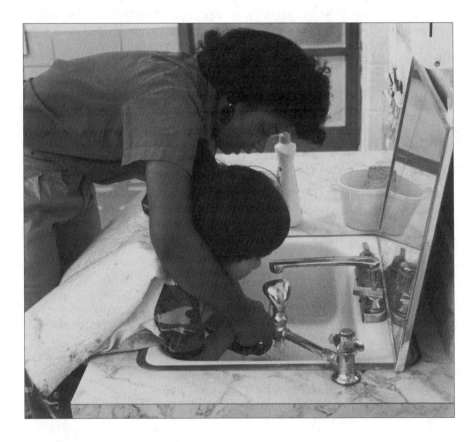

Teachers call less attention to children with disabilities when they find ways to meet their needs through adaptations of regular activities and routines.

instructional procedure with another behavior that the peer had displayed. Five times during each art activity, she assisted the child with disabilities in imitating his peers. Over time she delayed her assistance so that the children with disabilities had opportunities to imitate behaviors without adult help. All three boys who participated in the study learned to imitate their peers.

Embedding instruction in ongoing activities and routines has several advantages. It does not require changes in the classroom schedule or routine, and often no additional materials are needed. Nor does embedding instruction require additional staff members; it uses the teacher—and the children—who are already in the classroom. The adult can seize teachable moments (times when it is natural to provide help or other instruction). Embedding instruction does not interfere with the teacher's ongoing responsibilities; for example, in the art study described previously, if a child who was engaged in the activity needed help (additional materials, help hanging up his watercolor picture, getting his smock adjusted, etc.), the teacher was able to do these things and still provide the instruction. Instruction can be embedded in nearly all types of classroom activities and areas and used to help children develop many different skills. (For other examples of embedding instruction in ongoing activities and routines, see Schwartz, Anderson, & Halle 1989 and Fox & Hanline 1993.)

Adjust activities and routines by changing what children do in them

Staff with limited training may view too narrowly the functions of various activities for children. For example, they may see snack times only as opportunities for children to take refreshment rather than as times for promoting communicative exchanges between children (Venn, Wolery, Fleming, et al. 1993). They may see transitions only as times for children to move from one area to another rather than as instructional times (Werts et al. 1992; Wolery, Doyle, et al. 1993) or perceive circle time only as a time to sing songs rather than to learn specific skills or to engage in social interactions (McEvoy et al. 1988). Some may even fail to recognize that free play is a time to learn and to acquire skills (Chiara et al. 1993). Often, by changing what children do in an activity, different skills can be promoted.

During group activities children in early childhood settings often sing songs, engage in finger plays, listen to stories, "do the calendar and weather," and answer adults' questions. While reasons could be presented for these activities, such activities often involve children being in a group but not interacting with one another;

INCLUDING CHILDREN WITH SPECIAL NEEDS

in fact, peer interaction is often discouraged. McEvoy and colleagues (1988) adapted what children did during group activities and thereby promoted increases in social interactions within the group activity and during free play. Rather than having children simply sing songs and do the usual group activities, the teacher led a short discussion of the importance of friendships. Also, the songs and activities were adapted to include a large amount of physical contact between children (e.g., rather than singing, "If you're happy and you know it, clap your hands," they sang "If you're happy and you know it, shake your friend's hand, . . . give your friend a hug, . . . pat your friend on the back," etc.). These adaptations changed what children did in the activity. The result of this change was that children interacted more with one another during the immediate group activities as well as the next day during free play. Thus, simply changing what children did in one activity produced desirable changes within that activity as well as during another activity on another day.

Adapting activities in such ways has several advantages. The teacher does not need to add new activities or areas. Staffing assignments usually do not have to change to adapt the activity. Adults can continue in roles similar to their customary roles. The child with disabilities can receive the instruction that is needed for facilitating important goals without attention being called to the fact that the activity was adapted for that child. (For examples of how transitions have been adapted by changing what children do, see Werts et al. 1992 and Wolery, Doyle, et al. 1993.)

Adjust activities and routines by adapting the materials and their access

In most early childhood programs, a variety of activity centers and materials are readily accessible to the children (see chapter 5). Although children should have free access to materials and be allowed to make choices about the materials with which they wish to play, sometimes manipulating certain characteristics of toys and materials results in the promotion of desirable skills.

As noted in chapter 6, when using the naturalistic strategies (e.g., incidental teaching), restricting access to some preferred toys may result in children asking for those toys, which provides an opportunity for teachers to help them elaborate their use of language (Kaiser, Yoder, & Keetz 1992). Other adaptations of toys and materials may also facilitate specific skills. Some toys and materials appear to promote more manipulative play, others foster more constructive play, and still others promote more dramatic play (Musselwhite 1986). Further, some toys and materials appear to facilitate solitary play, and others appear to facilitate social

If a child avoids certain activity areas, such as dramatic play and blocks, the teacher may want to offer the child a choice between only these two areas during a portion of the free play period.

play (Odom & Strain 1984; Rettig, Kallam, & McCarthy-Salm 1993). Thus, if a child needs to learn and practice social play and interactions, then parts of free play time should give the child the opportunity to join a few friendly peers in playing with toys and materials that are likely to promote social exchanges. If, however, the child needs to learn to play with toys in sustained and independent ways, then toys and materials that foster solitary play should be used.

Adjust activities and routines by providing additional opportunities to participate

Sometimes children are engaged in group activities and have only a few opportunities to participate. For example, during circle time adults often ask questions and have children answer either individually or chorally. Although having two or three opportunities to answer may be sufficient for most children, it may not be enough for children with disabilities. A solution is to increase the number of questions for the child with disabilities and to embed a specific teaching procedure in the questioning (e.g., constant time delay). Fleming (1991) used this strategy and found that increasing the number of opportunities to respond and using the constant time delay procedure (see chapter 6) aided learning in children with disabilities during circle time activities.

Use shorter but more frequent activities to increase opportunities for instruction

Skills often are best promoted at the time they are needed. Some skills are quite important and are needed on a regular basis, but few opportunities exist for promoting those skills. For example, learning to put on one's coat is a difficult but important skill for many young children with disabilities. However, if this skill is taught only when it arises naturally, there may be only one or two opportunities to learn it in a day (e.g., when the child leaves home for the program, when she goes out to play, or when she goes home from the program). To increase the occasions for using this skill, the teacher could simply have the child go outside to play more often (two or three times) during the day and decrease the amount of time that the child spends outside. Azrin and Armstrong (1973) used the more-but-shorter adaptation to teach individuals with disabilities to feed themselves. Rather than having the usual number of meals per day, they increased the number of meals but provided less food. This arrangement resulted in rapid learning of self-feeding skills, such as spoon use.

When planning direct instructional activities for a child with a disability, include children without disabilities in the activities to avoid the possibility of stigmatizing the child.

Adjust activities by changing the rules of access to particular areas

In many early childhood programs, children have relatively free access to different activity areas, which gives them opportunities to make choices, to sample different areas as they are motivated to do so, and to engage in play that is appropriate to their developmental levels. However, some children avoid certain areas; unfortunately, some of the areas they avoid may provide them with opportunities to learn and practice valuable skills. Two adaptations of the rules of access to areas can deal with this problem.

Although free choice of areas is desirable, during some portions of the day the teacher may provide children with a restricted range of choices. Thus, if a child often avoids the dramatic play area and the block area, then providing the child (for a small portion of the day) with only those two choices will increase the probability that the child will go to those areas and get engaged in the activities there. Another adaptation has been illustrated in a couple of studies that focused on the children in a class who consistently avoided a particular area or activity (Jacobson, Bushell, & Risley 1969; Rowbury, Baer, & Baer 1976). In these studies a rule required that when children wanted to switch areas, they first had to go to the area they had avoided. After spending a few minutes there, they could go to the area of their choice. This rule produced two effects. First, children spent more time engaged in the areas they had avoided, and second, they switched activities fewer times per day. Thus, this adaptation may help children who avoid particular areas, who do not stay in a particular area very long, and who make several area switches in a short time period.

Adding activities for teaching skills that cannot be easily embedded

As evidenced by the preceding guidelines, there are many ways to adapt early childhood programs to increase children's engagement in activities and to increase the opportunities for children to learn and practice important skills. In most cases, using the guidelines for embedding instruction will ensure sufficient opportunities to promote children's learning and development in all of the important skills. In a few instances, however, there appears to be no natural time or adaptation for facilitating children's learning of selected and important skills.

Given that the team (including the child's family) has determined that the skill is beneficial and important for the child's independence and developmental progress, teaching the skill cannot be ignored. As a result, on some occasions it may be necessary to designate times to teach selected skills directly. When constructing such sessions, several guidelines are important.

• *First*, because specific behavior is desired, the strategies listed on the right side of figure 1 in chapter 5 (in which the teacher exerts more control of child-environment interactions) are often employed; however, this will vary depending upon the child, the skill, and the situation.

• *Second*, when direct instructional activities are added, they should be kept short—a few minutes in length. Generally, two or three short sessions per day are preferable to one long session each day.

• *Third*, when planning direct instructional activities for children with disabilities, including some children without disabilities is desirable (Collins et al. 1991). For the child with disabilities, this reduces the stigma of being singled out and makes it less obvious to the children without disabilities.

• *Fourth*, when direct instructional activities are used, the adults should make sure to provide opportunities for children to transfer the skills to other situations (Horner, Dunlap, & Koegel 1988). Children often learn some skills in very specific situations

When children with disabilities spend large amounts of time (10 to 15%) in unoccupied behavior or waiting, further adjustments are needed to promote their engagement in activities.

and then fail to use those skills in other situations in which they are appropriate. Such an outcome means that the instructional time has been wasted.

• *Fifth*, the instruction should be brisk, involve frequent reviews of previously taught skills, be monitored, be characterized by frequent and helpful feedback, and result in independent performance of the skills being taught (Wolery, Bailey, & Sugai 1988; Wolery, Ault, & Doyle 1992).

Monitor and adjust

Promoting children's engagement and facilitating their learning of particular skills are challenging tasks, but they are critical for people who care for and teach young children with disabilities. Making adaptations in early childhood programs to accomplish these goals is not an exact science. Sometimes the adaptations that are used reap many positive benefits (Bricker & Cripe 1992); at other times children do not benefit as had been anticipated. As a result, adults must monitor the effects of their program adaptations. This monitoring should occur on at least two levels.

First, children's engagement (participation) in the adapted activities and areas should be monitored on a regular basis; procedures for such monitoring have been described in a number of sources (e.g., Wolery, Bailey, & Sugai 1988; McWilliam 1991; McWilliam & Bailey 1992). Usually this involves direct observation of the child in different activities. Often the extent of engagement, nonengagement (unoccupied or inappropriate behavior), and waiting (waiting for a turn, waiting for materials, etc.) are measured. Engagement can be defined and measured in several ways (McWilliam & Bailey 1992), so the adults in the program need to select a system that is feasible and helpful. When children spend large amounts of time (10 to 15%) in unoccupied behavior or waiting, then further adjustments are needed. Although children's engagement in activities does not ensure that the children will benefit from them, the children cannot benefit unless they are engaged.

The second level of monitoring focuses on the behaviors and interaction patterns that are being promoted. Many systems exist for monitoring children's performance (Cooper 1980; Wolery 1989; Bailey & Wolery 1992), and the monitoring can vary greatly in terms of the information collected and its demands on adults' time. However, some system of keeping track of children's progress should be in place for each important goal for children with disabilities. Usually these monitoring systems involve direct observation of children in their usual activities. In most cases the monitoring is done on a regular basis (daily, weekly, every two weeks, etc.), with the frequency based on the importance of the skill and on the child's progress. The more important the skill, the more important it is to monitor often. Also, when children are not making progress, more frequent monitoring may be needed because the adults should be making changes in the program to make it work better.

The purpose of such monitoring is twofold. First, it will help the team make decisions about whether adequate progress is being made. Second, it will often suggest the types of changes that are needed (Haring, Liberty, & White 1980; Haring 1988). Of course, when an adaptation is not working, it should be adjusted and monitored. Planning an adaptation that does not work is not a sign of professional incompetence, but failing to note that the adaptation is not working and failing to adjust it so that it will work *are* signs of incompetence.

Summary

When planning adjustments of the classroom to implement instruction for children with developmental delays and disabilities, the early intervention team should follow several guidelines. Team members should use the assessment information collected on children and on the program. They should have a purpose for each activity and interaction in which children with disabilities participate, establishing a balance between activities that promote independence and those that ensure participation and inclusion. Each activity and classroom area should be used to promote multiple goals across various domains of development, and each goal should be addressed multiple times throughout the day. The team may find the activity/routine-by-skill matrix to be a useful mechanism for planning children's days. Instruction can be implemented in ongoing activities by embedding the instruction into existing activities and routines, changing the behaviors expected of children, adjusting the rules that govern children's access to materials, increasing the number of opportunities to participate, providing more frequent opportunities to practice certain skills, and/or adjusting the rules that govern access to given classroom areas. When these strategies do not allow important goals to be addressed, then the team can devise special instructional sessions. In all cases, children's engagement and participation and their acquisition and use of important skills must be monitored on a regular basis to determine whether the children are benefiting from the program and to identify whether additional changes are needed.

Chapter 8

Completing the Circle: Planning and Implementing Transitions to Other Programs

*Jane B. Atwater, Lois Orth-Lopes, Marleen Elliott,
Judith J. Carta, and Ilene S. Schwartz*

P ROFESSIONALS IN EARLY CHILDHOOD PROGRAMS are well aware of the remarkable developmental changes that children exhibit during their early years. In fact, those changes account for much of the delight and challenge of working with young children. As educators, we recognize the need to provide a progression of learning environments that effectively support children's developing skills and interests. The major transitions across early learning environments—from home, to infant–toddler programs, to preschool programs, to kindergarten—are critical points in this progression and require significant adjustments for all young children and their families.

For typically developing children, program transitions generally are expected to go smoothly as long as there is reasonable continuity between the "sending" and "receiving" programs and care in alleviating any uncertainties that the children and

Children with developmental delays and disabilities often have consid-erable difficulty transferring what they have learned to the unfamiliar activities, settings, people, and routines of a new program.

their families may have about the change (Bredekamp 1987). For example, the National Association for the Education of Young Children (NAEYC) offers the following recommendations: "Children need time to talk about their feelings and sensitive adults to listen and help prepare them for the exciting and positive changes that are a natural part of growing up. . . . If parents' tensions are soothed, children will also face the change more calmly and confidently" (Bredekamp 1987, p. 61).

While open communication and reassurance are equally important for children with special needs and their families, our concerns for those children must go beyond their initial emotional adjustment to the transition. Children with developmental delays and disabilities often have considerable difficulty transferring what they have learned to the unfamiliar activities, settings, people, and routines of a new program (Anderson-Inman, Walker, & Purcell 1984). Thus, the important gains that a child has made through an effective early childhood program may be lost in the course of a major transition. A child experiencing such difficulties is at a serious disadvantage for learning more complex skills, being a full participant in the activities of the new setting, and forming positive relationships with new teachers and peers. That child also is at increased risk for behavior problems, further delays and disabilities, and future placement in programs that restrict her or his opportunities to learn and interact with typically developing peers (Fowler 1982; Carden-Smith & Fowler 1983; Hanline 1993).

Understandably, parents of young children with special needs have identified transitions as times of particular stress for their families (Johnson et al. 1986; Hains, Fowler, & Chandler 1988). Not only must they help their children adjust to the change but they also have many related responsibilities, decisions, and adjustments to make. For example, when a child moves on to a new program, family members may lose or fear the loss of the support they received from the professionals in the child's former program. Teachers and other service providers face the challenging task of helping children and families manage transition demands and benefit from the new opportunities that the transition will provide.

Over the past decade, educators and researchers have begun to identify the issues of transition for children with special needs and to develop comprehensive transition models to address the needs of young children, families, and professionals. System-atic transition planning is now a major component of best practice in early childhood special education (ECSE) (Wolery, Strain, & Bailey 1992) and is, in fact, mandated for early intervention services under Public Law 99-457 (Education of the Handicapped Amendments of 1986). Although more research is needed, investigators are begin-ning to document specific factors that place children at risk during transition and to demonstrate effective strategies for countering those risks (e.g., Carta, Sainato, & Greenwood 1988; Rule, Fiechtl, & Innocenti 1990; Noonan et al. 1992).

Transitions are a collaborative effort involving the child's family, the sending and receiving teachers, and other professionals who plan and provide services for the child and family.

Despite this progress, one limitation in the current transition literature has been its predominant focus on transitions to mainstream classrooms from programs that serve only children with special needs. Thus, teachers in traditional early childhood programs may have difficulty deriving clear implications for their own teaching from the ECSE transition literature. In this chapter, our goal is to address that need with an overview of the research on transitions of young children with special needs, the implications of that research for early childhood educators, and specific examples for translating those implications into practice. The information presented here applies to two major transitions in early childhood: (a) from infant–toddler programs (birth to age 3) to preschool programs (ages 3 through 5); and (b) from preschool programs to kindergarten. After a brief description of the transition process, we focus on one component of that process: the interrelated tasks of preparing children for program transitions and preparing programs to support the successful inclusion of children with special needs.

The transition process

Current perspectives emphasize that the transition is not a single event but rather an ongoing process that begins 6 to 12 months before a child leaves a program (the "sending" program) and continues throughout the child's period of adjustment to a new program (the "receiving" program) (Noonan & Kilgo 1987; Diamond, Spiegel-McGill, & Hanrahan 1988; Hains, Rosenkoetter, & Fowler 1991). This process is a collaborative effort involving the child's family, the sending and receiving teachers, and other professionals who plan and provide services for the child and family. Hanline (1993) outlined the important contributions of the child's present and future teachers:

The role of the professional (usually the teacher) from the sending program is to: (1) prepare the child for a successful transition through the implementation of an appropriate individualized program and classroom curriculum, (2) collaborate with family members by acknowledging the role they have chosen and supporting them in that role, and (3) act as a liaison with professionals in the receiving program. The receiving teacher must: (1) learn about the strengths, needs, and background of the child who is making the transition; (2) adjust the demands of the classroom to facilitate the child's transition; (3) begin to establish a relationship and communication pattern with parents; and (4) act as liaison with professionals in the sending program. (p. 140)

Additional key features of a well-planned transition, which require the contributions of other professionals, include (a) development of a comprehensive transition plan that serves as a blueprint for collaboration across providers and agencies; (b) inclusion of parents as active participants in planning; (c) assessment of the family's needs for education and support related to the transition; (d) administrative support for the teachers' collaborative efforts; and (e) follow-up to determine whether the transition plan was successful. Although a complete discussion of the entire transition process is beyond the scope of this chapter, several sources detail the components, goals, and recommended practices of early childhood transition models (Noonan & Kilgo 1987; Polloway 1987; Diamond, Spiegel-McGill, & Hanrahan 1988; Wolery 1989b; Conn-Powers, Ross-Allen, & Holburn 1990; Rice & O'Brien 1990; Fowler, Schwartz, & Atwater 1991; Hanline 1993; Rosenkoetter, Hains, & Fowler 1994). Other sources focus on family involvement, education, and support during the transition process (Fowler et al. 1988; Hains, Fowler, & Chandler 1988; Hanline 1988; Hanline & Knowlton 1988; Kilgo, Richard, & Noonan 1989; Hamblin-Wilson & Thurman 1990; Spiegel-McGill et al. 1990; Hains, Rosenkoetter, & Fowler 1991). Clearly, too, the concerns of the preceding chapters in this volume—working with families, collaborating with other disciplines, designing supportive learning environments, assessing and teaching children effectively—all become especially salient at times of transition.

Research on early childhood transitions

The majority of the studies on early childhood transitions relate to the goal of preparing children with special needs to function successfully in new, typically more demanding learning environments. The implications of this research must be considered carefully because they raise important, but possibly difficult, issues for teachers in general early childhood programs. As Hanline (1993) observed, teachers usually have the primary responsibility for activities to prepare children for the future environment, tasks that are considered essential to a well-planned transition (Vincent et al. 1980; Conn-Powers, Ross-Allen, & Holburn 1990; Chandler 1992). Although the most recent NAEYC guidelines (Bredekamp & Rosegrant 1992) did not directly address the issue of teaching children the skills they will need in the next environment, sometimes this practice raises questions of developmental appropriateness (Hanline 1993; Atwater et al. 1994). For example, is it appropriate to teach preschool children the skills they will need to function in kindergarten? In addition, teachers might well be concerned about whether their time and resources can be stretched to include transition activities. We will consider these issues as we review two of the major questions that have been addressed in the current research literature.

What skills should we teach children to prepare them for transitions?

Two groups of studies assist us in answering this question. First, several researchers asked experienced teachers in mainstream preschool and kindergarten programs to identify child behaviors that are important for successful functioning in their classrooms. The rationale was that by identifying important skills in the child's future program, one can develop curricula that are most effective in preparing

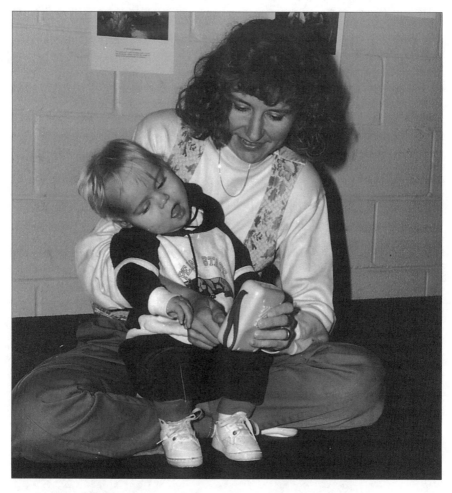

a child with special needs to do well in the new program. General findings were remarkably consistent across these studies. Rather than citing preacademic readiness skills, kindergarten teachers pointed to children's general skills for independence (e.g., completing a task with minimal teacher supervision), group participation (e.g., attending and following instructions during group activities), and social interaction (e.g., playing cooperatively) as being most essential for successful inclusion in mainstream kindergarten classrooms (Vincent et al. 1980; Walter & Vincent 1982; Beckoff & Bender 1989; Hains et al. 1989; Sainato & Lyon 1989); see Chandler 1992 for a compilation of specific behaviors. Comparable research with early childhood teachers, although rare, revealed similar themes. Teachers in integrated preschools identified 30 essential skills for 3-year-olds, most of which fall within the areas of appropriate classroom behavior, social/play skills, and self-help skills (Noonan et al. 1992). Similarly, early childhood care providers identified skills for communication and independence as being most important and preacademic skills as being least important for successful performance in integrated child care programs (Murphy & Vincent 1989).

In a second group of studies, classroom observations have confirmed that in mainstream kindergartens, children often take part in activities that require skills for working independently and participating in groups. These studies reported consistently that kindergarten children spent most of their time in large instructional groups or in independent tasks with little, if any, individual teacher direction (Vincent et al. 1980; Hoier, McConnell, & Pallay 1987; Carta, Sainato, & Greenwood 1988; Carta et al. 1990; Rule, Fiechtl, & Innocenti 1990). In contrast, children in early childhood special education (ECSE) programs spent most of their time in small groups or in one-to-one interactions with the teacher and received much higher rates of teacher prompting and feedback during instructional activities. Thus, although the ECSE programs may have been very effective in promoting many of the children's developmental objectives, they were providing few opportunities for children to learn and practice skills that would foster independence and group participation in their future classrooms. Further research will be needed to determine how children's learning environments change as they move from *integrated* preschools to kindergarten and as they move *into* integrated preschools from center-based infant–toddler programs or home-based services.

Despite these general findings, observational studies also found considerable variability across classrooms at both the preschool and kindergarten levels. In fact, within classrooms, individual children's activities and interactions with their teachers often varied greatly (Carta, Greenwood, & Robinson 1987; Hoier, McConnell, & Pallay 1987; Carta, Sainato, & Greenwood 1988; Sainato & Lyon 1989). Thus, a

INCLUDING CHILDREN WITH SPECIAL NEEDS

Teacher surveys and classroom observations indicate that functional skills for independence, group participation, and social interaction are essential for children with special needs to succeed in mainstream kindergarten classrooms.

child in transition across early childhood programs may experience environmental changes that are quite different from changes described for groups of children in the research literature.

Taken together, teacher surveys and classroom observations provide consistent evidence that preparing a child with special needs for early childhood transitions does not entail teaching specific preacademic or readiness skills that may not be developmentally or individually appropriate for that child. Rather, it involves teaching generic, functional skills that move a child toward increasing independence and increasingly active, appropriate engagement, alongside typically developing peers, in the instructional, play, and social activities of early childhood programs. This conclusion leads us to the question of how we might accomplish that goal successfully.

What teaching strategies are effective in facilitating early childhood transitions?

Although we need a broader base of research to answer this question fully, recent work demonstrates that systematic teaching strategies to facilitate early childhood transitions can benefit children with special needs. Based on their observations in kindergarten and first grade classrooms, Rule and her colleagues (Rule, Fiechtl, & Innocenti 1990) developed a curriculum to teach skills for participating appropriately and independently in nine common classroom activities (e.g., group circle, individual tasks, child-selected activities), with systematic strategies to help children use their skills across different settings and situations. To examine the effectiveness of the curriculum, a special education teacher conducted daily activities with children from two mainstream child care centers over 22 to 29 weeks. The regular child care providers, who did not have information about the curriculum, reported improvements in children's skills after the intervention; and in the following year, kindergarten teachers evaluated positively the children's abilities to participate independently.

Other investigators have demonstrated the effectiveness of specific strategies that were designed to facilitate transitions by promoting children's appropriate engagement during (a) group instruction activities (Sainato, Strain, & Lyon 1987), (b) independent activities (Sainato et al. 1990; Hains 1992), and (c) in-class transitions (Sainato, Strain, Lefebvre, & Rapp 1987; Connell et al. 1993). For each of these studies, teachers structured typical preschool activities in ways that would provide increased opportunities for children to participate actively and with minimal teacher direction. The ultimate goal was to prepare the children for successful transitions to kindergarten.

Children with disabilities who have been in early childhood programs designed to facilitate transition are more likely to receive regular kindergarten placement and favorable teacher ratings than children from other classrooms.

Building on this work by Sainato and her colleagues, Carta, Atwater, and Schwartz (1991, 1992) developed an intervention program composed of teaching strategies to foster children's active, appropriate engagement during typical group activities, independent activities, and in-class transitions. Instead of teaching specific content, these strategies focused on structural characteristics of activities, such as pacing, teacher prompting, and physical setting, and thus could be blended with teachers' existing curricula and instructional plans. For example, during group instruction activities, teachers alternated prompts to individual children with prompts directed to the entire group. This strategy fostered children's engagement by giving them many opportunities for active participation and by giving them practice in responding to group-directed prompts, which typically are more difficult for children with special needs. The same strategies were used at the preschool level to prepare children for mainstream kindergarten environments and at the kindergarten level to support the inclusion of children with special needs.

In a three-year study of the effectiveness of this intervention, four ECSE teachers and eight kindergarten teachers learned to restructure typical classroom activities so that children would have opportunities to practice skills for group participation and for independent performance. Although children with special needs were the focus of this research, all strategies were implemented on a classwide basis in both the ECSE classrooms and the mainstream kindergartens. To assess the effects of the intervention, the researchers not only monitored the progress of children whose teachers were using the intervention strategies but also tracked the progress of children from the same school district whose teachers were not participating in the intervention. When compared with children who had not received the intervention, participating children had (a) greater gains over the school year in their active engagement in classroom activities; (b) greater reductions in teacher direction during independent activities; (c) greater improvements in their teachers' ratings of their classroom skills; and (d) greater reductions in teachers' ratings of problem social behavior. Furthermore, in mainstream kindergartens, teachers indicated that typically developing children, as well as children with special needs, benefited from the strategies. Upon exit from the ECSE program, children who had received the intervention were less likely than were nonintervention children to be placed in special education kindergarten programs. In fact, in those ECSE classrooms in which teachers had followed intervention guidelines closely, the percentage of children receiving regular kindergarten placement (75%) was almost twice that for other classrooms. The following fall, regular kindergarten and first grade teachers, who did not know which children had received the intervention, gave higher classroom skill ratings and lower behavior problem ratings to the children who had participated in the intervention program.

Together, these intervention studies support the results of teacher surveys and classroom observations by demonstrating that, given facilitative classroom environments, many young children with special needs can learn skills for independence and group participation. Furthermore, systematic strategies to foster such skills can assist children in making successful transitions to inclusive educational settings. Rather than supplanting existing curricula, these strategies can be incorporated to strengthen the ongoing activities of both the sending and the receiving classrooms.

Implications for early childhood education

Research on early childhood transitions, although still incomplete, provides direction for activities to prepare children for successful transitions and to create receiving environments that facilitate inclusion. Drawing from this research and current standards of best practice, we offer the following recommendations for incorporating effective transition instruction and support in a manner that is developmentally and individually appropriate and that is manageable within the many competing demands of an early childhood program.

Skills identified as important for success in inclusive programs should NOT be viewed as prerequisites for those programs. Instead, they represent goals for teaching and intervention, as well as standards for evaluating the effectiveness of services provided to the child (Salisbury & Vincent 1990; Fowler, Schwartz, & Atwater 1991; Hanline 1993). Thus, the burden does not fall on the child to demonstrate "readiness" for an inclusive program; rather, the burden falls on the sending and receiving programs to provide experiences that prepare and support the child's inclusion effectively.

Skills selected for transition activities should be functional (useful) for children in their current and future environments. Transition skills that are most functional for a child may be identified by some or all of the following criteria.

• First, they are useful to the child across diverse settings and situations and will continue to be useful as the child moves to new educational programs. For example, the ability to locate and replace one's own materials is functional at home, in classrooms, during play and educational activities, and throughout the lifespan.

• Second, they are "keystone skills" that enable a child to learn a number of more complex skills (Wolery 1991). For instance, the ability to attend and follow instructions in group activities enables a child to acquire new knowledge, to expand linguistic skills, and to learn interactive skills, such as turn taking with peers.

• Third, they move a child toward increasing independence in inclusive environments. The ability to interact socially with peers, for example, provides the child with natural opportunities to observe and practice age-appropriate play skills rather than being dependent on direct instruction by adults.

*Teaching strategies to facilitate transitions can be incorpo-
rated into ongoing activities rather than taking the place of
the regular curriculum.*

• Fourth, they facilitate a child's active engagement in learning activities. The ability to complete tasks without frequent teacher prompting enables a child to spend more time actively engaged in child-directed tasks and less time passively attending to teacher direction. The critical importance of active engagement to a child's optimal development has been well documented (McWilliam & Bailey 1992; Carta et al. 1993).

Because of diversity in classroom environments and in children's needs, a universal set of transition skills is not likely to be found (Fowler, Schwartz, & Atwater 1991). The functional skills selected for transition activities will vary depending on specific areas of discrepancy and similarity between the sending and receiving programs, the current skills of children who are making the transition, and relevance to children's communities and cultures. In addition, early childhood and kindergarten programs themselves are in a state of transition because they are affected by legislation, societal changes, and shifts in educational philosophy. Currently, for example, there are efforts to make early childhood and kindergarten programs more inclusive (Salisbury 1991), to decrease the emphasis on didactic teaching and academics (Salisbury & Vincent 1990), and to accommodate cultural diversity (Hanson & Lynch 1992; Barrera 1993). All of these trends are likely to produce changes in specific transition goals. Thus, to ensure a child's successful transition, it is critical that the sending and receiving teachers have practical, systematic methods for sharing relevant information about their programs and that administrators provide teachers with the release time required to exchange such information.

Teaching strategies to facilitate transitions can be incorporated into ongoing activities rather than taking the place of the regular curriculum and, when appropriate, can be implemented classwide to benefit all children. Thus, preparing the child for the next educational environment does not require teachers to reproduce activities from the next environment in their classroom. Rather, within the context of developmentally appropriate activities, a teacher can provide opportunities for the child to learn functional skills (as defined above) that are natural precursors of skills needed in the next environment (Noonan & Ratokalau 1991; Noonan et al. 1991). For example, preschool children can learn to find and replace their own materials to prepare for the increasing independence that will be needed during activity transitions and independent learning activities in kindergarten. These skills can be taught within the regular curriculum, including the transformational curriculum described by Rosegrant and Bredekamp (1992). In addition, transitions will be facilitated by effective teaching strategies throughout the year, especially those that permit children with diverse abilities to participate in functional activities together (e.g., Bricker & Cripe 1992).

Transition activities should include strategies for helping children transfer skills to the future environment. One such strategy is to arrange for common features in the sending and receiving environments (Stokes & Baer 1977). Familiar materials, routines, and teaching strategies provide the child with clear opportunities to use acquired skills and thus to participate actively and successfully in the new classroom. Both the sending and receiving teachers can adapt their activities to maximize common features, especially during the weeks just before and just after the child's transition. A second effective strategy is to include activities in the receiving environment that give children opportunities to review and extend the skills that they learned in the sending program (Carta, Atwater, & Schwartz 1991, 1992). Some children, because of specific disabilities, may have difficulties in the typical activities of the new program. Thus, a third essential strategy for the receiving teacher is to adapt and modify classroom activities so that these children can be included as full participants with their peers (Noonan et al. 1992; Thompson et al. 1993). Specific examples of each of these strategies are described in the section, "Increasing the child's familiarity with the next environment," beginning on page 179 of this book. Chandler (1992) describes additional strategies that could be used to support children's transfer of skills to inclusive environments.

Children's families should be included, to the extent they choose, in planning and implementing activities to facilitate successful transitions for their children. Family-focused strategies are important to the transition process, just as they are to other components of early childhood programs for children with special needs. To assist their child and to make informed decisions about the transition plan, parents need information about differences between the sending and receiving programs, how those differences might affect their family, skills that are important for their child's success in the future program, and the programs' plans for supporting the child's successful transition (Kilgo, Richard, & Noonan 1989; Hanline 1993). Parents also have the right to be informed about the rationale for a program's policies and practices relative to transition planning. For example, do a program's policies and recommendations conform to standards of best practice, and do they reflect a consideration of current research findings? Furthermore, families can be a valuable resource in the planning and implementation of strategies to facilitate the transition (Chandler 1992). Family members, for example, may be in the best position to identify skills that are likely to be functional and appropriate within the child's home and community—outside the classroom—and to identify supports and adaptations that the child and family may need in the future program. In addition, parents might help their child transfer skills to the future program by

Including the family in planning and implementing transition activities helps to ensure that the transition plan focuses on functional, culturally relevant objectives and that the child, the family, and the future program are prepared for a successful transition.

planning family activities that provide opportunities for the child to practice previously learned skills and that incorporate such elements as new songs, new routines, and unfamiliar terms that will be typical in the future program. Thus, inclusion of the family can be a powerful strategy for ensuring that transition plans focus on functional, culturally relevant objectives and that the child, the family, and the future program are prepared for a successful transition.

Practical applications in early childhood programs

The specific strategies described in this section are offered as examples of how teachers might translate the general recommendations derived from research into practice. Such strategies can be adapted to meet individual child and family needs, as well as the constraints of the sending and receiving programs, and might serve as a mechanism for incorporating transition goals into the child's Individualized Family Service Plan or Individualized Education Plan. The strategies that we describe fall into two general categories: (a) procedures for increasing familiarity with the receiving program prior to the transition, and (b) techniques for teaching functional skills that are developmentally appropriate and useful in any educational environment.

Increasing the child's familiarity with the next environment

Strategies to increase the child's familiarity with the next environment enable teachers and families to identify functional transition goals for the child and to support the child's adjustment and transfer of skills to the new setting.

Sharing information across programs. To address a child's individual transition needs, communication among the child's parents and the sending and receiving teachers is essential. Ideally, teachers would have release time to visit each other's programs during typical activities. The sending teacher and the child's parents could visit the receiving program to observe the skill levels of children in the program, the content and structure of activities, the materials available, the physical setting, and any obstacles that might inhibit the child's full participation. The receiving teacher could visit the sending program to make similar observations. If visits to the receiving program occur at the end of a school year, teachers and parents should

Because children with special needs often have difficulty with changes in familiar routines, teachers may find it helpful to give some advance preparation when introducing a change or a new activity.

keep in mind that their observations of children's skill levels and classroom activities may not be representative of those that their child will encounter at the beginning of the year. If possible, a visit early in the year also would be helpful.

If visits during a typical program day are not possible, teachers might schedule on-site visits after school hours, attend each other's open-house activities or parents' night, or communicate by phone or letter. Families also might be invited to special events in the receiving program. Specific examples of questions one might ask to identify significant features of a child's future program are listed in table 1. Bennett and colleagues (1991) provide a checklist to assist parents in learning about preschool programs, while Chandler (1992) and Fowler (1982) detail differences that might exist between preschool and kindergarten classrooms. With such information, teachers and parents can work together to plan how best to prepare the child for the new program and to minimize differences between programs prior to the child's transition. Essentially the two programs would become more alike at the time of the transition than might be typical at other times during the year.

Arranging child visits. To help a child become familiar with the new environment, the receiving teacher can invite the child and her parents to visit the classroom. Depending on the child, the first visit might occur when other children are not present, followed by a visit during a typical day. Photographs of such visits help children remember the new classroom and teachers and to see themselves as part of that setting; audio tapes might be used for children who have visual impairments. Child visits also provide an opportunity for the receiving teacher to learn more about the child. For example, the teacher can observe the child manipulating materials or interacting with a peer who has been selected to play with the child (Haymes, Fowler, & Cooper 1991). Through such observations and conversations with the parents, the teacher can determine whether activity areas and materials are accessible to the child and identify adaptations that might be needed to support the child's inclusion. The parents also can provide useful information about the child's favorite activities and special interests and should be given opportunities to express any concerns they might have about the transition.

Adapting familiar activities. Several activities—such as free play, snacktime, and storytime—are common to most early childhood programs and child care settings; however, the format of such activities in the receiving program may be unfamiliar to a child. Although most teachers allow for a period of adjustment to new activities, children with special needs often have difficulty with changes to familiar routines. Some advance preparation may help them keep pace with their peers as they are introduced to new activities. For example, before they enter preschool, many

INCLUDING CHILDREN WITH SPECIAL NEEDS

Table 1. Sample Questions for the Child's Future Program

For transitions to early childhood programs

— How many adults and children will be present in the child's classroom?

— What self-help skills are emphasized? What type of assistance is provided?

— If children take naps, how much flexibility is possible for individual naptimes?

— How much time do children spend in various activity formats, such as group circle, free play, snack, activity centers, and preacademics?

— What type of regular or adaptive seating is used for these activities?

— Do children manage some of their own toys and materials?

— Are transportation services available? How is the child seated, moved, and supervised for transportation?

— How are parents involved in and kept informed of classroom activities?

For transitions to kindergarten

— How many children with and without special needs are likely to attend the child's kindergarten?

— What is the adult/child ratio?

— How much time do children spend in various activity formats, such as large-group instruction, small-group instruction, independent tasks, cooperative tasks with peers, and free play?

— What is the seating arrangement during group and independent activities?

— What are the appropriate ways for children to gain teacher attention or to ask for assistance?

— What types of consequences do teachers provide for appropriate and inappropriate child behavior?

— What types of supportive services are available at the school?

— What are the methods of communication between home and school? What is the procedure for arranging family visits to the classroom?

Source: Many of these questions were adapted from S.A. Fowler, Transition from preschool to kindergarten for children with special needs. In *Early childhood education: Special problems, special solutions*, eds. K.E. Allen & E.M. Goetz (Rockville, MD: Aspen, 1982), 309–35.

young children are accustomed to having a parent serve snacks to them individually, and many have not had an opportunity to help with setup or cleanup tasks. In contrast, preschool teachers typically ask children to take turns serving themselves during snacks and then to take part in cleanup. Thus, some children might benefit from experience with the new format a few weeks prior to the transition. At home, for example, a child might learn to take one item, such as a carrot stick, from a plate and then pass the plate to other members of the family. Following meals or snacks, the child might be given simple cleanup tasks, such as throwing napkins in the trash; siblings might act as cleanup partners for children who need physical assistance. In this way, new activity formats can be introduced within familiar settings and can become an opportunity for family members to help the child prepare for increasing independence.

Following the transition, the receiving teacher can incorporate familiar activities, such as the child's favorite story or song, into the activities of the new program. Most young children enjoy repeating familiar songs, stories, and games. In addition, this strategy will give the child an opportunity to be the class "expert" for a particular activity. Parents might be invited to visit the classroom as guest experts on topics that may or may not be related to their child's special needs. Activities that are traditional in a child's culture are especially appropriate for teaching all children in the classroom to value the special contributions of each individual.

Introducing new activities. A teacher or parent also can prepare a child for a transition by introducing simple activities that are typical in the future program. Before a transition to preschool, for example, the teacher or parent might teach the child songs and finger plays that are preschool standards (e.g., "The Itsy Bitsy Spider" or "Head, Shoulders, Knees, and Toes"). If the child currently attends a group program, other children can easily join in these activities. If parents want to work on such songs with their child, the preschool teacher might recommend commercial recordings or send home tapes of the children singing in their classrooms. Similarly, as a sending teacher, a preschool teacher might introduce elements of typical kindergarten activities. For example, the child's future kindergarten program may include a daily group activity in which the date and the weather are discussed. A similar activity, at a simpler level, can become part of opening circle in the child's preschool. As an alternative the preschool teacher might teach a song about days of the week so that relevant terms become familiar.

Introducing new responsibilities. In typical kindergarten classrooms, children are responsible for managing their own materials. To prepare children for this responsibility, the preschool teacher might have children decorate boxes in which

"Affection activities"—songs and games that encourage friendship between children—may help eliminate the social barriers that might exist for children with disabilities in an early childhood program.

their own materials—such as crayons, scissors, and glue—can be kept. A few weeks prior to the transition, the teacher might introduce tabletop activities that require the child to use the box of supplies and then return it to a specific shelf. For some kindergarten activities, children may use materials from a large box of shared supplies; thus, the preschool teacher also might give the child opportunities to share materials, as well as responsibility for putting them away correctly. Learning to manage materials responsibly under different circumstances will strengthen the

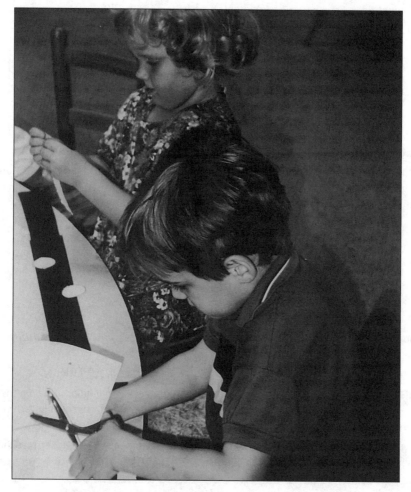

Table 2. Resources for Teaching Skills to Facilitate Transition

Preschool Preparation and Transition Project: Hawaii Preparing for Integrated Preschool (PIP) Curriculum

Authors: Mary Jo Noonan, Lynn Yamashita, Marjie A. Graham, & Dean Nakamoto

Skills Focus: Self-help, communication and social skills, and skills required for classroom routines

Target Population: Young children with disabilities who are entering regular preschool programs, with special adaptations for children with sensory or physical disabilities

Source: Preschool Preparation and Transition Outreach Project
Department of Special Education
University of Hawaii at Manoa
1776 University Avenue, WIST 211
Honolulu, HI 96822
Fax: 808-956-5713

Handbook for the Inclusion of Young Children with Severe Disabilities

Authors: Barbara Thompson, Donna Wickham, Jane Wegner, Marilyn Mulligan Ault, Pamela Shanks, & Barbara Reinertson

Skills Focus: Communication and social skills

Target Population: Young children with severe disabilities and their peers in preschool

Source: Learner Managed Designs, Inc.
P.O. Box 3067
Lawrence, KS 66046
Phone: 913-842-9088
Fax: 913-842-6881

Bridging Early Services for Children with Special Needs and Their Families: A Practical Guide for Transition Planning

Authors: Sharon E. Rosenkoetter, Ann Higgins Hains, & Susan A. Fowler

Skills Focus: Preschool focus is on communication, social, self-help, and cognitive skills; kindergarten focus is on playing and working independently and collaboratively, interacting with peers, and following directions, routines, and classroom rules.

Target Population: Young children with disabilities who are entering regular preschool or kindergarten programs

Source: Paul H. Brookes Publishing Co.
P.O. Box 10624
Baltimore, MD 21285-0624
Phone: 410-337-9580
Fax: 410-337-8539

Effective Instructional Strategies to Facilitate In-Class Transitions, Group Instruction, and Independent Performance Activities

Authors: Judith J. Carta, Marleen Elliott, Lois Orth-Lopes, Holly Scherer, Ilene S. Schwartz, & Jane B. Atwater

Skills Focus: Skills required for in-class transitions, group responding, and independent performance

Target Population: Young children with special needs who are entering regular kindergarten programs

Source: Project SLIDE
Juniper Gardens Children's Project
1614 Washington Blvd.
Kansas City, KS 66102
Phone: 913-321-3143
Fax: 913-371-8522

Project STEPS: Instructional Strategies for the Helpful Entry Level Skills Checklist (2nd edition)

Authors: Rita Bryd & Beth Rous

Skills Focus: Communication, social behavior, and self-management; classroom rule following and work-related skills

Target Population: Young children with disabilities who are about to enter regular kindergarten programs

Source: Project STEPS (Sequenced Transition to Education in the Public Schools)
Child Development Centers of the Bluegrass, Inc.
465 Springhill Drive
Lexington, KY 40503
Phone: 606-278-0549

child's flexibility in adapting to the demands of the new setting. Of course, the receiving teacher must be able to adapt material storage systems to meet the child's needs. If the child has physical disabilities, for example, the teacher might change the location of materials or develop a system of buddies who share responsibilities for gathering materials for an activity. Parents might have suggestions on storage arrangements that have worked at home, and they in turn also might appreciate suggestions on how to increase their child's responsibility in the home.

Teaching functional skills that facilitate transitions

Research has identified skills that facilitate successful transitions and inclusion in the early childhood years: self-help skills, social interaction skills, and skills that promote independence and group participation. In this section we briefly describe strategies for teaching these skills. Readers who would like more specific, detailed information are referred to the resources listed in table 2. All of these resources represent efforts to translate research evidence and best-practice guidelines into practical, effective curricula and instructional strategies for classroom teachers.

Self-help skills. Most typically developing preschool children have acquired basic self-help skills, including toileting, hand washing, eating, and dressing; but because of their complexity, these skills can be particularly difficult for many children with disabilities. For example, eating finger foods involves several component skills, including the ability to grasp small pieces of food, move a hand to the mouth, place food in the mouth, chew, and swallow. Bailey and Wolery (1992) and Campbell (1987) suggest various techniques for teaching eating, dressing, and toileting skills to young children with disabilities.

The Hawaii Preparing for Integrated Preschool (PIP) Curriculum (Noonan et al. 1991) identifies the components of several complex self-help skills that are important for successful inclusion in regular preschool programs. Five strategies are used to teach skills in natural settings and during related play activities:

• demonstrating the skill for the child;

• encouraging the child to take part in an activity that involves the skill;

• physically guiding or assisting the child, if needed;

• providing opportunities to practice the skill in pretend play activities and in actual situations; and

• reinforcing the child's efforts to use the skill independently.

For a child with a disability that limits his self-help skills, the curriculum suggests relevant adaptations for accommodating the child's needs in an inclusive program. Even if the child has acquired self-help skills, the receiving teacher might need to help the child become more fluent with the skills or to use these skills in the new setting.

Parent and family needs also must be considered when setting goals for teaching self-help skills. Parents' priorities will be influenced by the child's special needs but also by the needs of other family members. For example, if a child's eating difficulties cause more family tension than do toileting problems, the family might place a higher priority on self-feeding skills. It is important for the sending teacher to balance the child's needs, the parents' priorities, and the expectations of the receiving program.

Social interaction skills. Many children with disabilities lack the social skills that are so critical for interactions with peers and adults (McEvoy, Odom, & McConnell 1992; Odom, McConnell, & McEvoy 1992a). Without these skills, many opportunities to learn from peers are lost. As with self-help skills, there are many prerequisite skills involved in complex social interactions, such as looking at a speaker (when this is culturally acceptable), expressing needs, sharing, and taking turns. The Hawaii PIP Curriculum (Noonan et al. 1991) provides specific guidelines for identifying and promoting prerequisite skills that are basic to positive social interactions in preschool.

Other strategies are useful for eliminating the social barriers that might exist for a child with disabilities in an early childhood program. For example, "affection activities" are songs and games that encourage friendship between children (McEvoy et al. 1988; McEvoy, Twardosz, & Bishop 1990). As peers become more comfortable around the child with disabilities through these activities, the teacher can encourage social interaction at other times. In fact, McEvoy and colleagues (1988) found that friendship activities facilitated children's interactions during subsequent free play periods.

Many effective strategies promote the social inclusion of a child with special needs by teaching classmates to accept and get to know the child. For example, the receiving teacher might help classmates interact with a child who has disabilities by modeling strategies for getting the child's attention, greeting the child, and recognizing the child's response to a greeting (e.g., Strain & Timm 1974; Strain & Odom 1986; Sasso & Rude 1987; Odom & Watts 1991). Peers also can be encouraged to invite the child with special needs to play and to share materials. Such activities must be structured so that the child with special needs is not always the recipient of help from the peer but rather is a contributing partner in play and learning.

Skills that promote independence and group participation. The most consistently documented finding from current transition research is the critical importance of independence and group participation skills for successful transition to kindergarten. One comprehensive model for promoting these skills has been developed by Project SLIDE (Skills for Learning Independence in Diverse Environments) (Carta, Elliott, et al. 1992). Based on previous research by Carta and her colleagues (Carta, Atwater, & Schwartz 1991, 1992), Project SLIDE focuses on strategies for promoting children's active, independent engagement within the context of typical preschool and kindergarten activities. The original intervention program, described earlier in this chapter, has been refined and expanded to facilitate its application across diverse educational settings. Project SLIDE's core components include strategies for (a) identifying individual and classwide transition goals; (b) teaching functional skills and promoting active engagement during group instruction, independent activities, and in-class transitions; and (c) facilitating parent involvement and interagency collaboration in transition planning. Each component incorporates planned flexibility to permit adaptation to the needs, concerns, and resources of a particular school district or educational program. In addition, the model places a strong emphasis on teaching practices that are effective throughout the school year, such as using clear, concise instructions; providing many natural opportunities for children to practice skills; evaluating activities to determine how well they are working for individual children; and modifying activities as indicated by ongoing evaluations. Currently, Project SLIDE is providing technical assistance to school districts from 10 states, as district personnel adapt, implement, and evaluate the project's intervention model in their early childhood and kindergarten programs.

Summary

Current research on early childhood transitions, although still incomplete, has clear implications for early childhood programs that serve children with special needs. The research demonstrates that early childhood educators can prepare young children for transitions with curricula focused on functional skills, appropriate learning activities, and effective teaching strategies. In children's future programs, the same strategies can be used to prepare educational environments that effectively support the inclusion of children with diverse needs and abilities. With planning, such activities not only provide a critical service for children with special needs but also enrich learning experiences for all children.

Chapter 9

Conclusions and Future Directions

Mark Wolery

THE 1992–1993 SCHOOL YEAR witnessed a landmark event for 3- through 5-year-old children with disabilities. For the first time in the history of the United States, every state in the nation mandated that preschoolers with disabilities have a right to a free, appropriate public education in the least restrictive appropriate environment (U.S. Department of Education 1993). This event is a major accomplishment of advocacy by parents and other concerned individuals and of public responsibility; it is cause for celebration. And it did not occur overnight. Some states and local school districts have provided these services for many years, and others joined the effort more recently. The mandate is the result of a long history of legislation and litigation. It has been slow in coming, but it is here! In addition, continued progress is being made in developing early intervention services for infants and toddlers with developmental delays and disabilities and their families.

Although these achievements are recent, infants, toddlers, and preschoolers with disabilities have not been ignored by the federal government. As noted in chapter 1, several federal initiatives (e.g., P.L. 90-538, P.L. 94-142, P.L. 99-457) resulted in a considerable amount of experience and research. Thus, much is known about how to provide services to young children with disabilities and their families. In this monograph we have addressed the knowledge base as it applies to practice in several areas; however, many other resources (cited in the respective chapters) include more complete discussions of the relevant issues.

In this summary chapter, three questions are addressed briefly: (a) Do we know how to provide high-quality services to young children with disabilities and their families? (b) What barriers exist to ensuring high-quality services? and (c) What issues need to be addressed in the future? These questions are addressed for families, for general service delivery issues, and for classroom-based services for children.

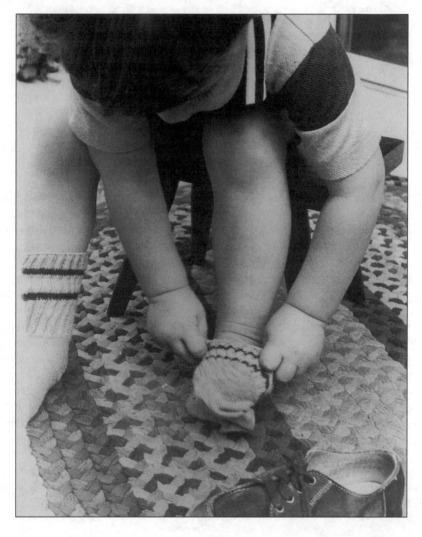

Including Children with Special Needs

The field of early childhood special education has learned a great deal about how to support families of young children with disabilities.

Services for families of children with disabilities

The field of early childhood special education has learned a great deal about how to support families of young children with disabilities (Dunst et al. 1993; Bailey, this volume, chapter 2). We now understand more clearly that

• families exist within larger and interrelated social systems;

• having a child with a disability does not make a family dysfunctional;

• we must attend to families' goals and priorities for their child and for the family;

• some families may have very different priorities and resources from other families;

• one of our primary roles is to assist families in accessing their informal and existing resources; and

• *how* we provide help is a critical variable in how effective that help will be (cf. Dunst, Trivette, & Deal 1988; Brown, Thurman, & Pearl 1993).

Several potential barriers exist to providing effective early childhood services for families; two of these barriers deserve mention. First, the manner in which programs (i.e., early intervention programs, early childhood programs for typically developing children, and public schools) have interacted with families in the past is often quite at odds with what we know about how best to interact with families. Traditionally, families have been perceived as outsiders, were given relatively few choices about what services were provided or about how those services were delivered, and were seen as extensions of the programs (i.e., to help the program meet its goals for the child). We clearly recognize that such perspectives are counterproductive. Nonetheless, tradition in most areas of human services has always been a formidable barrier to change. To change these program–family roles, a shift in the balance of power is required. Families must become participants in decision making rather than recipients of information about decisions made by professionals. Second, and closely related to the first barrier, is the issue of the level of staff preparation and training in family-related issues (Bailey, this volume, chapter 2). Current perspectives on how to interact with and support families require a different set of skills from those commonly taught in university personnel preparation programs. Thus, practitioners have likely acquired a new set of skills in school or through training and then had to try implementing those skills in contexts that do not support or encourage their use.

Four particularly important issues remain unresolved. First, substantial research is needed to identify, implement, and evaluate mechanisms for causing changes in the family-related policies and practices of educational programs. Second, resources

Despite efforts to combat poverty, it continues to be a major factor in how a lot of families function and how education is implemented— including early childhood services for families of young children with disabilities.

and personnel are needed to implement widespread, effective staff development related to family services. Third, programs must determine how to provide effective support and assistance to families when their young children with disabilities are enrolled in classroom-based services for small parts of the week (e.g., two mornings per week). When such children are in inclusive community programs, how should those programs be organized to support families and to ensure that the families' goals and priorities are addressed and the child's development is promoted? Fourth, many families with young children live in pervasive poverty, and an increasing proportion of families in the United States are culturally and linguistically different from the majority culture (Lynch & Hanson 1992). Despite efforts to combat poverty, it continues to be a major factor in how a lot of families function and how education is implemented—including early childhood services for families of young children with disabilities. Similarly, the extent to which effective practices for some groups (e.g., Caucasian families from middle-class backgrounds) apply to other groups remains, for the most part, an unstudied issue. Also, research is needed to understand the variations in services that may be required for each family and child within diverse groups.

Service delivery issues

The three aspects of service delivery discussed in this section include (a) the relationship of early childhood personnel with families, (b) the issues involved in team functioning, and (c) the placement of children in inclusive early childhood services.

Collaborative relationships with families

Services for families have been discussed, and the relationship between families and the program staff is noted below. The importance of collaborating with families is stressed in each chapter of this monograph that focuses on classroom-based practices (e.g., chapters 3 through 8). In chapter 3 the family is seen as a vital member of the intervention team. Through membership on the team, family members play an important role in planning and implementing assessment activities and in taking action based on the results of the assessment activities (chapter 4). Although families are not responsible for designing early childhood classrooms (chapter 5), selecting instructional strategies (chapter 6), or implementing those strategies in classrooms (chapter 7), their views about the goals of classroom-

No single discipline sufficiently prepares its members to provide effective early childhood services to families and children with disabilities without the assistance of individuals from other disciplines.

---

based services and about the manner in which programs operate are critical. Also, families play a central role in selecting post-preschool placements and in the transition of children into those new placements (Atwater et al., this volume, chapter 8).

Some of the barriers to establishing collaborative relationships between families and early childhood staff were noted in the previous section. Another substantial barrier that affects both families and program staff is the time required to establish and maintain such relationships. Many families are busy with childrearing, employment, and other important activities; thus, their time for communicating and interacting with program staff may be limited. Likewise, program staff have extensive demands on their time and energy that are often complicated by high child-to-staff ratios (Wolery, Huffman, Holcombe, et al., n.d.). Establishing and maintaining collaborative relationships with families also requires shifts in the roles of early childhood personnel, and they may not perceive themselves as having the skills to fulfill those roles (Buysse & Wesley 1993). Finally, as noted earlier, the traditional interaction patterns that families and schools have adopted may be a barrier to collaborative relationships.

Future research should document the contextual factors that influence the viability of collaborative relationships. For example, the effects of reducing child-to-staff ratios on the time available to staff for collaborating with families should be studied, as should the effects of more flexible meeting times and places on families' perceptions of programs' responsiveness to their schedules and other demands. If such adjustments are found to produce more collaborative relationships, then mechanisms should be studied for making such changes in preschool programs. Finally, research is needed to find ways to conduct some of the important functions (e.g., assessment, IFSP/IEP planning) more efficiently while maintaining effectiveness and fostering collaboration.

Transdisciplinary team issues

No single discipline (e.g., early childhood special education, early childhood education, speech-language pathology, physical and occupational therapy, psychology, medicine) sufficiently prepares its members to provide effective early childhood services to families and children with disabilities without the assistance of individuals from other disciplines. Services must be delivered in the context of a team because the benefits of team-based planning and implementation are clear. Experience and research suggest that several factors may facilitate effective team functioning, including adequate preparation within one's own discipline; a philosophy, a mission, and goals that are shared by team members; defined decision-making processes; clearly identified roles; and effective team leadership (Bailey & Wolery 1992; Rainforth, York, & Macdonald 1992; Bruder & Bologna 1993).

Several barriers exist to establishing collaborative, well-functioning teams. First, some disciplines have historically had a shortage of personnel who are trained to work with young children. In some disciplines, their members are trained to provide services across a wide age range (e.g., from children to geriatric patients); thus, they may have limited expertise in working with young children and families. Also, some disciplines offer many competing job opportunities that often pay higher salaries than do positions in early childhood programs. Although shortages of adequately prepared personnel may be most acute in the related-service areas (e.g., physical and

INCLUDING CHILDREN WITH SPECIAL NEEDS

occupational therapy), many of the personnel who work in early childhood programs (public and private) are not trained in early childhood education or early childhood special education (Wolery, Martin, et al., n.d.). Second, some programs—particularly non–public school, community-based programs—may not employ and may not have the resources to employ members of related-service disciplines (Wolery, Venn, et al., n.d.). Thus, related-service personnel may be employed either as private therapists or by agencies that are contracted to provide services to multiple programs. Third, when children with disabilities are integrated into community programs that do not employ their own related-service staff, logistical problems may arise in delivering those services (Odom & McEvoy 1990). Teams may have few opportunities to meet, communicate, and work together in developing and implementing truly integrated service plans. Other barriers include the absence of the factors that facilitate team functioning (e.g., lack of team goals; failure of teams to define roles or to establish decision-making processes).

Clearly, a central issue that needs to be addressed is ensuring that an adequate supply of appropriately trained personnel in each relevant discipline are readily available. This, of course, is less a research issue than a policy and resource-allocation issue. Research is needed to address administrative and programmatic variables that can promote team functioning. Research is also needed to resolve issues such as how related-service personnel provide effective consultation to educators, how families are integrated into teams, and how therapy goals can be integrated into ongoing classroom activities (McWilliam & Bailey n.d.).

Placement of children in inclusive programs

One of the provisions of the Individuals with Disabilities Education Act (IDEA) is that children must be placed in the least restrictive appropriate environment (Turnbull 1990). For young children with disabilities, many individuals perceive this to mean enrollment in programs designed for typically developing children, including their chronological agemates (Buysse & Bailey 1993; Peck, Odom, & Bricker 1993; Wolery, Werts, & Holcombe 1994). The rationale and potential benefits of inclusive placements are clearly known and were discussed in chapter 1. To date, the precise number and percentage of young children with disabilities who receive their early childhood services in programs designed for typically developing children is not known (Wolery, Werts, & Holcombe 1994). However, many preschoolers (3- through 5-year-old children) are served in regular school buildings—although not necessarily with their typically developing peers (U.S. Department of Education 1993)—and many programs (public and private) that were designed for typically

Future efforts should focus on identifying which policy barriers are actually impeding inclusive placements of young children, and research should evaluate mechanisms for addressing those barriers.

developing preschoolers report enrolling at least one child with a diagnosed disability (Wolery, Holcombe, et al. 1993). Further, many families of young children with and without disabilities generally view integration as a positive practice (Bailey & Winton 1987; Peck, Carlson, & Helmstetter 1992). Reliable information is lacking on the extent to which infants and toddlers with disabilities are served in integrated group-care programs.

Barriers to inclusive placements of young children with disabilities have been discussed in several sources, including chapter 1 of this book. These barriers include policy barriers (Odom & McEvoy 1990; Smith & Rose 1993), general trends in society (e.g., emphasis on academic rather than social outcomes; Strain & Smith 1993), philosophic differences between general and special early educators (Odom & McEvoy 1990), and programmatic variables such as high child-to-staff ratios and lack of adequate training and consultation (Wolery, Huffman, Brookfield, et al., n.d.; Wolery, Huffman, Holcombe, et al., n.d.).

Future efforts should focus on identifying which policy barriers are actually impeding inclusive placements of young children, and research should evaluate mechanisms for addressing those barriers. Similarly, the programmatic factors that function as barriers should be studied, both in terms of the extent to which they actually are barriers and the effectiveness of various strategies for addressing the factors that are barriers. Clearly, continued research on models of staff development, as well as resources for addressing staff development needs, is important (Kontos & File 1993).

Classroom issues

In the past 25 years, tremendous activity has focused on providing early education to young children with disabilities, particularly regarding assessment practices, instructional and intervention practices, and general service delivery issues (DEC Task Force on Recommended Practices 1993). Early intervention for young children with disabilities has occurred in a range of different settings, including clinics, hospitals, the children's homes, private preschools, and public preschools (Bailey & Wolery 1992). Currently, the majority of preschool-age children with disabilities seem to be served in some type of classroom-based program (U.S. Department of Education 1993); some infants and toddlers with disabilities also are served in center-based programs. Thus, the status of assessment and intervention practices in classroom-based programs deserves discussion.

Assessment activities in classrooms

Accepted practices for assessing young children with disabilities illustrate several themes. First, assessment activities should be conducted for specific purposes, and different purposes require different measurement strategies (Wolery, Strain, & Bailey 1992). Second, families should be involved (to the extent they desire) in the entire assessment process, including planning the assessment, gathering information, validating that information, and making consequent decisions (Bailey 1989b). Third, for planning interventions, naturalistic observation coupled with professional and parental judgment and interviews are accepted practices (Barnett, Carey, & Hall 1993). Fourth, assessment and curriculum activities should be interrelated and ongoing so that one informs the other (Neisworth 1993). Finally, assessment activities require a team of individuals who each bring unique sets of knowledge to the task (Linder 1993). As noted in chapter 4, many of the recommended practices for young children with disabilities are consistent with those recommended for all young children (NAEYC & NAECS/SDE 1991).

Despite a considerable amount of agreement on the acceptability of these practices (Neisworth 1993), several barriers exist to their implementation. One of the perceived barriers is the limited amount of time allowed for developing the initial Individualized Education Plan (IEP) or Individualized Family Service Plan (IFSP). However, if program personnel realize that the IEP and the IFSP can be revised, then assessment activities can continue and appropriate revisions can be made to reflect the knowledge that is acquired from greater opportunities to observe and interact with the child. Another barrier is the excessive confidence that traditionally has been placed in standardized testing, often with a concomitant lack of confidence in direct observation and judgment-based methods. A third barrier is the skill, time, and effort required to conduct ecologically valid assessments that occur outside classroom contexts. A final barrier is the complexity of development and the host of variables that can influence it, including the types of disabilities. For example, determining the cognitive skills of young children with physical and language disabilities is no simple task (Dunst & McWilliam 1986).

Several tasks require attention. A substantial need exists for understanding ways to involve families meaningfully in instructional planning assessments without imposing excessive demands on them. Similarly, there is a need to investigate ways for integrating assessment information from different domains and from different team members into cohesive understandings of children's developmental needs and abilities. As noted, there is a need to further understand the effects of various disabilities on children's development. Although substantial progress has been made in assessing the effects of environmental factors on children's behavior (i.e., eco-behavior analysis; Carta, Sainato, & Greenwood 1988; Barnett, Carey, & Hall 1993), strategies for making such procedures more efficient and simpler to use and analyze are needed.

Curriculum issues

For several years, the curriculum content for young children with disabilities has come from two sources: typical development and the unique demands of children's environments (Bailey & Wolery 1989). These approaches were often presented as being more or less applicable to different groups of children—the developmental model was seen as appropriate for children with mild and moderate delays and disabilities, and the ecological approach (focusing on enabling children to function in their particular environments) was viewed as appropriate for children with severe disabilities. Both approaches, however, can be applicable for all children, although perhaps with varying levels of emphasis. In addition, other models may be emerging (Mallory 1992).

Educational methods have originated from a number of theoretical perspectives, including constructivist (e.g., Dunst 1981), behavioral (Strain et al. 1992), and ecological (Barnett & Carey 1992). As a result, an impressive array of strategies have emerged for nearly all areas of development, including social skills (Odom, McConnell, & McEvoy 1992b), motor skills (Horn 1991; Demchak 1993), cognitive skills (Dunst 1981; Wolery & Wolery 1992), adaptive skills (Wolery, Ault, & Doyle 1992), and communication skills (Warren & Reichle 1992; Kaiser & Gray 1993). These methods occur on a continuum from material selection and arrangements of the physical space (Sainato & Carta 1992) to systematized prompting procedures (Wolery, Ault, & Doyle 1992). Some, but not all, of the strategies were developed initially in segregated programs serving children with disabilities; however, many were developed and evaluated in inclusive programs. Recently, considerable attention has been given to the relevance of the developmentally appropriate practice guidelines (Bredekamp 1987) to young children with disabilities (Carta, Schwartz, et al. 1991; Wolery, Strain, & Bailey 1992; Bredekamp 1993; Carta et al. 1993; McLean & Odom 1993). The general conclusion is that programs following the guidelines are suitable placements for children with disabilities, but adaptations and modifications of the guidelines are required for many of the children with developmental delays and disabilities.

The barriers to implementing curricular strategies for young children with disabilities in integrated programs lie primarily in three areas. First, philosophic

Substantial agreement exists between early childhood education and special education on many issues.

differences may exist between general and special early educators about the content and methods of the curriculum (Odom & McEvoy 1990). However, philosophic differences exist within both disciplines (Wolery & Bredekamp n.d.), and substantial agreement exists between disciplines on many issues (Bredekamp 1993; Carta, Atwater, et al. 1993; McLean & Odom 1993). Second, many early childhood programs have high child-to-staff ratios. Third, caregivers of children with disabilities may need more adequate training and more opportunities for consultation with the other parties involved in providing special education and related services (Wolery, Huffman, Holcombe, et al., n.d.). The programmatic barriers (child-to-staff ratios, training, and consultation) are primarily resource-allocation issues.

Future research should focus on issues related to curriculum content and methods. In terms of content, attention should be given to analyzing children's dispositions toward learning and patterns of responding (e.g., persistence, flexibility, problem solving); such skills have been underinvestigated with young children who have disabilities. Research related to instructional methods should focus on the adaptations and modifications that are required in the developmentally appropriate practice guidelines for young children with disabilities and on how various effective educational strategies can be implemented in programs that follow the guidelines. Perhaps the most critical area of curricular research deals with the issue of individualization, including how to plan individualized programs, how to implement them within the ongoing activities and routines of the classroom, and how to monitor and evaluate children's progress on their individualized goals.

Closing thoughts

Preschool children with disabilities now have the right to a free, appropriate public education in the least restrictive environment, and many of these children appear to be receiving such an early education. Comprehensive services for infants and toddlers with disabilities and their families also are becoming a reality. Previous research and experience have produced a large body of information with direct implications for practice. Thus, much is known about interacting with families of young children with disabilities, arranging services for them, and assessment and instructional practices for early childhood programs. When applied appropriately, this information is likely to result in positive benefits for young children with disabilities and for their families. However, as many individuals and groups will attest, having a right to high-quality services and receiving them are separate issues. Ensuring that validated practices are implemented in appropriate ways in most preschool programs throughout the nation remains a challenging task; many things

Teachers are an indispensable source of information and insight for researchers.

have yet to be learned, and many implementation issues have yet to be resolved. It has been our intention in writing this monograph to draw from the existing research implications for practice that will be useful in providing early childhood services to young children with developmental delays and disabilities in programs with their typically developing peers; to provide personnel in those programs with additional sources to help them in improving their practices; and to emphasize that much remains to be learned about providing high-quality and effective services to young children with developmental delays and disabilities and their families.

Teachers themselves are an indispensable source of information and insight for researchers. Along with parents, they are in a prime position to know the kinds of issues that arise for children with disabilities in inclusive settings, as well as to evolve and improve strategies that work for these children and their typically developing peers. Researchers should make a point of drawing on this wealth of knowledge and daily, firsthand experience in determining key issues for further study.

References

Achenbach, T.M., & C.S. Edelbrock. 1983. *Manual for the child behavior checklist and revised child behavior profile*. Burlington: University of Vermont, Department of Psychiatry.

Affleck, G., H. Tennen, J. Rowe, B. Roscher, & L. Walker. 1989. Effects of formal support on mothers' adaptation to the hospital-to-home transition of high-risk infants: The benefits and costs of helping. *Child Development* 60: 488–501.

Albano, M. 1983. *Transdisciplinary teaming in special education: A case study*. Urbana: University of Illinois–Urbana/Champaign.

Allen, K.E. 1992. *The exceptional child: Mainstreaming in early childhood education*. 2nd ed. Albany, NY: Delmar.

Alpern, G.D., T.J. Boll, & M.S. Shearer. 1980. *Manual: Developmental profile II*. Aspen, CO: Psychological Development Publications.

Alpert, C.L., & A.P. Kaiser. 1992. Training parents as milieu language teachers. *Journal of Early Intervention* 16: 31–52.

American Occupational Therapy Association. 1989. *Guidelines for occupational therapy services in the public schools*. 2nd ed. Rockville, MD: Author.

American Physical Therapy Association. 1990. *Physical therapy practice in educational environments*. Alexandria, VA: Author.

American Speech-Language-Hearing Association. 1991. A model for collaborative service delivery for students with language-learning disorders in the public schools. *Asha* 33 (Supplement 5): 44–50.

Anderson-Inman, L., H.W. Walker, & J. Purcell. 1984. Promoting the transfer of skills across settings: Transenvironmental programming for handicapped students in the mainstream. In *Focus on behavior analysis in education*, eds. W.L. Heward, T.E. Heron, D.S. Hill, & J. Trap-Porter, 17–37. Columbus, OH: Merrill.

Apolloni, T., S.A. Cooke, & T.P. Cooke. 1977. Establishing a normal peer as a behavioral model for delayed toddlers. *Perceptual and Motor Skills* 44: 231–41.

Arndorfer, R.E., R.G. Miltenberger, S.H. Woster, A.K. Rortvedt, & T. Gaffaney. 1994. Home-based descriptive and experimental analysis of problem behavior in children. *Topics in Early Childhood Special Education* 14: 66–87.

Atwater, J.B., J.J. Carta, I.S. Schwartz, & S.R. McConnell. 1994. Blending developmentally appropriate practice and early childhood special education: Redefining best practice to meet the needs of all children. In *Diversity and developmentally appropriate practices: Challenges for early childhood education*, eds. B.L. Mallory & R.S. New, 185–201. New York: Teachers College Press.

Ayllon, T. 1963. Intensive treatment of psychotic behavior by stimulus satiation and food reinforcement. *Behaviour Research and Therapy* 1: 53–61.

Azrin, N.H., & P.M. Armstrong. 1973. The "mini-meal": A method for teaching eating skills to the profoundly retarded. *Mental Retardation* 11: 9–13.

Babcock, N.L., & W.B. Pryzwansky. 1983. Models of consultation: Preferences of educational professionals at five stages of service. *Journal of School Psychology* 21: 359–66.

Baer, D.M., R.F. Peterson, & J.A. Sherman. 1967. The development of imitation by reinforcing behavioral similarity of a model. *Journal of the Experimental Analysis of Behavior* 10: 405–16.

Baer, R.A. 1990. Correspondence training: Review and current issues. *Research in Developmental Disabilities* 11: 379–93.

Bagnato, S.J., S. Kontos, & J. Neisworth. 1987. Integrated day care as special education: Profiles of programs and children. *Topics in Early Childhood Special Education* 7 (1): 28–47.

Bagnato, S.J., J.T. Neisworth, & S.M. Munson. 1989. *Linking developmental assessment and early intervention: Curriculum-based prescriptions*. 2nd ed. Rockville, MD: Aspen.

Bailey, D.B. 1984. A triaxial model of the interdisciplinary team and group process. *Exceptional Children* 5 (1): 17–25.

Bailey, D.B. 1987. Collaborative goal-setting with families: Resolving differences in values and priorities for services. *Topics in Early Childhood Special Education* 7 (2): 59–71.

Bailey, D.B. 1989a. Assessing environments. In *Assessing infants and preschoolers with handicaps*, eds. D.B. Bailey & M. Wolery, 97–118. Columbus, OH: Merrill.

Bailey, D.B. 1989b. Assessment and its importance in early intervention. In *Assessing infants and preschoolers with handicaps*, eds. D.B. Bailey & M. Wolery, 1–21. Columbus, OH: Merrill.

Bailey, D.B. 1989c. Issues and directions in preparing professionals to work with young handicapped children and their families. In *Policy implementation and P.L. 99-457: Planning for young children with special needs*, eds. J. Gallagher, P. Trohanis, & R. Clifford, 97–132. Baltimore: Paul H. Brookes.

Bailey, D.B. 1991. Issues and perspectives on family assessment. *Infants and Young Children* 4 (1): 26–34.

Bailey, D.B., & P. Blasco. 1990. Parents' perspectives on a written survey of family needs. *Journal of Early Intervention* 14: 1–9.

Bailey, D.B., & H.A. Brochin. 1989. Tests and test development. In *Assessing infants and preschoolers with handicaps*, eds. D.B. Bailey & M. Wolery, 22–46. Columbus, OH: Merrill.

Bailey, D.B., & R.A. McWilliam. 1990. Normalizing early intervention. *Topics in Early Childhood Special Education* 10 (2): 33–47.

Bailey, D.B., & R.J. Simeonsson. 1988a. Assessing needs of families with handicapped infants. *Journal of Special Education* 22: 117–27.

Bailey, D.B. & R.J. Simeonsson. 1988b. *Family assessment in early intervention.* Columbus, OH: Merrill.

Bailey, D.B., & P.J. Winton. 1987. Stability and change in parents' expectations about mainstreaming. *Topics in Early Childhood Special Education* 7 (1): 73–88.

Bailey, D.B., & M. Wolery. 1984. *Teaching infants and preschoolers with handicaps.* Columbus, OH: Merrill.

Bailey, D.B., & M. Wolery. 1989. *Assessing infants and preschoolers with handicaps.* Columbus, OH: Merrill.

Bailey, D.B., & M. Wolery. 1992. *Teaching infants and preschoolers with disabilities.* 2nd ed. Columbus, OH: Merrill.

Bailey, D.B., P.M. Blasco, & R.J. Simeonsson. 1992. Needs expressed by mothers and fathers of young children with disabilities. *American Journal of Mental Retardation* 97: 1–10.

Bailey, D.B., M.R. Burchinal, & R.A. McWilliam. 1993. Age of peers and early child development. *Child Development* 64: 848–62.

Bailey, D.B., S. Palsha, & G. Huntington. 1990. Preservice preparation of special education to serve infants with handicaps and their families: Current status and training needs. *Journal of Early Intervention* 14 (1): 43–54.

Bailey, D.B., S.A. Palsha, & R.J. Simeonsson. 1991. Professional skills, concerns, and perceived importance of work with families in early intervention. *Exceptional Children* 58: 156–65.

Bailey, D.B., V. Buysse, R. Edmondson, & T.M. Smith. 1992. Creating family-centered services in early intervention: Perceptions of professionals in four states. *Exceptional Children* 58: 298–307.

Bailey, D.B., V. Buysse, T. Smith, & J. Elam. 1992. The effects and perceptions of family involvement in program decisions about family-centered practices. *Evaluation and Program Planning* 15: 23–32.

Bailey, D.B., R.A. McWilliam, W.B. Ware, & M.A. Burchinal. 1993. The social interactions of toddlers and preschoolers in same-age and mixed-age groups. *Journal of Applied Developmental Psychology* 14: 261–76.

Bailey, D.B., P.J. McWilliam, P.J. Winton, & R.J. Simeonsson. 1992. *Implementing family-centered services in early intervention: A team-based model for change.* Cambridge, MA: Brookline.

Bailey, D.B., R.J. Simeonsson, D.E. Yoder, & G.S. Huntington. 1990. Preparing professionals to serve infants and toddlers with handicaps and their families: An integrative analysis across eight disciplines. *Exceptional Children* 57: 26–35.

Bailey, D.B., R.J. Simeonsson, P.J. Winton, G.S. Huntington, M. Comfort, P. Isbell, K.J. O'Donnell, & J.M. Helm. 1986. Family-focused intervention: A functional model for planning, implementing, and evaluating individualized family services in early intervention. *Journal of the Division for Early Childhood* 10: 156–71.

Bambara, L., P. Spiegel-McGill, R.E. Shores, & J.J. Fox. 1984. A comparison of reactive and nonreactive toys on severely handicapped children's manipulative play. *The Journal of the Association for Persons with Severe Handicaps* 9: 142–49.

Barnett, D.W., & K.T. Carey. 1991. Intervention design for young children: Assessment concepts and procedures. In *The psychoeducational assessment of preschool children*, ed. B.A. Bracken, 529–44. Boston: Allyn & Bacon.

Barnett, D.W., & K.T. Carey. 1992. *Designing interventions for preschool learning and behavior problems.* San Francisco, CA: Jossey-Bass.

Barnett, D.W., K.T. Carey, & J.D. Hall. 1993. Naturalistic intervention design for young children: Foundations, rationales, and strategies. *Topics in Early Childhood Special Education* 13: 430–44.

Barona, A. 1991. Assessment of multicultural preschool children. In *The psychoeducational assessment of preschool children*, ed. B.A. Bracken, 379–91. Boston: Allyn & Bacon.

Barrera, I. 1993. Effective and appropriate instruction for all children: The challenge of cultural/ linguistic diversity and young children with special needs. *Topics in Early Childhood Special Education* 13: 461–87.

Batshaw, M.L., & Y.M. Perret. 1992. *Children with disabilities: A medical primer.* 3rd. ed. Baltimore: Paul H. Brookes.

Baumeister, A.A., F. Kupstas, & L.M. Klindworth. 1990. New morbidity: Implications for prevention and children's disabilities. *Exceptionality* 1: 1–16.

Beckoff, A.G., & W.N. Bender. 1989. Programming for mainstream kindergarten success in preschool: Teachers' perceptions of necessary prerequisite skills. *Journal of Early Intervention* 13: 269–80.

Benner, S.M. 1992. *Assessing young children with special needs: An ecological perspective.* White Plains, NY: Longman.

Bennett, T., M. Raab, & D. Nelson. 1991. The transition process for toddlers with special needs and their families. *Zero to Three* 11 (3): 17–21.

Bergan, J.R., & T.R. Kratochwill. 1990. *Behavioral consultation in applied settings.* New York: Plenum.

Bijou, S.W., & D.M. Baer. 1961. *Child development: A systematic and empirical theory.* Vol 1. Englewood Cliffs, NJ: Prentice Hall.

Bijou, S.W., & D.M. Baer. 1965. *Child development: Universal stage of infancy.* Vol 2. Englewood Cliffs, NJ: Prentice Hall.

Bijou, S.W., & D.M. Baer. 1978. *Behavior analysis of child development.* Englewood Cliffs, NJ: Prentice Hall.

Billingsley, F.F., & L. Romer. 1983. Response prompting and the transfer of stimulus control: Methods, research, and a conceptual framework. *Journal of the Association for the Severely Handicapped* 8 (2): 3–12.

Blackhurst, A.E., & W.H. Berdine, eds. 1993. *An introduction to special education.* 3rd. ed. Boston: Little, Brown.

Blackman, J.A. 1990. *Medical aspects of developmental disabilities in children birth to three.* 2nd ed. Rockville, MD: Aspen.

Blasco, P.M., D.B. Bailey, & M.A. Burchinal. 1993. Dimensions of mastery in same-age and mixed-age integrated classrooms. *Early Childhood Research Quarterly* 8: 193–206.

Bloom, B.S. 1964. *Stability and change in human characteristics.* New York: Wiley.

Bracken, B.A. 1991a. The assessment of preschool children with the McCarthy Scales of Children's Abilities. In *The psychoeducational assessment of preschool children*, ed. B.A. Bracken, 53–85. Boston: Allyn & Bacon.

Bracken, B.A. 1991b. *The psychoeducational assessment of preschool children.* 2nd ed. Boston: Allyn & Bacon.

Bradley, R.H. 1985. Social-cognitive development and toys. *Topics in Early Childhood Special Education* 5 (3): 11–30.

Bredekamp, S., ed. 1987. *Developmentally appropriate practice in early childhood programs serving children from birth through age 8.* Exp. ed. Washington, DC: NAEYC.

Bredekamp, S. 1993. The relationship between early childhood education and early childhood special education: Healthy marriage or family feud? *Topics in Early Childhood Special Education* 13: 258–73.

Bredekamp. S., & T. Rosegrant, eds. 1992. *Reaching potentials: Appropriate curriculum and assessment for young children,* Vol. 1. Washington, DC: NAEYC.

Brewer, E.J., M. McPherson, P.R. Magrab, & V.L. Hutchins. 1989. Family-centered, community-based, coordinated care for children with special health care needs. *Pediatrics* 83: 1055–60.

Bricker, D. 1978. A rationale for the integration of handicapped and nonhandicapped preschool children. In *Early intervention and the integration of handicapped and nonhandicapped children,* ed. M.J. Guralnick, 3–26. Baltimore: University Park Press.

Bricker, D., & W.A. Bricker. 1973. *Infant, toddler and preschool research and intervention project report: Year III.* IMRID Behavioral Science Monograph 23. Nashville, TN: Institute on Mental Retardation and Intellectual Development.

Bricker, D., & J.J.W. Cripe. 1992. *An activity-based approach to early intervention.* Baltimore: Paul H. Brookes.

Bricker, W.A. 1970. Identifying and modifying behavioral deficits. *American Journal of Mental Deficiency* 75: 16–21.

Bricker, W.A., & D. Bricker. 1974. An early language training strategy. In *Language perspectives— acquisition, retardation, and intervention,* eds. R.L. Schiefelbusch & L.L. Lloyd, 431–68. Baltimore: University Park Press.

Brickerhoff, J.L., & L.J. Vincent. 1986. Increasing parental decision making at the individualized educational program meeting. *Journal of the Division for Early Childhood* 11 (1): 46–58.

Bristol, M.M., J.J. Gallagher, & E. Schopler. 1988. Mothers and fathers of young developmentally disabled and nondisabled boys: Adaptation and spousal support. *Developmental Psychology* 24: 441–51.

Broman, B. 1982. *The early years in childhood education.* Boston: Houghton Mifflin.

Bronfenbrenner, U. 1977. Toward an experimental ecology of human development. *American Psychologist* 32: 513–31.

Bronfenbrenner, U. 1979. *The ecology of human development: Experiments by nature and design.* Cambridge: Harvard University Press.

Brown, J., & J.A. Ritchie. 1990. Nurses' perceptions of parent and nurse roles in caring for hospitalized children. *Children's Health Care* 19: 28–36.

Brown, W.H., E.U. Ragland & N. Bishop. 1989. *A socialization curriculum for preschool programs that integrate children with handicaps.* Nashville, TN: Vanderbilt University.

Brown, W.H., E.U. Ragland, & J.J. Fox. 1988. Effects of group socialization procedures on the social interactions of preschool children. *Research in Developmental Disabilities* 9: 359–76.

Brown, W., S.K. Thurman, & L.F. Pearl. 1993. *Family-centered early intervention with infants and toddlers: Innovative cross-disciplinary approaches.* Baltimore: Paul H. Brookes.

Bruder, M.B. 1993. The provision of early intervention and early childhood special education within community early childhood programs: Characteristics of effective service delivery. *Topics in Early Childhood Special Education* 13 (1) :19–37.

Bruder, M.B., & T. Bologna. 1993. Collaboration and service coordination for effective early intervention. In *Family-centered early intervention with infants and toddlers: Innovative cross-disciplinary approaches,* eds. W. Brown, S.K. Thurman, & L.F. Pearl, 103–51. Baltimore: Paul H. Brookes.

Bryen, D.N., & D. Gallagher. 1991. Assessment of language and communication. In *The psychoeducational assessment of preschool children*, ed. B.A. Bracken, 187–240. Boston: Allyn & Bacon.

Burton, C.B., A.H. Hains, M.F. Hanline, M. McLean, & K. McCormick. 1992. Early childhood intervention and education: The urgency of professional unification. *Topics in Early Childhood Special Education* 11 (4): 53–69.

Buysse, V., & D.B. Bailey. 1993. Behavioral and developmental outcomes in young children with disabilities in integrated and segregated settings: A review of comparative studies. *Journal of Special Education* 26: 434–61.

Buysse, V., & P.W. Wesley. 1993. The identity crisis in early childhood special education: A call for professional role clarification. *Topics in Early Childhood Special Education* 13: 418–29.

Campbell, P.H. 1987. Physical management and handling procedures with students with movement dysfunction. In *Systematic instruction of persons with severe handicaps*, ed. M.E. Snell, 174–87. Columbus, OH: Merrill.

Campbell, P.H., W. McInerney, & M. Cooper. 1984. Therapeutic programming for students with severe handicaps. *American Journal of Occupational Therapy* 38 (9): 594–602.

Carden-Smith, L.K., & S.A. Fowler. 1983. An assessment of student and teacher behavior in treatment and mainstreamed classes for preschool and kindergarten. *Analysis and Intervention in Developmental Disabilities* 3: 35–37.

Carr, E.G., & M. Darcy. 1990. Setting generality of peer modeling in children with autism. *Journal of Autism and Developmental Disorders* 20: 45–59.

Carta, J.J., J.B. Atwater, & I.S. Schwartz. 1991. *Early classroom survival skills: A training approach.* Paper presented at conference, New Directions in Child and Family Research: Shaping Head Start in the 90s, June 25, Arlington, VA.

Carta, J.J., J.B. Atwater, & I.S. Schwartz. 1992. *Classroom survival skills interventions: Demonstration of short- and long-term effects.* Poster presented at the meeting of the Association for Behavior Analysis, May 28, San Francisco, CA.

Carta, J.J., C.R. Greenwood, & S.L. Robinson. 1987. Application of an ecobehavioral approach to the evaluation of early intervention programs. In *Advances in behavioral assessment of children and families*, ed. R.J. Prinz, Vol. 3, 123–55. Greenwich, CT: JAI Press.

Carta, J.J., D.M. Sainato, & C.R. Greenwood. 1988. Advances in the ecological assessment of classroom instruction for young children with handicaps. In *Early intervention for infants and children with handicaps: An empirical base*, eds. S.L. Odom & M.B. Karnes, 217–39. Baltimore: Paul H. Brookes.

Carta, J.J., J.B. Atwater, I.S. Schwartz, & S.R. McConnell. 1993. Developmentally appropriate practices and early childhood special education: A reaction to Johnson and McChesney Johnson. *Topics in Early Childhood Special Education* 13: 243–54.

Carta, J.J., J.B. Atwater, I.S. Schwartz, & P.A. Miller. 1990. Application of ecobehavioral analysis to the study of transitions across early education settings. *Education and Treatment of Children* 13: 298–311.

Carta, J.J., I.S. Schwartz, J.B. Atwater, & S.R. McConnell. 1991. Developmentally appropriate practice: Appraising its usefulness for young children with disabilities. *Topics in Early Childhood Special Education* 11 (1): 1–20.

Carta, J.J., M. Elliott, L. Orth-Lopes, H. Scherer, I.S. Schwartz, & J.B. Atwater. 1992. *Effective instructional strategies to facilitate in-class transitions, group instruction, and independent performance activities.* 2nd ed. Kansas City, KS: Juniper Gardens Children's Project, University of Kansas.

Carter, J.F. 1989. The fact and fiction of consultation. *Academic Therapy* 25: 231–42.

Chandler, L.K. 1992. Promoting children's social/survival skills as a strategy for transition to mainstreamed kindergarten programs. In *Social competence of young children with disabilities: Issues and strategies for intervention*, eds. S.L. Odom, S.R. McConnell, & M.A. McEvoy, 245–76. Baltimore: Paul H. Brookes.

Chiara, L., J.W. Schuster, J. Bell, & M. Wolery. 1993. *Comparison of distributed trials and small group instruction with constant time delay.* Manuscript submitted for publication.

Cohn, M.E. 1992. Screening measures. In *Assessing and screening preschoolers: Psychological and educational dimensions,* eds. E.V. Nuttall, I. Romero, & J. Kalesnik, 83–98. Boston: Allyn & Bacon.

Collins, B.C., D.L. Gast, M.J. Ault, & M. Wolery. 1991. Small group instruction: Guidelines for teachers of students with moderate to severe handicaps. *Education and Training in Mental Retardation* 26: 18–32.

Connell, M.C., J.J. Carta, S. Lutz, C. Randall, & J. Wilson. 1993. Building independence during in-class transitions: Teaching in-class transition skills to preschoolers with developmental delays through choral-response-based self-assessment and contingent praise. *Education and Treatment of Children* 16 (2): 160–74.

Conn-Powers, M.C., J. Ross-Allen, & S. Holburn. 1990. Transition of young children into the elementary education mainstream. *Topics in Early Childhood Special Education* 9 (4): 91–105.

Cooper, C.S., & K.W. Allred. 1992. A comparison of mothers' versus fathers' needs for support in caring for a young child with special needs. *Infant-Toddler Intervention* 2: 205–21.

Cooper, J.O. 1980. *Measuring behavior.* 2nd. ed. Columbus, OH: Merrill.

Cooper, J.O., T.E. Heron, & W.L. Heward. 1987. *Applied behavior analysis.* Columbus, OH: Merrill.

Courtnage, L., & J. Smith-Davis. 1987. Interdisciplinary team training: A national survey of special education teacher training programs. *Exceptional Children* 53 (5): 451–58.

Crocker, A.C. 1992. Data collection for the evaluation of mental retardation prevention activities: The fateful forty-three. *Mental Retardation* 30: 303–17

Cutler, B.C. 1993. *You, your child, and "special" education: A guide to making the system work.* Baltimore: Paul H. Brookes.

Cybriwsky, C.A., M. Wolery, & D.L. Gast. 1990. Use of a constant time delay procedure in teaching preschoolers in a group format. *Journal of Early Intervention* 14: 99–116.

Davis, C.A., & M.P. Brady. 1993. Expanding the utility of behavioral momentum with young children: Where we've been and where we need to go. *Journal of Early Intervention* 17: 211–23.

DEC Task Force on Recommended Practices. 1993. *DEC recommended practices: Indicators of quality in programs for infants and young children with special needs and their families.* Reston, VA: Council for Exceptional Children.

DeKlyen, M., & S.L. Odom. 1989. Activity structure and social interactions with peers in developmentally integrated play groups. *Journal of Early Intervention* 13: 342–52.

Demchak, M.A. 1990. Response prompting and fading methods: A review. *American Journal on Mental Retardation* 94: 603–15.

Demchak, M.A. 1993. A review of behavioral procedures to teach motor skills to individuals with severe disabilities. *Journal of Behavioral Education* 3: 339–61.

Diamond, K.E., P. Spiegel-McGill, & P. Hanrahan. 1988. Planning for school transition: An ecological-developmental approach. *Journal of the Division for Early Childhood* 12: 245–52.

Dunn, W. 1990. A comparison of service provision models in school-based occupational therapy services: A pilot study. *Occupational Therapy Journal of Research* 10: 300–20.

Dunn, W. 1991. Integrated related services. In *Critical issues in the lives of people with severe disabilities,* eds. L.H. Meyer, C.A. Peck, & L. Brown, 353–77. Baltimore: Paul H. Brookes.

Dunn, W. 1992. Assessment of sensorimotor and perceptual development. In *Assessing and screening preschoolers: Psychological and educational dimensions,* eds. E.V. Nuttall, I. Romero, & J. Kalesnik, 213–31. Boston: Allyn & Bacon.

Dunst, C. 1990. Assessment of social support in early intervention programs. In *Handbook of early childhood intervention,* eds. S.J. Meisels & J.P. Shonkoff, 326–49. Cambridge: Cambridge University Press.

Dunst, C.J. 1981. *Infant learning: A cognitive-linguistic intervention strategy.* Hingham, MA: Teaching Resources.

Dunst, C.J. 1985. Rethinking early intervention. *Analysis and Intervention in Developmental Disabilities* 5: 165–201.

Dunst, C.J., & R.A. McWilliam. 1986. Cognitive assessment of multiply handicapped young children. In *Assessment of young developmentally disabled children,* eds. T.D. Wachs & R. Sheehan, 213–38. New York: Plenum.

Dunst, C.J., C. Trivette, & A. Deal. 1988. *Enabling and empowering families: Principles and guidelines for practice.* Cambridge, MA: Brookline.

Dunst, C.J., C.M. Trivette, A.L. Starnes, D.W. Hamby, & N.J. Gordon. 1993. *Building and evaluating family support initiatives: A national study of programs for persons with developmental disabilities.* Baltimore: Paul H. Brookes.

Dunst, C.J., J.J. Lesko, K.A. Holbert, L.L. Wilson, K.L. Sharpe, & R.F. Liles. 1987. A systematic approach to infant intervention. *Topics in Early Childhood Special Education* 7 (2): 19–37.

Dyer, K., G. Dunlap, & V. Winterling. 1990. Effects of choice making on the serious problem behaviors of students with severe handicaps. *Journal of Applied Behavior Analysis* 23: 515–24.

Dyer, W. 1977. *Team building: Issues and alternatives.* Reading, MA: Addison-Wesley.

Education of the Handicapped Act Amendments of 1986. U.S. Statutes at Large 100: 1145–77.

Fallen, N.H., & W. Umansky. 1985. *Young children with special needs.* 2nd ed. Columbus, OH: Merrill.

Federal Register. 1993, January 21. 58 (12): 5502–18.

Fewell, R.R. 1991. Assessment of visual functioning. In *The psychoeducational assessment of preschool children,* ed. B.A. Bracken, 317–40. Boston: Allyn & Bacon.

Fewell, R.R., & P.L. Oelwein. 1990. The relationship between time in integrated environments and developmental gains in young children with special needs. *Topics in Early Childhood Special Education* 10 (2): 104–16.

Field, T. 1982. Interactive coaching for high-risk infants and their parents. In *Early intervention programs for infants,* eds. H.A. Moss, R. Hess, & C. Swift, 5–24. New York: Haworth.

File, N., & S. Kontos. 1992. Indirect service delivery through consultation: Review and implications for early intervention. *Journal of Early Intervention* 16 (3): 221–33.

Fleming, L.A. 1991. *Using constant time delay during circle time.* Doctoral dissertation, University of Kentucky, Lexington.

Fleming, L.A., M. Wolery, C. Weinzierl, M.L. Venn, & C. Schroeder. 1991. Model for assessing and adapting teachers' roles in mainstreamed settings. *Topics in Early Childhood Special Education* 11 (1): 85–98.

Fowler, S.A. 1982. Transition from preschool to kindergarten for children with special needs. In *Early childhood education: Special problems, special solutions,* eds. K.E. Allen & E.M. Goetz, 309–35. Rockville, MD: Aspen.

Fowler, S.A., I. Schwartz, & J. Atwater. 1991. Perspectives on the transition from preschool to kindergarten for children with disabilities and their families. *Exceptional Children* 58: 136–45.

Fowler, S.A., L.K. Chandler, T.E. Johnson, & M.E. Stella. 1988. Individualizing family involvement in school transitions. *Journal of the Division for Early Childhood* 12: 208–16.

Fox, L., & M.F. Hanline. 1993. A preliminary evaluation of learning within developmentally appropriate early childhood settings. *Topics in Early Childhood Special Education* 13: 308–27.

Foxx, R.M., & N.H. Azrin. 1973. *Toilet training the retarded: A rapid program for day and nighttime independent toileting.* Champaign, IL: Research Press.

Garbarino, J. 1990. The human ecology of early risk. In *Handbook of early childhood intervention,* eds. S.J. Meisels & J.P. Shonkoff, 78–96. Cambridge: Cambridge University Press.

Garwood, S.G., & S. Sheehan. 1989. *Designing a comprehensive early intervention system: The challenge of public law 99-457.* Austin, TX: PRO-ED.

Gesell, A., H.M. Halverson, H. Thompson, F.L. Ilg, B.M. Castner, & L.B. Ames. 1940. *The first five years of life: A guide to the study of the preschool child.* New York: HarperCollins.

Giangreco, M. 1986. Effects of integrated therapy: A pilot study. *Journal of The Association for Persons with Severe Handicaps* 11 (3): 205–08.

Gillespie-Silver, P., & S. Scarpati. 1992. Academic readiness in preschool children. In *Assessing and screening preschoolers: Psychological and educational dimensions,* eds. E.V. Nuttall, I. Romero, & J. Kalesnik, 233–45. Boston: Allyn & Bacon.

Goldstein, H., & T.M. Gallagher. 1992. Strategies for promoting the social-communicative competence of young children with specific language impairment. In *Social competence of young children with disabilities: Issues and strategies for intervention,* eds. S.L. Odom, S.R. McConnell, & M.A. McEvoy, 189–213. Baltimore: Paul H. Brookes.

Goldstein, H., & S. Wickstrom. 1986. Peer intervention effects on communicative interaction among handicapped and nonhandicapped preschoolers. *Journal of Applied Behavior Analysis* 19: 209–14.

Green, C.W., D.H. Reid, L.K. White, R.C. Halford, D.P. Brittain, & S.M. Gardner. 1988. Identifying reinforcers for persons with profound handicaps: Staff opinion versus systematic assessment of preferences. *Journal of Applied Behavior Analysis* 20: 243–52.

Gresham, F.M., & G.K. Kendall. 1987. School consultation research: Methodological critique and future research directions. *School Psychology Review* 16: 306–16.

Guess, D., H.A. Benson, & E. Siegel-Causey. 1985. Concepts and issues related to choice-making and autonomy among persons with severe disabilities. *Journal of the Association for Persons with Severe Handicaps* 10: 79–86.

Guralnick, M.J. 1981. The efficacy of integrating handicapped children in early education settings: Research implications. *Topics in Early Childhood Special Education* 1 (1): 57–71.

Gutkin, T.B., & M.J. Curtis. 1982. School-based consultation: Theory and techniques. In *The handbook of school psychology,* eds. C.R. Reynolds & T.B. Gutkin, 796–828. New York: Wiley.

Gyurke, J.S. 1991. The assessment of preschool children with the Wechsler Preschool and Primary Scale of Intelligence-Revised. In *The psychoeducational assessment of preschool children,* ed. B.A. Bracken, 86–106. Boston: Allyn & Bacon.

Hains, A.H. 1992. Strategies for preparing preschool children with special needs for the kindergarten mainstream. *Journal of Early Intervention* 16: 320–33.

Hains, A.H., S.A. Fowler, & L.K. Chandler. 1988. Planning school transitions: Family and professional collaboration. *Journal of the Division for Early Childhood* 12: 108–15.

Hains, A.H., S.E. Rosenkoetter, & S.A. Fowler. 1991. Transition planning with families in early intervention programs. *Infants and Young Children* 3 (4): 38–47.

Hains, A.H., S.A. Fowler, I.S. Schwartz, E. Kottwitz, & S. Rosenkoetter. 1989. A comparison of preschool and kindergarten teacher expectations for school readiness. *Early Childhood Research Quarterly* 4: 75–88.

Hall, G., & S. Loucks. 1978. Teacher concerns as a basis for facilitating and personalizing staff development. *Teachers College Record* 80 (1): 36–53.

Halle, J.W., D.M. Baer, & J.E. Spradlin. 1981. Teachers' generalized use of delay as a stimulus control procedure to increase language use in handicapped children. *Journal of Applied Behavior Analysis* 14: 389-409.

Halle, J.W., C.L. Alpert, & S.R. Anderson. 1984. Natural environment language assessment and intervention with severely impaired preschoolers. *Topics in Early Childhood Special Education* 4 (3): 36–56.

Hamblin-Wilson, C., & S.K. Thurman. 1990. The transition from early intervention to kindergarten: Parental satisfaction and involvement. *Journal of Early Intervention* 14: 55–61.

Hanline, M.F. 1988. Making the transition to preschool: Identification of parent needs. *Journal of the Division for Early Childhood* 12: 98–104.

Hanline, M.F. 1990. Project Profile: A consulting model for preschool children with disabilities. *Journal of Early Intervention* 14 (4): 360–66.

Hanline, M.F. 1993. Facilitating integrated preschool service delivery transitions for children, families, and professionals. In *Integrating young children with disabilities into community programs: Ecological perspectives on research and implementation*, eds. C.A. Peck, S.L. Odom, & D. Bricker, 133–46. Baltimore: Paul H. Brookes.

Hanline, M.F., & A. Knowlton. 1988. A collaborative model for providing support to parents during their child's transition from infant intervention to preschool special education public school programs. *Journal of the Division for Early Childhood* 12: 116–25.

Hanson, M.J., & M.F. Hanline. 1989. Integration options for the young child. In *Integration strategies for students with handicaps*, ed. R. Gaylord-Ross, 177–94. Baltimore,: Paul H. Brookes.

Hanson, M.J., & A. Widerstrom. 1993. Consultation and collaboration: Essentials of integration efforts for young children. In *Integrating young children with disabilities into community programs*, eds. C.A. Peck, S.L. Odom, & D. Bricker, 149–68. Baltimore: Paul H. Brookes.

Hanson, M.J., & E.W. Lynch. 1992. Family diversity: implications for policy and practice. *Topics in Early Childhood Special Education* 12: 283–306.

Haring, N.G., ed. 1988. *Generalization for students with severe handicaps: Strategies and solutions.* Seattle: University of Washington Press.

Haring, N.G., & L. McCormick, eds. 1994. *Exceptional children and youth.* 6th ed. Columbus, OH: Merrill.

Haring, N.G., K.A. Liberty, & O.R. White. 1980. Rules for data-based strategy decisions in instructional programs. In *Methods of instruction for severely handicapped students*, eds. W. Sailor, B. Wilcox, & L. Brown, 159–92. Baltimore: Paul H. Brookes.

Haring, T.G. 1992. The context of social competence: Relations, relationships, and generalization. In *Social competence of young children with disabilities: Issues and strategies for intervention*, eds. S.L. Odom, S.R. McConnell, & M.A. McEvoy, 307–20. Baltimore: Paul H. Brookes.

Harms, T., & R.M. Clifford. 1980. *Early Childhood Environment Rating Scale.* New York: Teachers College Press.

Harris, F.R., M.M. Wolf, & D.M. Baer. 1964. Effects of adult social reinforcement on child behavior. *Young Children* 20: 8–17.

Harrison, P.L. 1991. Assessment of adaptive behavior. In *The psychoeducational assessment of preschool children*, ed. B.A. Bracken, 168–86. Boston: Allyn & Bacon.

Hart, B., & T.R. Risley. 1968. Establishing the use of descriptive adjectives in the spontaneous speech of disadvantaged preschool children. *Journal of Applied Behavior Analysis* 1: 109–20.

Hart, B., & T.R. Risley. 1975. Incidental teaching of language in the preschool. *Journal of Applied Behavior Analysis* 7: 411–20.

Hart, B., & T.R. Risley. 1980. In vivo language intervention: Unanticipated general effects. *Journal of Applied Behavior Analysis* 8: 407–32.

Hart, B., & T.R. Risley. 1992. American parenting of language-learning children: Persisting differences in family-child interactions observed in natural home environments. *Developmental Psychology* 28: 1096–105.

Haskins, R. 1989. Beyond metaphor: The efficacy of early childhood education. *American Psychologist* 44: 274–82.

Haymes, L.K., S.A. Fowler, & A.Y. Cooper. 1991. *Assessing the transition and adjustment of preschoolers with special needs to an integrated program.* University of Kansas, Kansas Early Childhood Research Institute, Lawrence. Unpublished manuscript.

Heinicke, C.M., L. Beckwith, & A. Thompson. 1988. Early intervention in the family system: A framework and review. *Infant Mental Health Journal* 9: 111–41.

Higgins-Hains, A. 1992. Strategies for preparing preschool children with special needs for the kindergarten mainstream. *Journal of Early Intervention* 16: 320–33.

Hoier, T.S., S.R. McConnell, & A.G. Pallay. 1987. Observational assessment for planning and evaluating educational transitions: An initial analysis of template matching. *Behavioral Assessment* 9: 9–18.

Holcombe, A., M. Wolery, & E. Snyder. 1994. Effects of two levels of procedural fidelity with constant time delay on children's learning. *Journal of Behavioral Education* 4: 49–73.

Horn, E.M. 1991. Basic motor skills instruction for children with neuromotor delays: A critical review. *Journal of Special Education* 25: 168–97.

Horn, E., A.J. Hazel, & C. Hamlet. 1991. An investigation of the feasibility of a video game system for developing scanning and selecting skills. *Journal of the Association for Persons with Severe Handicaps* 16: 108–15.

Horner, R.H., G. Dunlap, & R.L. Koegel, eds. 1988. *Generalization and maintenance: Life-style changes in applied settings.* Baltimore: Paul H. Brookes.

Hunt, J.McV. 1961. *Intelligence and experience.* New York: Ronald Press.

Hutchinson, D. 1978. The transdisciplinary approach. In *Mental retardation: Nursing approaches to care,* eds. J. Curry & K. Peppe, 65–74. St. Louis, MO: Mosby.

Idol, L. 1993. *Special educator's consultation handbook.* 2nd ed. Austin, TX: PRO-ED.

Idol, L., P. Paolucci-Whitcomb, & A. Nevin. 1986. *Collaborative consultation.* Austin, TX: PRO-ED.

Inge, K., & M. Snell. 1985. Teaching positioning and handling techniques to public school personnel through inservice training. *Journal of the Association for Persons with Severe Handicaps* 10 (2): 105–10.

Jacobson, J.M., D. Bushell, & T.R. Risley. 1969. Switching requirements in a Head Start classroom. *Journal of Applied Behavior Analysis* 2: 43–47.

Johnson, J.E., & K.M. Johnson. 1992. Clarifying the developmental perspective in response to Carta, Schwartz, Atwater, and McConnell. *Topics in Early Childhood Special Education* 12: 439–57.

Johnson, K.M., & J.E. Johnson. 1993. Rejoinder to Carta, Atwater, Schwartz, and McConnell. *Topics in Early Childhood Special Education* 13: 255–57.

Johnson, L.J., & M.C. Pugach. 1991. Continuing the dialogue: Recognizing barriers to consultation and expanding our conceptualization of collaborative relationships. In *Controversial issues in special education,* eds. W. Stainback & S. Stainback. Boston: Allyn & Bacon.

Johnson, L.J., M.C. Pugach, & D.J. Hammitte. 1988. Barriers to effective special education consultation. *Remedial and Special Education* 9 (6): 41–47.

Johnson, T.E., L.K. Chandler, G.M. Kerns, & S.A. Fowler. 1986. What are parents saying about family involvement in school transitions? A retrospective transition interview. *Journal of the Division for Early Childhood* 11: 10–17.

Jones, K.L. 1988. *Smith's recognizable patterns of human malformation.* 4th ed. Philadelphia: Saunders.

Jones, S., & S. Meisels. 1987. Training family day care providers to work with special needs children. *Topics in Early Childhood Special Education* 7 (1): 1–12.

Kagan, S. 1991. *United we stand: Collaboration for child care and early intervention and education services.* New York: Teachers College Press.

Kaiser, A.P., & D.B. Gray. 1993. *Enhancing children's communication: Research foundations for interventions.* Baltimore: Paul H. Brookes.

Kaiser, A.P., & M.C. Hemmeter. 1989. Value-based approaches to family intervention. *Topics in Early Childhood Special Education* 8 (4): 72–86.

Kaiser, A.P., C.L. Alpert, & S.F. Warren. 1987. Teaching functional language: Strategies for language intervention. In *Systematic instruction of persons with severe handicaps*, 3rd. ed., ed. M.E. Snell, 247–72. Columbus, OH: Merrill.

Kaiser, A.P., P. Yoder, & A. Keetz. 1992. Evaluating milieu teaching. In *Causes and effects in communication and language intervention*, eds. S.F. Warren & J. Reichle, 9–47. Baltimore: Paul H. Brookes.

Kaiser, A.P., P.P. Hester, C.L. Alpert, & B.C. Whiteman. 1994. *Training parent trainers: Effects on trainers, parents and children.* Manuscript submitted for publication.

Kamphaus, R.W., & A.S. Kaufman. 1991. The assessment of preschool children with the Kaufman assessment battery for children. In *The psychoeducational assessment of preschool children*, ed. B.A. Bracken, 154–67. Boston: Allyn & Bacon.

Kennedy, C.H., & T.G. Haring. 1993. Teaching choice making during social interactions to students with profound multiple disabilities. *Journal of Applied Behavior Analysis* 26: 63–76.

Kilgo, J.L., N. Richard, & M.J. Noonan. 1989. Teaming for the future: Integrating transition planning with early intervention services for young children with special needs and their families. *Infants and Young Children* 2 (2): 37–48.

Klein, M., & R. Sheehan. 1987. Staff development: A key issue in meeting the needs of young handicapped children in day care settings. *Topics in Early Childhood Special Education* 7 (1): 13–27.

Knoff, H.M. 1992. Assessment of social-emotional functioning and adaptive behavior. In *Assessing and screening preschoolers: Psychological and educational dimensions*, eds. E.V. Nuttall, I. Romero, & J. Kalesnik, 121–44. Boston: Allyn & Bacon.

Koegel, R.L., K. Dyer, & L.K. Bell. 1987. The influence of child-preferred activities on autistic children's social behavior. *Journal of Applied Behavior Analysis* 20: 243–52.

Kohl, F.L., & P. Beckman. 1984. A comparison of handicapped and non-handicapped preschoolers' interactions across classroom activities. *Journal of the Division for Early Childhood* 8: 49–56.

Kohler, F.W., & P.S. Strain. 1990. Peer-assisted interventions: Early promises, notable achievements, and future aspirations. *Clinical Psychology Review* 10: 441–52.

Kontos, S. 1988. Family day care as an integrated early intervention. *Topics in Early Childhood Special Education* 8 (2): 1–14.

Kontos, S., & N. File. 1993. Staff development in support of integration. In *Integrating young children with disabilities into community programs: Ecological perspectives on research and implementation*, eds. C.A. Peck, S.L. Odom, & D. Bricker, 169–86. Baltimore: Paul H. Brookes.

Kratochwill, T.R., S.M. Sheridan, & K.R. VanSomeren. 1988. Research in behavioral consultation: Current status and future directions. In *School consultation: Interdisciplinary perspectives on theory, research, training, and practice*, ed. J.R. West, 77–102. Austin, TX: Association for Educational and Psychological Consultants.

Lamorey, S., & D.D. Bricker. 1993. Integrated programs: Effects on young children and their parents. In *Integrating young children with disabilities into community programs: Ecological perspectives on research and implementation*, eds. C.A. Peck, S.L. Odom, & D. Bricker, 249–70. Baltimore: Paul H. Brookes.

Lane, H. 1979. *The wild boy of Aveyron.* Cambridge, MA: Harvard University Press.

Langley, M.B. 1985. Selecting, adapting, and applying toys as learning tools for handicapped children. *Topics in Early Childhood Special Education* 5 (3): 101–18.

Langley, M.B., & N. Harris. 1989. Assessing infant cognitive development. In *Assessing infants and preschoolers with handicaps*, eds. D.B. Bailey & M. Wolery, 249–74. Columbus, OH: Merrill.

Lichtenstein, R., & H. Ireton. 1991. Preschool screening for developmental and educational problems. In *The psychoeducational assessment of preschool children*, ed. B.A. Bracken, 485–513. Boston: Allyn & Bacon.

Linder, T.W. 1990. *Transdisciplinary play-based assessment*. Baltimore: Paul H. Brookes.

Linder, T.W. 1993. *Transdisciplinary play-based assessment: A functional approach to working with young children*. Rev. ed. Baltimore: Paul H. Brookes.

Lowe, J., & M. Herranen. 1982. Understanding teamwork: Another look at the concepts. *Social Work in Health Care* 7 (2): 1–11.

Lynch, E.W., & M.J. Hanson. 1992. *Developing cross-cultural competence: A guide for working with young children and their families*. Baltimore: Paul H. Brookes.

Lyon, S., & G. Lyon. 1980. Team functioning and staff development: A role release approach to providing integrated educational services for severely handicapped students. *Journal of the Association for the Severely Handicapped* 5 (3): 250–63.

MacDonald, J.D., & Y. Gillette. 1988. Communicating partners: A conversational model for building parent-child relationships with handicapped children. In *Parent-child interaction and developmental disabilities: Theory, research, and intervention*, ed. K. Marfo, 220–41. New York: Praeger.

Mace, F.C., M.L. Hock, J.S. Lalli, B.J. West, P.J. Belfiore, E. Pinter, & D.K. Brown. 1988. Behavioral momentum in the treatment of noncompliance. *Journal of Applied Behavior Analysis* 21: 123–41.

Mace, F.C., J.S. Lalli, M.C. Shea, E. Pinter-Lalli, B.J. West, M. Roberts, & J.A. Nevin. 1990. The momentum of human behavior in a natural setting. *Journal of the Experimental Analysis of Behavior* 54: 163–72.

Maddux, R.B. 1988. *Team building: An exercise in leadership*. Los Altos, CA: Crisp.

Mahoney, G., & A. Powell. 1986. *The transactional intervention program teacher's guide*. Rock Hill, SC: Center for Excellence in Early Childhood Education.

Mahoney, G., & P.S. O'Sullivan. 1990. Early intervention practices with families of children with handicaps. *Mental Retardation* 28: 169–76.

Mahoney, G., P.S. O'Sullivan, & S. Fors. 1989. The family practices of service providers for young handicapped children. *Infant Mental Health Journal* 10 (2): 75–83.

Mallory, B.L. 1992. Is it always appropriate to be developmental? Convergent models for early intervention practice. *Topics in Early Childhood Special Education* 11 (4): 1–12.

Mason, S.A., G.G. McGee, V. Farmer-Dougan, & T.R. Risley. 1989. A practical strategy for ongoing reinforcer assessment. *Journal of Applied Behavior Analysis* 22: 171–79.

McCollum, J., & M. Hughes. 1988. Staffing patterns and team models in infancy programs. In *Early childhood special education: Birth to three*, eds. J. Jordon, J. Gallagher, P. Hutinger, & M. Karnes, 129–46. Reston, VA: Council for Exceptional Children.

McCollum, J., & V. Stayton. 1985. Infant/parent interaction: Studies and intervention guidelines based on the SIAI model. *Journal of the Division for Early Childhood* 9 (2): 125–35.

McCormick, L., & R. Goldman. 1979. The transdisciplinary model: Implications for service delivery and personnel preparation for the severely and profoundly handicapped. *AAESPH Review* 4: 152–62.

McEvoy, M.A. 1990. The organization of caregiving environments: Critical issues and suggestions for future research. *Education and Treatment of Children* 13: 269–73.

McEvoy, M.A., S.L. Odom, & S.R. McConnell. 1992. Peer social competence interventions for young children with disabilities. In *Social competence of young children with disabilities: Issues and strategies for intervention*, eds. S.L., Odom, S.R. McConnell, & M.A. McEvoy, 113–33. Baltimore: Paul H. Brookes.

McEvoy, M.A., S. Twardosz, & N. Bishop. 1990. Affection activities: Procedures for encouraging young children with handicaps to interact with their peers. *Education and Treatment of Children* 13: 159–67.

McEvoy, M.A., V.M. Nordquist, S. Twardosz, K.A. Heckman, J.H. Wehby, & R.K. Denny. 1988. Promoting autistic children's peer interaction in an integrated early childhood setting using affection activities. *Journal of Applied Behavior Analysis* 21: 193–200.

McGee, G.G., T. Daly, S.G. Izeman, L.H. Mann, & T.R. Risley. 1991. Use of classroom materials to promote preschool engagement. *Teaching Exceptional Children* 23: 44–47.

McGonigel, M. 1988. *Guidelines for family-centered research.* Washington, DC: Association for the Care of Children's Health.

McLaren, J., & S.E. Bryson. 1987. Review of recent epidemiological studies of mental retardation: Prevalence, associated disorders, and etiology. *American Journal of Mental Retardation* 92: 243–54.

McLean, M.E., & S.L. Odom. 1993. Practices for young children with and without disabilities: A comparison of DEC and NAEYC identified practices. *Topics in Early Childhood Special Education* 13: 274–92.

McLean, M.E., D.B. Bailey, & M. Wolery. n.d. *Assessing infants and preschoolers with disabilities.* 2nd ed. Columbus, OH: Merrill. In press.

McWilliam, R.A. 1991. Targeting teaching at children's use of time: Perspectives on preschoolers' engagement. *Teaching Exceptional Children* 23 (4): 42–43.

McWilliam, R.A., & D.B. Bailey. 1992. Promoting engagement and mastery. In *Teaching infants and preschoolers with disabilities,* eds. D.B. Bailey & M. Wolery, 229–55. 2nd ed. Columbus, OH: Merrill.

McWilliam, R.A., & D.B. Bailey. n.d. Perceptions of integrated services in early intervention. *Exceptional Children.* In press.

Medway, F.J. 1982. School consultation research: Past trends and future directions. *Professional Psychology* 13: 422–30.

Medway, F., & J. Updyke. 1985. Meta-analysis of consultation outcome studies. *American Journal of Community Psychology* 13: 489–504.

Meisels, S.J., & S. Provence. 1989. *Screening and assessment: Guidelines for identifying young disabled and developmentally vulnerable children and their families.* Washington, DC: National Center for Clinical Infant Programs.

Meisels, S.J., & B.A. Wasik. 1990. Who should be served? Identifying children in need of early intervention. In *Handbook of early childhood intervention,* eds. S.J. Meisels & J.P. Shonkoff, 605–32. New York: Cambridge University Press.

Melaville, A.I., & M.J. Blank. 1991. *What it takes: Structuring interagency partnerships to connect children and families with comprehensive services.* Washington, DC: Education and Human Services Consortium.

Meyers, J., L.M. Gelzheiser, & G. Yelich. 1991. Do pull-in programs foster teacher collaboration? *Remedial and Special Education* 12 (2): 7–15.

Miller, J.F. 1981. *Assessing language production in children.* Austin, TX: PRO-ED.

Miller, P.S. 1992. Segregated programs of teacher education in early childhood: Immoral and inefficient practice. *Topics in Early Childhood Special Education* 11 (4): 39–52.

Miller, T.L., & D.A. Sabatino. 1978. An evaluation of the teacher consultation model as an approach to mainstreaming. *Exceptional Children* 45 (2): 86–91.

Mudd, J., & M. Wolery. 1987. Teaching Head Start teachers to use incidental teaching. *Journal of the Division for Early Childhood* 11: 124–34.

Murphy, M., & L.J. Vincent. 1989. Identification of critical skills for success in day care. *Journal of Early Intervention* 13: 221–29.

Musselwhite, C.R. 1986. *Adaptive play for special needs children: Strategies to enhance communication and learning.* Boston: College Hill Press.

National Association for the Education of Young Children and National Association of Early Childhood Specialists in State Departments of Education. 1991. Guidelines for appropriate curriculum content and assessment in programs serving children ages 3 through 8. *Young Children* 46 (3): 21–38.

Neisworth, J.T. 1993. Assessment. In DEC Task Force on Recommended Practices, *DEC recommended practices: Indicators of quality in programs for infants and young children with special needs and their families,* 11–18. Reston, VA: Council for Exceptional Children.

References

Noonan, M.J., & J.L. Kilgo. 1987. Transition services for early age individuals with severe mental retardation. In *Transition issues and directions*, eds. R.N. Ianacone & R.A. Stodden, 25–37. Reston, VA: Council for Exceptional Children.

Noonan, M.J., & N.B. Ratokalau. 1991. PPT: The Preschool Preparation and Transition Project. *Journal of Early Intervention* 15: 390–98.

Noonan, M.J., N.B. Ratokalau, L. Lauth-Torres, L. McCormick, C.A. Esaki, & K.W. Claybaugh. 1992. Validating critical skills for preschool success. *Infant-Toddler Intervention: The Transdisciplinary Journal* 2: 187–203.

Noonan, M.J., L. Yamashita, M.A. Graham, & D. Nakamoto. 1991. *Hawaii Preparing for Integrated Preschool (PIP) Curriculum*. Honolulu: Department of Special Education & University Affiliated Program, University of Hawaii at Manoa.

Nordquist, V.M., & S. Twardosz. 1992. Environmental analysis: The preschool setting. In *Assessing young children with special needs: An ecological perspective*, ed. S.M. Benner, 143–67. White Plains, NY: Longman.

Norris, J.A. 1991. Providing developmentally appropriate intervention to infants and young children with handicaps. *Topics in Early Childhood Special Education* 11 (1): 21–35.

Notari, A., & K. Cole. 1993. Language intervention: Research and implications for service delivery. In *Integrating young children with disabilities into community programs: Ecological perspectives on research and implementation*, eds. C.A. Peck, S.L. Odom, & D. Bricker, 17–37. Baltimore: Paul H. Brookes.

Nuttall, E.V., I. Romero, & J. Kalesnik. 1992. *Assessing and screening preschoolers: Psychological and educational dimensions*. Boston: Allyn & Bacon.

Odom, S.L., & W.H. Brown. 1993. Social interaction skills interventions for young children with disabilities in integrated settings. In *Integrating young children with disabilities into community programs: Ecological perspectives on research and implementation*, eds. C.A. Peck, S.L. Odom, & D. Bricker, 39–64. Baltimore: Paul H. Brookes.

Odom, S.L., & S.R. McConnell. 1989. Assessing social interaction skills. In *Assessing infants and preschoolers with handicaps*, eds. D.B. Bailey & M. Wolery, 390–427. Columbus, OH: Merrill.

Odom, S.L., & M.A. McEvoy. 1988. Integration of young children with handicaps and normally developing children. In *Early intervention for infants and children with handicaps: An empirical base*, eds. S.L. Odom & M.B. Karnes, 241–67. Baltimore: Paul H. Brookes.

Odom, S.L., & M.A. McEvoy. 1990. Mainstreaming at the preschool level: Potential barriers and tasks for the field. *Topics in Early Childhood Special Education* 10 (2): 48–61.

Odom, S.L., & P.S. Strain. 1984. Classroom-based social skills instruction for severely handicapped preschool children. *Topics in Early Childhood Special Education* 4, 97–116.

Odom, S.L., & E. Watts. 1991. Reducing teacher prompts in peer-mediated interventions for young children with autism. *Journal of Special Education* 25: 26–43.

Odom, S.L., S.R. McConnell, & M.A. McEvoy. 1992a. Peer-related social competence and its significance for young children with disabilities. In *Social competence of young children with disabilities*, eds. S.L. Odom, S.R. McConnell, & M.A. McEvoy, 3–35. Baltimore: Paul H. Brookes.

Odom, S.L., S.R. McConnell, & M.A. McEvoy. 1992b. *Social competence of young children with disabilities: Issues and strategies for intervention*. Baltimore: Paul H. Brookes.

Odom, S.L., M. Hoyson, B. Jamieson, & P.S. Strain. 1985. Increasing handicapped preschoolers' peer social interactions: Cross setting and component analysis. *Journal of Applied Behavior Analysis* 18: 3–16.

Odom, S.L., C. Peterson, S.R. McConnell, & M.M. Ostrosky. 1990. Eco-behavioral analysis of early education/specialized classroom settings and peer social interactions. *Education and Treatment of Children* 13: 316–30.

Odom, S.L., M.K. Bender, M.L. Stein, L.P. Doran, P.M. Houden, M. McInnes, M.M. Gilbert, M. DeKlyen, M.L. Speltz, & J.R. Jenkins. 1988. *The integrated preschool curriculum: Procedures for socially integrating young handicapped and normally developing children.* Seattle, WA: University of Washington Press.

Ogbu, J.U. 1987. Cultural influences on plasticity in human development. In *The malleability of children,* eds. J.J. Gallagher & C.T. Ramey, 155–69. Baltimore: Paul H. Brookes.

Orelove, F., & M. Sobsey. 1991. *Educating children with multiple disabilities.* Baltimore: Paul H. Brookes.

Ostrosky, M.M., & A.P. Kaiser. 1991. Preschool classroom environments that promote communication. *Teaching Exceptional Children* 23 (4): 6–10.

Paniagua, F.A. 1990. A procedural analysis of correspondence training techniques. *The Behavior Analyst* 13: 107–19.

Parker, F.L., C.S. Piotrkowski, & L. Peay. 1987. Head Start as a social support for mothers: The psychological benefits of involvement. *American Journal of Orthopsychiatry* 57: 220–33.

Peck, C.A., C. Killen, & D. Baugmart. 1989. Increasing implementation of special education instruction on mainstreaming preschools: Direct and generalized effects on nondirective consultation. *Journal of Applied Behavior Analysis* 22: 1913–25.

Peck, C.A. 1993. Ecological perspectives on the implementation of integrated early childhood programs. In *Integrating young children with disabilities into community programs: Ecological perspectives on research and implementation,* eds. C.A. Peck, S.L. Odom, & D. Bricker, 3–15. Baltimore: Paul H. Brookes.

Peck, C.A., & T.P. Cooke. 1983. Benefits of mainstreaming at the early childhood level: How much can we expect? *Analysis and Intervention in Developmental Disabilities* 3: 1–22.

Peck, C.A., P. Carlson, & E. Helmstetter. 1992. Parent and teacher perceptions of outcomes for typically developing children enrolled in integrated early childhood programs: A statewide survey. *Journal of Early Intervention* 16: 53–63.

Peck, C.A., S.L. Odom, & D. Bricker, eds. 1993. *Integrating young children with disabilities into community programs: Ecological perspectives on research and implementation.* Baltimore: Paul H. Brookes.

Peck, C.A., T. Apolloni, T.P. Cooke, & S.A. Raver. 1978. Teaching retarded preschoolers to imitate the free-play behavior of nonretarded classmates: Trained and generalized effects. *Journal of Special Education* 12: 195–207.

Peterson, C., J. Peterson, & G. Scriven. 1977. Peer imitation by nonhandicapped and handicapped preschoolers. *Exceptional Children* 43: 223–25.

Piaget, J. 1951. *Play, dreams and imitation in childhood.* New York: Norton.

Piaget, J. 1952. *Origins of intelligence in children.* New York: Norton.

Piaget, J. 1954. *The construction of reality in the child.* New York: Basic.

Polloway, E.A. 1987. Transition services for early age individuals with mild mental retardation. In *Transition issues and directions,* eds. R.N. Ianacone & R.A. Stodden, 11–24. Reston, VA: Council for Exceptional Children.

Pope, A.M. 1992. Preventing secondary conditions. *Mental Retardation* 30: 347–54.

Pryzwansky, W., & G. White. 1983. The influences of consultee characteristics on preferences for consultation approaches. *Professional Psychology: Research and Practice* 14 (4): 457–61.

Pugach, M.C., & L.J. Johnson. 1989. The challenge of implementing collaboration between general and special education. *Exceptional Children* 56: 232–35.

Quiltich, H.R., E.R. Christopherson, & T.R. Risley. 1977. The evaluation of children's play materials. *Journal of Applied Behavior Analysis* 10: 501–02.

Rainforth, B., J. York, & C. Macdonald. 1992. *Collaborative teams for students with severe disabilities: Integrating therapy and educational services.* Baltimore: Paul H. Brookes.

Ramey, C.T., & S.L. Ramey. 1992. Effective early intervention. *Mental Retardation* 30: 337–45.

REFERENCES   **215**

Ramey, C.T., D.M. Bryant, B.H. Wasik, J.J. Sparling, K.H. Fendt, & L.M. LaVange. 1992. Infant health and development program for low birth weight, premature infants: Program elements, family participation, and child intelligence. *Pediatrics* 3: 454–65.

Rettig, M., M. Kallam, & K. McCarthy-Salm. 1993. The effect of social and isolate toys on social interactions of preschool-aged children. *Education and Training in Mental Retardation* 28: 252–56.

Rice, M.L., & M. O'Brien. 1990. Transitions: Times of change and accommodation. *Topics in Early Childhood Special Education* 9 (4): 1–14.

Risley, T.R. 1968. The effects and side effects of punishing the autistic behavior of a deviant child. *Journal of Applied Behavior Analysis* 1: 21–34.

Roberts, J.E., & E.R. Crais. 1989. Assessing communication skills. In *Assessing infants and preschoolers with handicaps*, eds. D.B. Bailey & M. Wolery, 339–89. Columbus, OH: Merrill.

Roberts, J.E., M.R. Burchinal, & D.B. Bailey. n.d. Communication among preschoolers with and without disabilities in same-age and mixed-age classes. *American Journal on Mental Retardation.* In press.

Rogers-Warren, A., & S.F. Warren. 1980. Mands for verbalization: Facilitating the display of newly taught language. *Behavior Modification* 4: 361–82.

Rosegrant, T., & S. Bredekamp. 1992. Reaching individual potentials through transformational curriculum. In *Reaching potentials: Appropriate curriculum and assessment for young children*, eds. S. Bredekamp & T. Rosegrant, Vol. 1, 66–73. Washington, DC: NAEYC.

Rosenkoetter, S.E., A.H. Hains, & S.A. Fowler. 1994. *Bridging early services for children with special needs and their families: A practical guide for transition planning.* Baltimore: Paul H. Brookes.

Rowbury, T.G., A.M. Baer, & D.M. Baer. 1976. Interactions between teacher guidance and contingent access to play in developing preacademic skills of deviant preschool children. *Journal of Applied Behavior Analysis* 9: 85–104.

Rule, S., B.J. Fiechtl, & M.S. Innocenti. 1990. Preparation for transition to mainstreamed post-preschool environments: Development of a survival skills curriculum. *Topics in Early Childhood Special Education* 9 (4): 78–90.

Rule, S., J.J. Stowitschek, M. Innocenti, S. Striefel, J. Killoran, K. Swezey, & C. Boswell. 1987. The social integration program: An analysis of the effects of mainstreaming handicapped children into day care centers. *Education and Treatment of Children* 10: 175–92.

Rushton, C.H. 1990. Family-centered care in the critical care setting: Myth or reality? *Children's Health Care* 19 (2): 68–77.

Safford, P.L. 1989. *Integrated teaching in early childhood: Starting in the mainstream.* White Plains, NY: Longman.

Sainato, D.M., & J.J. Carta. 1992. Classroom influences on the development of social competence in young children with disabilities. In *Social competence of young children with disabilities: Issues and strategies for intervention*, eds. S.L. Odom, S.R. McConnell, & M.A. McEvoy, 93–109. Baltimore: Paul H. Brookes.

Sainato, D.M., & S.R. Lyon. 1989. Promoting successful mainstreaming transitions for handicapped preschool children. *Journal of Early Intervention* 13: 305–14.

Sainato, D.M., H. Goldstein, & P.S. Strain. 1992. Effects of self-evaluation on preschool children's use of social interaction strategies with their classmates with autism. *Journal of Applied Behavior Analysis* 25: 127–41.

Sainato, D.M., P.S. Strain, & S.R. Lyon. 1987. Increasing academic responding of handicapped preschool children during group instruction. *Journal of the Division for Early Childhood* 12: 23–30.

Sainato, D.M., P.S. Strain, D. Lefebvre, & N. Rapp. 1987. Facilitating transition times with handicapped preschool children: A comparison between peer-mediated and antecedent prompt procedures. *Journal of Applied Behavior Analysis* 20: 285–91.

INCLUDING CHILDREN WITH SPECIAL NEEDS

Sainato, D.M., P.S. Strain, D. Lefebvre, & N. Rapp. 1990. Effects of self-evaluation on the independent work skills of preschool children with disabilities. *Exceptional Children* 56: 540–49.

Salisbury, C.L. 1991. Mainstreaming during the early childhood years. *Exceptional Children* 58: 146–55.

Salisbury, C.L., & L.J. Vincent. 1990. Criterion of the next environment and best practices: Mainstreaming and integration 10 years later. *Topics in Early Childhood Special Education* 10 (2): 78–89.

Sameroff, J.J., & B.H. Fiese. 1990. Transactional regulation and early intervention. In *Handbook of early childhood intervention*, eds. S.J. Meisels & J.P. Shonkoff, 119–49. Cambridge: Cambridge University Press.

Sasso, G.M., & H.A. Rude. 1987. Unprogrammed effects of training high-status peers to interact with severely handicapped children. *Journal of Applied Behavior Analysis* 20: 35–44.

Schnell, R.R., & K. Workman-Daniels. 1992. Intellectual assessment of preschoolers. In *Assessing and screening preschoolers: Psychological and educational dimensions*, eds. E.V. Nuttall, I. Romero, & J. Kalesnik, 145–92. Boston: Allyn & Bacon.

Schulte, A.C., S.S. Osborne, & J.D. McKinney. 1990. Academic outcomes for students with learning disabilities in consultation and resource programs. *Exceptional Children* 57 (2): 162–72.

Schwartz, I.S., S.R. Anderson, & J.W. Halle. 1989. Training teachers to use naturalistic time delay: Effects on teacher behavior and on the language of students. *Journal of the Association for Persons with Severe Handicaps* 14: 48–57.

Seifer, R., G.N. Clark, & A.J. Sameroff. 1991. Positive effects of interaction coaching on infants with developmental disabilities and their mothers. *American Journal on Mental Retardation* 96: 1–11.

Seymour, H.N., & T. Wyatt. 1992. Speech and language assessment of preschool children. In *Assessing and screening preschoolers: Psychological and educational dimensions*, eds. E.V. Nuttall, I. Romero, & J. Kalesnik, 193–212. Boston: Allyn & Bacon.

Shah, C.P., & M.F.H. Boyden. 1991. Assessment of auditory functioning. In *The psychoeducational assessment of preschool children*, ed. B.A. Bracken, 341–78. Boston: Allyn & Bacon.

Shelton, T.L., E.S. Jeppson, & B.H. Johnson. 1987. *Family-centered care for children with special health care needs.* Washington, DC: Association for the Care of Children's Health.

Shenet, M.A. 1982. *State education coordination efforts: Summary.* (Project Report No. 1449). Washington, DC: Urban Institute.

Shonk, J.H. 1982. *Working in teams: A practical manual for improving work groups.* New York: AMACOM.

Sibley, S. 1986. *A meta-analysis of school consultation research.* Unpublished doctoral dissertation, Texas Woman's University, Denton.

Simeonsson, R.J. 1986. *Psychological and developmental assessment of special children.* Boston: Allyn & Bacon.

Smith, B.J. 1988. Early intervention public policy: Past, present, and future. In *Early childhood special education: Birth to three*, eds. J.B. Jordon, J.J. Gallagher, P.L. Hutinger, & M.B. Karnes, 213–28. Reston, VA: Council for Exceptional Children.

Smith, B.J., & D. Rose. 1993. *Administrator's policy handbook for preschool mainstreaming.* Cambridge, MA: Brookline.

Smith, P.D. 1989. Assessing motor skills. In *Assessing infants and preschoolers with handicaps*, eds. D.B. Bailey & M. Wolery, 301–38. Columbus, OH: Merrill.

Spiegel-McGill, P., D.J. Reed, C.S. Konig, & P.A. McGowan. 1990. Parent education: Easing the transition to preschool. *Topics in Early Childhood Special Education* 9 (4): 66–77.

Starcevich, M., & S. Stowell. 1990. Team effectiveness questionnaire. In *Teamwork: We have met the enemy and they are us*, eds. M. Starcevich & S. Stowell. Bartlesville, OK: The Center for Management and Organization Effectiveness.

Stayton, V.D., & P.S. Miller. 1993. Combining general and special early childhood education standards in personnel preparation programs: Experiences from two states. *Topics in Early Childhood Special Education* 13: 372–87.

Stokes, T.F., & D.M. Baer. 1977. An implicit technology of generalization. *Journal of Applied Behavior Analysis* 10: 349–67.

Stoneman, Z. 1993. The effects of attitude on preschool integration. In *Integrating young children with disabilities into community programs: Ecological perspectives on research and implementation,* eds. C.A. Peck, S.L. Odom, & D. Bricker, 223–48. Baltimore: Paul H. Brookes.

Strain, P.S., & S.L. Odom. 1986. Peer social initiations: Effective intervention for social skills development of exceptional children. *Exceptional Children* 52: 543–51.

Strain, P.S., & B.J. Smith. 1993. Comprehensive education, social, and policy forces that affect preschool integration. In *Integrating young children with disabilities into community programs: Ecological perspectives on research and implementation,* eds. C.A. Peck, S.L. Odom, & D. Bricker, 209–22. Baltimore: Paul H. Brookes.

Strain, P.S., & M.A. Timm. 1974. An experimental analysis of social interaction between a behaviorally disordered preschool child and her classroom peers. *Journal of Applied Behavior Analysis* 7: 583–90.

Strain, P.S., S.R. McConnell, J.J. Carta, S.A. Fowler, J.T. Neisworth, & M. Wolery. 1992. Behaviorism in early intervention. *Topics in Early Childhood Special Education* 12 (1): 121–41.

Surr, J. 1992. Early childhood programs and the Americans with Disabilities Act. *Young Children* 47 (5): 18–21.

Swan, W., & J. Morgan. 1992. *Collaborating for comprehensive services for young children and their families.* Baltimore: Paul H. Brookes.

Tannock, R., L. Girolametto, & L.S. Siegel. 1992. Language intervention with children who have developmental delays: Effects of an interactive approach. *American Journal on Mental Retardation* 97: 145–60.

Templeman, T.P., H.D. Fredericks, & T. Udell. 1989. Integration of children with moderate and severe handicaps into a day care center. *Journal of Early Intervention* 13: 315–28.

Tharp, R., & R. Wertzel. 1969. *Behavior modification in the natural environment.* New York: Academic.

Thompson, B., D. Wickham, J. Wegner, M.M. Ault, B. Shanks, & B. Reinertson. 1993. *Handbook for the inclusion of young children with severe disabilities.* Lawrence, KS: Learner Managed Designs.

Thousand, J.S., & R.A. Villa. 1990. Sharing expertise and responsibilities through teaching teams. In *Support networks for inclusive schooling,* eds. S. Stainback & W. Stainback, 151–66. Baltimore: Paul H. Brookes.

Thurlow, M.L. 1992. Issues in the screening of preschool children. In *Assessing and screening preschoolers: Psychological and educational dimensions,* eds. E.V. Nuttall, I. Romero, & J. Kalesnik, 67–82. Boston: Allyn & Bacon.

Tindal, G., M.R. Shinn, & K. Rodden-Nord. 1990. Contextually-based school consultation: Influential variables. *Exceptional Children* 56: 324–36.

Turnbull, A.B., J.A. Summers, & M.J. Brotherson. 1984. *Working with families with disabled members: A family systems approach.* Lawrence, KS: University of Kansas University Affiliated Facility.

Turnbull, H.R. 1990. *Free appropriate public education: The law and children with disabilities.* 3rd ed. Denver: Love.

U.S. Department of Education. 1993. *To assure the free appropriate public education of all children with disabilities: Fifteenth Annual Report to Congress on the Implementation of the Individuals with Disabilities Education Act.* Washington, DC: U.S. Department of Education.

Vandercook, T., & J. York. 1990. A team approach to program development and support. In *Support networks for inclusive schooling,* eds. S. Stainback & W. Stainback, 95–122. Baltimore: Paul H. Brookes.

Venn, M.L., & M. Wolery. 1992. Increasing day care staff members' interactions during caregiving routines. *Journal of Early Intervention* 16: 304–19.

Venn, M.L., M. Wolery, L.A. Fleming, L.D. DeCesare, A. Morris, & M.H. Sigesmund. 1993. Effects of teaching preschool peers to use the mand-model procedure during snack activities. *American Journal of Speech-Language Pathology* 2 (1): 38–46.

Venn, M.L., M. Wolery, M.G. Werts, A. Morris, L.D. DeCesare, & M.S. Cuffs. 1993. Embedding instruction in art activities to teach preschoolers with disabilities to imitate their peers. *Early Childhood Research Quarterly* 8: 277–94.

Vincent, L.J., C. Salisbury, G. Walter, P. Brown, L.J. Gruenwald, & M. Powers. 1980. Program evaluation and curriculum development in early childhood/special education: Criteria for the next environment. In *Methods of instruction for severely handicapped students*, eds. W. Sailor, B. Wilcox, & L. Brown, 303–38. Baltimore: Paul H. Brookes.

Vygotsky, L. 1978. *Mind in society: The development of psychological processes.* Cambridge, MA: Harvard University Press.

Wachs, T.D. 1988. Environmental assessment of developmentally disabled infants and preschoolers. In *Assessment of young developmentally disabled children*, eds. T.D. Wachs & R. Sheehan, 321–46. New York: Plenum.

Wachs, T.D., & R. Sheehan. 1988. *Assessment of young developmentally disabled children.* New York: Plenum.

Walter, G., & L. Vincent. 1982. The handicapped child in the regular classroom. *Journal of the Division for Early Childhood* 6: 84–95.

Walton, J.R., & E.V. Nuttall. 1992. Preschool evaluation of culturally different children. In *Assessing and screening preschoolers: Psychological and educational dimensions*, eds. E.V. Nuttall, I. Romero, & J. Kalesnik, 281–99. Boston: Allyn & Bacon.

Wandersman, L.P. 1982. An analysis of the effectiveness of parent-infant support groups. *Journal of Primary Prevention* 3 (2): 99–115.

Warren, S.F. 1992. Facilitating basic vocabulary acquisition with milieu teaching procedures. *Journal of Early Intervention* 16: 235–51.

Warren, S.F., & G. Gazdag. 1990. Facilitating early language development with milieu intervention procedures. *Journal of Early Intervention* 14: 62–86.

Warren, S.F., & A.P. Kaiser. 1988. Research in early language intervention. In *Early intervention for infants and children with handicaps: An empirical base*, eds. S.L. Odom & M.B. Karnes, 89–108. Baltimore: Paul H. Brookes.

Warren, S.F., & J. Reichle, eds. 1992. *Causes and effects in communication and language intervention.* Baltimore: Paul H. Brookes.

Warren, S.F., R.J. McQuarter, & A. Rogers-Warren. 1984. The effects of mands and models on the speech of unresponsive socially isolated children. *Journal of Speech and Hearing Disorders* 47: 42–52.

Weeks, Z.R., & B. Ewer-Jones. 1991. Assessment of perceptual-motor and fine motor functioning. In *The psychoeducational assessment of preschool children*, ed. B.A. Bracken, 259–83. Boston: Allyn & Bacon.

Wenger, R.D. 1979. Teacher response to collaborative consultation. *Psychology in the Schools* 16: 127–31.

Werts, M.G., M. Wolery, A. Holcombe, M.A. Vassilaros, & S.S. Billings. 1992. Efficacy of transition-based teaching with instructive feedback. *Education and Treatment of Children* 15: 320–34.

West, J.F., & G.S. Cannon. 1988. Essential collaborative consultation competencies for regular and special educators. *Journal of Learning Disabilities* 21: 56–63.

West, J.F., & L. Idol. 1987. School consultation (Part I): An interdisciplinary perspective on theory, models and research. *Journal of Learning Disabilities* 20 (7): 388–408.

White, K.R., M.J. Taylor, & V.D. Moss. 1992. Does research support claims about the benefits of involving parents in early intervention programs? *Review of Educational Research* 62: 91–125.

Williams, H.G. 1991. Assessment of gross motor functioning. In *The psychoeducational assessment of preschool children*, ed. B.A. Bracken, 284–316. Boston: Allyn & Bacon.

Winton, P.J. 1986. The consequences of mainstreaming for families of young handicapped children. In *Mainstreamed handicapped children: Outcomes, controversies, and new directions*, ed. S.J. Meisel, 129–48. Hillsdale, NJ: Erlbaum.

Winton, P.J. 1988. The family-focused interview: An assessment measure and goal-setting mechanism. In *Family assessment in early intervention*, eds. D.B. Bailey & R.J. Simeonsson, 185–205. Columbus, OH: Merrill.

Winton, P.J. 1990. A systemic approach for planning inservice training related to Public Law 99–457. *Infants and Young Children* 3: 51–60.

Winton, P.J., & D.B. Bailey. 1993. Communicating with families: Examining practices and facilitating change. In *Children with special needs: Family, culture, and society*, eds. J. Paul and R.J. Simeonsson, 210–30. Orlando, FL: Harcourt Brace.

Winton, P.J., P.J. McWilliam, T. Harrison, A.M. Owens, & D.B. Bailey. 1992. Lessons learned from implementing a team-based model for change. *Infants and Young Children* 5 (1): 49–57.

Wolery, M. 1989a. Child find and screening issues. In *Assessing infants and preschoolers with handicaps*, eds. D.B. Bailey & M. Wolery, 117–43. Columbus, OH: Merrill.

Wolery, M. 1989b. Transitions in early childhood special education: Issues and procedures. *Focus on Exceptional Children* 22 (2): 1–16.

Wolery, M. 1989c. Using assessment information to plan instructional programs. In *Assessing infants and preschoolers with handicaps*, eds. D.B. Bailey & M. Wolery, 478–95. Columbus, OH: Merrill.

Wolery, M. 1989d. Using direct observation in assessment. In *Assessing infants and preschoolers with handicaps*, eds. D.B. Bailey & M. Wolery, 64–96. Columbus, OH: Merrill.

Wolery, M. 1991. Instruction in early childhood special education: "Seeing through a glass darkly . . . knowing in part." *Exceptional Children* 58: 127–35.

Wolery, M., & D.B. Bailey. 1989. Assessing play skills. In *Assessing infants and preschoolers with handicaps*, eds. D.B. Bailey & M. Wolery, 428–46. Columbus, OH: Merrill.

Wolery, M., & S. Bredekamp. n.d. Developmentally appropriate practice and young children with special needs: Contextual issues and a framework for convergence. *Journal of Early Intervention*. In press.

Wolery, M., & L.A. Fleming. 1993. Implementing individualized curriculum in integrated settings. In *Integrating young children with disabilities into community programs: Ecological perspectives on research and implementation*, eds. C.A. Peck, S.L. Odom, & D. Bricker, 109–32. Baltimore: Paul H. Brookes.

Wolery, M., & D.M. Sainato. n.d. General curriculum and intervention strategies. In *Recommended practices in early intervention/early childhood special education*, eds. S.L. Odom & M.E. McLean. Austin, TX: PRO-ED. In press.

Wolery, M., & P.D. Smith. 1989. Assessing self-care skills. In *Assessing infants and preschoolers with handicaps*, eds. D.B. Bailey & M. Wolery, 447–77. Columbus, OH: Merrill.

Wolery, M., & R.A. Wolery. 1992. Promoting functional cognitive skills. In *Teaching infants and preschoolers with disabilities*, eds. D.B. Bailey & M. Wolery, 2nd ed., 521–72. Columbus, OH: Merrill.

Wolery, M., M.J. Ault, & P.M. Doyle. 1992. *Teaching students with moderate and severe disabilities: Use of response prompting strategies*. White Plains, NY: Longman.

Wolery, M., D.B. Bailey, & G.M. Sugai. 1988. *Effective teaching: Principles and procedures of applied behavior analysis with exceptional students*. Boston: Allyn & Bacon.

Wolery, M., P.S. Strain, & D.B. Bailey. 1992. Reaching potentials of children with special needs. In *Reaching potentials: Appropriate curriculum and assessment for young children*, Vol. 1, eds. S. Bredekamp & T. Rosegrant, 92-111. Washington, DC: NAEYC.

Wolery, M., M.G. Werts, & A. Holcombe. 1994. Current practices with young children who have disabilities: Issues of placement, assessment, and instruction. *Focus on Exceptional Children* 26 (6): 1-12.

Wolery, M., L. Anthony, K. Heckathorn, A. Filla, & R. Bell. n.d. *Promoting preschoolers' conversations at snack and mealtimes.* Manuscript submitted for publication.

Wolery, M., P.M. Doyle, D.L. Gast, M.J. Ault, & S.L. Simpson. 1993. Comparison of progressive time delay and transition-based teaching with preschoolers who have developmental delays. *Journal of Early Intervention* 17: 160-76.

Wolery, M., J. Brookfield, K. Huffman, C. Schroeder, C.G. Martin, M.L. Venn, & A. Holcombe. 1993. Preparation in preschool mainstreaming as reported by general early education faculty. *Journal of Early Intervention* 17: 298-308.

Wolery, M., A. Holcombe, C.A. Cybriwsky, P.M. Doyle, J.W. Schuster, M.J. Ault, & D.L. Gast. 1992. Constant time delay with discrete responses: A review of effectiveness and demographic, procedural, and methodological parameters. *Research in Developmental Disabilities* 13: 239-66.

Wolery, M., K. Huffman, A. Holcombe, C.G. Martin, J. Brookfield, C. Schroeder, & M.L. Venn. n.d. Preschool mainstreaming: Perceptions of barriers and benefits by faculty in general early childhood education. *Teacher Education and Special Education.* In press.

Wolery, M., K. Huffman, J. Brookfield, C. Schroeder, M.L. Venn, A. Holcombe, L.A. Fleming, & C.G. Martin. n.d. Benefits and barriers to preschool mainstreaming: Perceptions of general early childhood educators. *Exceptional Children.* In press.

Wolery, M., C.G. Martin, C. Schroeder, K. Huffman, M.L. Venn, A. Holcombe, J. Brookfield, & L.A. Fleming. n.d. Employment of educators in preschool mainstreaming: A survey of general early educators. *Journal of Early Intervention.* In press.

Wolery, M., M.L. Venn, A. Holcombe, J. Brookfield, C.G. Martin, K. Huffman, C. Schroeder, & L.A. Fleming. n.d. Availability of related services in preschool mainstreaming: A survey of general early educators. *Exceptional Children.* In press.

Wolery, M., M.L. Venn, C. Schroeder, A. Holcombe, K. Huffman, C.G. Martin, J. Brookfield, & L.A. Fleming. 1994. A survey of the extent to which speech-language pathologists are employed in preschool programs. *Language, Speech, and Hearing Services in the Schools* 25: 2-8.

Wolery, M., A. Holcombe, J. Brookfield, K. Huffman, C. Schroeder, C.G. Martin, M.L. Venn, M.G. Werts, & L.A. Fleming. 1993. The extent and nature of preschool mainstreaming: A survey of general early educators. *Journal of Special Education* 27: 222-34.

Wolf, M.M., T.R. Risley, & H.L. Mees. 1964. Application of operant conditioning procedures to the behaviour problems of an autistic child. *Behaviour Research and Therapy* 1: 305-12.

Woodruff, G., & M. McGonigel. 1988. Early intervention team approaches: The transdisciplinary model. In *Early childhood special education: Birth to three*, eds. J. Jordon, J. Gallagher, P. Hutinger, & M. Karnes. Reston, VA: Council for Exceptional Children.

York, J., J. Nietupski, & S. Hamre-Nietupski. 1985. A decision-making process for using microswitches. *Journal of the Association for Persons with Severe Handicaps* 10: 214-23.

Zigler, E., & K.B. Black. 1989. America's family support movement: Strengths and limitations. *American Journal of Orthopsychiatry* 59: 6-19.

Subject Index

A

activities
  adapting
    by adapting materials 161
    by changing rules of access 163
    by changing what children do 160-161
    by embedding instruction 158, 160, 163
    by providing opportunities to
      participate 162
    by using shorter but more frequent
      activities 162
  new, introducing 182
activities, assessment. *See* assessment
activity/routine-by-skill matrix 157, 166
adaptations
  in response to
    children's abilities 87
    children's interests and preferences 115
    children's needs 87
  of classroom activities 178
  of classroom practices 158
  of toys and materials 109, 110
adult-targeted behavior versus child-
  initiated behavior 105
affection training (friendship training) 118
Americans with Disabilities Act (P.L. 101-
  336). *See* legislation
assessment 71-96
  activities 28, 44, 72, 84, 89, 91-95,
    192, 197
  information 82, 84, 89, 94, 152, 166,
    197, 221
  purposes of
    abilities, child's, determining 81
    diagnosis 70, 72, 76, 92
    environment, identifying the child's 85
    instructional programs, planning 72,
      77, 78, 81, 86, 91-93
    intervention planning 86
    placement 74, 77
    program effects, evaluating 74, 80
    progress, monitoring 73, 74, 77, 78,
      80, 89-91, 94, 96
    screening 7, 72-79, 96
    special services, eligibility for,
      determining 72, 74, 76, 96

assessment *(cont'd)*
  strategies
    interviews 21, 69, 72, 73, 80, 82, 84,
      86, 93, 95, 96, 197
    observation 21, 72, 73, 79, 80, 82,
      84-86, 90-93, 95, 96, 197
    testing 21, 73, 92, 96, 197
audiology, field of 47, 52, 68

B

behavior
  patterns of, teaching 119-140
  reinforced, generalizing 124

C

child care 39
child-environment interactions. *See*
  environment
child visits to a new program, arranging.
  See transitions
children's abilities, interests, needs,
  preferences. *See* adaptations
classification of children with special needs
  3-5
collaboration
  between parents and professionals 42, 43
  interagency, barriers to 55
  models for 54
  with families 192-193. *See also* teams,
    early intervention
collaborative consultation for problem
  solving 17, 54, 55, 57-59, 62, 65-67
collaborative service delivery team 59-63,
  192-195
communication skills, children's, increasing
  114, 141-144, 156, 198
community and financial services 41
consultation. *See* collaboration

D

developmentally appropriate practice 37,
  41, 98-102, 106, 177, 179, 198, 199
diagnosis. *See* assessment, purposes of
differential reinforcement strategies. *See*
  strategies (instructional)

E

early childhood education, field of 50–53
early childhood personnel/staff, role of 80, 86, 87, 91, 94, 101, 169
Early Education Program for Children with Disabilities. *See* legislation, P.L. 90-538 Handicapped Children's Early Education Program
early intervention programs 24, 31, 33, 35, 37, 41, 42
eligibility for 3, 4, 7
early intervention team. *See* teams
Education for All Handicapped Children Act (P.L. 94-142). *See* legislation
educational enhancement programs 24, 25, 27, 36, 37, 38
embedding instruction. *See* activities, adapting
engagement, active 20, 85, 99, 103, 111, 114, 115, 151, 163, 165, 166, 173, 174, 177, 188
environment
    child's interactions with 24, 98, 99, 101, 102, 105
    home 24, 25, 36
    increasing child's familiarity with 179, 180
    preschool, designing of 107

F

families 23–44, 191–193
    assessment of 30, 34
    communicating with 37, 42,
    needs 30, 34–40, 43
        for information 35, 36
        for special services 36–39
    participation in decisions 28, 31, 32, 42, 84
    resources, priorities, and concerns of 20, 29, 33, 34, 42, 44
    and social support 38
    support services for 25–27, 31–34, 38
free, appropriate education 17, 19, 189, 199. *See also* inclusion
friendship training 118

G

grouping
    mixed-age 114
    same-age 114
groups. *See* collaboration; teams

H

Handicapped Children's Early Education Program (P.L. 90-538). *See* legislation
Hawaii Preparing for Integrated Preschool (PIP) curriculum 184, 186
Head Start 16, 18, 24, 45, 58
home environment. *See* environment

I

IEP. *See* Individualized Education Plan
IFSP. *See* Individualized Family Service Plan
imitation, children's
    of adult models 143
    of peers 111, 113, 114, 115, 158–159
in-class transitions. *See* transitions
inclusion 8–13. *See also* least restrictive (appropriate) environment
    barriers to 2, 12, 13
    curriculum issues relevant to 198–199
    potential benefits of 2, 9, 11, 195
    preschool 9–13
independence, child's
    principle of 154
    with tasks 172–175, 186, 188
individual differences. *See* adaptations
Individualized Education Plan (IEP) 18, 19, 21, 29, 46, 54, 66, 81, 86–89, 91, 95, 105, 109, 111, 118, 152, 156, 193, 197
Individualized Family Service Plan (IFSP) 18, 19, 21, 29–31, 34, 41, 66, 81, 86, 88, 89, 91, 95, 105, 111, 118, 152, 156, 193, 197
individualizing. *See* adaptations
Individuals with Disabilities Education Act (IDEA). *See* legislation
infant–toddler program to preschool program. *See* transitions
instruction, embedding. *See* strategies (instructional), naturalistic/milieu
integration 8, 10, 13, 14. *See also* inclusion

Project STEPS (Sequenced Transition to Education in the Public Schools) 185
prompting strategies. *See* strategies (instructional)
prompts 103, 108, 135–139, 147, 174
  advantages of 139
  combining 137
  timing of 137
  types of
    gestural 136, 137
    model 136, 137
    physical 136, 138, 139, 147
    pictorial (two-dimensional) 137
    verbal 136, 137
  use of 137–139
  withdrawing 138
psychology, field of 50, 69, 193

Q

"qualified personnel" 47, 68, 69. *See also* legislation; related services; special education, field of

R

readiness (for an inclusive program) 175
reinforcement
  behavior–reinforcer relationships 122–125
  definition 121
  external 121, 128
  justification for using 125
  positive 120–122, 139
  types of
    behavioral momentum 103, 130, 131, 140, 206
    correspondence training 103, 129–131, 140
    differential reinforcement 103, 106, 128, 129, 131, 135, 140
reinforcers
  adult approval as 126
  as determined by child preferences 126
  combining weak and strong 125
  definition 122
  effectiveness of 122, 124
  frequency of 123

reinforcers (cont'd)
  identifying 120, 126, 127
  individualizing 124
  natural 127, 128, 131
  rules for using 120, 127, 138
  sources of 122
  timing of 123
  uses of 120, 128, 131, 140
related services 10, 12, 13, 48, 50–53, 68–70
response-prompting strategies, response-prompting procedures. *See* strategies (instructional)
role release 60
routines, adapting. *See* adaptations of classroom practices

S

same-age grouping. *See* grouping, same-age
screening. *See* assessment, purposes of
self-help skills, teaching children 186–187
sending and receiving programs. *See* transitions
Sequenced Transition to Education in the Public Schools. *See* Project STEPS
service coordination. *See* service delivery, coordinated
service delivery 31, 46, 48, 54, 56, 58–60, 62, 63, 65–67, 190, 192–196
  coordinated 26, 29, 30, 31, 34
  issues 190, 196
  team 54, 59, 62, 63, 65, 66, 67, 192–195
sharing information across programs. *See* collaboration; teams
skills
  social interaction 12, 83, 108, 109, 111–114, 117, 118, 156, 160, 161, 172, 186, 187
  teaching
    new responsibilities, introducing 182
    sequence of steps 148
    single-behavior 148
    specific 119–140
  transfer 130, 131, 164
  for transitions (functional "keystone" skills) 171–173

Author Index

Information about NAEYC

NAEYC is . . .

. . . a membership-supported organization of people committed to fostering the growth and development of children from birth through age 8. Membership is open to all who share a desire to serve and act on behalf of the needs and rights of young children.

NAEYC provides . . .

. . . educational services and resources to adults who work with and for children, including
- *Young Children,* the journal for early childhood educators
- **Books, posters, brochures,** and **videos** to expand your knowledge and commitment to young children, with topics including infants, curriculum, research, discipline, teacher education, and parent involvement
- An **Annual Conference** that brings people from all over the country to share their expertise and advocate on behalf of children and families
- **Week of the Young Child** celebrations sponsored by NAEYC Affiliate Groups across the nation to call public attention to the needs and rights of children and families
- **Insurance plans** for individuals and programs
- **Public affairs information** for knowledgeable advocacy efforts at all levels of government and through the media
- The **National Academy of Early Childhood Programs,** a voluntary accreditation system for high-quality programs for children
- The **National Institute for Early Childhood Professional Development,** providing resources and services to improve professional preparation and development of early childhood educators
- The **Information Service,** a centralized source of information sharing, distribution, and collaboration

For free information about membership, publications, or other NAEYC services . . .
- call NAEYC at 202-232-8777 or 1-800-424-2460,
- or write to the National Association for the Education of Young Children, 1509 16th Street, N.W., Washington, DC 20036-1426.